MY MOTHER'S
FAVORITE
SONG

MY MOTHER'S FAVORITE SONG

Tender Stories of Home to Deepen Your Faith

JOHN WILLIAM SMITH

HOWARD
PUBLISHING CO.

West Monroe, Louisiana

Our purpose at Howard Publishing is:

- *Instructing* believers toward a deeper faith in Jesus
  Christ
- *Inspiring* holiness in the lives of believers
- *Instilling* hope in the hearts of struggling people
  everywhere

Because he's coming again

Howard Publishing Co., Inc.,
3117 North 7th Street, West Monroe, Louisiana 71291-2227

My Mother's Favorite Song
© 1995 by John William Smith
All rights reserved. Published 1995
Printed in the United States of America

Cover Design by LinDee Loveland
Manuscript editing by Philis Boultinghouse

ISBN 1-878990-46-2

This book is dedicated
To You

❧

    To those who made the first book possible, financially and spiritually. To my good and faithful friend, Mark McInteer, to the Herb Underwoods, the Clyde Joneses, the Sid Smiths, the Fred Odoms, the Joe Donaldsons, the Jim Fairs, Johnie Lou Timms, the Ed Parks, the Wayne Wrights, Mae Matthews, the Louie Moores, the Bill Sanfords and the Tenth Street Church of Christ.

To all of you who bought the first book
and wrote and called and told me
that it meant something to you
and changed your life.

To those who laughed
and cried
and remembered
and were made better.
I pray you will be made
better still.

To my wife,
who has borne with my moods –
my depression –
my long periods of absence from her
when I was traveling
but especially when I was home –
but absent.

To the praise, glory, honor,
and everlasting dominion
of the only true and living God
and Jesus Christ the Messiah.

And once again –

To You.

CONTENTS

Contents

♦

viii

Contents

♦

ix

TWELVE — Heaven   *269*

Contents

♦

x

PREFACE

"Of making many books
there is no end,
and much study
is a weariness of the flesh."
—Ecclesiastes 12:12

The wise man Solomon was never more wise than when he wrote the words above. If he had foreseen the advent of computers and desktop publishing, which has resulted in the incredible proliferation of books that have wearied, confused, and discouraged the average reader, I doubt he would have had the heart to write the book of Ecclesiastes. Everybody who is anybody and some who are nobodies – yes, even people who can neither read, write, nor spell – have written a book.

This is now my second attempt to write a book. I wrote the first book initially because I wanted to preserve something of myself and my childhood for my children and grandchildren. I wanted them to know who I was and what I believed. I wanted them to know who they were and something of their history, both the flesh and the faith. I have written this one because God gave me the gift and I felt compelled to do so. Writing has become therapeutic for me, sort of an ongoing introspective, internal cleansing and examination that never reaches a culmination.

One of the great problems I face as a writer is that I do not wish to be misunderstood or to unnecessarily offend. I go over and over each page, each line, each word, searching for a better way of expression. Every time I go over it, I change something. I also want to make sure that I have said exactly what I mean. If I say what I mean and cause offense, that does not bother me so much, but there is nothing I fear more than misunderstanding. Words are fragile things, easily broken, and easily lead astray. There is nothing I strive for more and have less hope of achieving than understanding.

As I reach back and reproduce old scenes, I find much in my writing, and in my life, that is not only inconsistent but contradictory. Writing has helped me understand Ralph Waldo Emerson's statement about "foolish consistency being the hobgoblin of small minds." At times I feel a need to remove those contradictions and make a neatly wrapped, consistently progressive package with a warm beginning and a happy end. But my life was not, is not, and will never be a nice, neat, consistent package – although I believe with all my heart that it will have a happy ending. So I bring it to you as it was, and as it is – full of ups and downs and inconsistencies.

This book is about life, love, happiness, sorrow, loneliness, death, and final victory. This bitter-sweet mix we call "life" is an experience shared by men and women the world over. The overall purpose of this book is to take you through a progression of experiences that are common to us all, ending with death and heaven. As you see the potential for ultimate joy in the midst of your own personal struggles, you can begin to understand how Jesus endured the cross – he endured it "for the joy set before him."

This book is brutally honest in places – painfully honest in others. At its roots, it is the story of my life, my experience, my struggle, but in a broader sense, it is the story of every man and woman – for we all experience the same basic ingredients of life. I am terribly embarrassed and ashamed by much of it and somewhat satisfied with a little of it. If you haven't struggled with sin and doubt, if you have never been honest with your feelings, this book will probably make you uncomfortable at times. If you're one of those special people who have never known the depths of depression – who have lived from one sunny, blissful day to the next – this book will be totally incomprehensible to you.

There are things in this book that I would disclaim or apologize for in advance. There is much to be misunderstood, but that is the risk that all authors take. If I offend, let it be because I believe too much – and not because I believe too little.

And so I bring you this book – unfinished and flawed. I hope you will read with grace in your heart and know that my intent is good, even if my words seem to at times belie my heart.

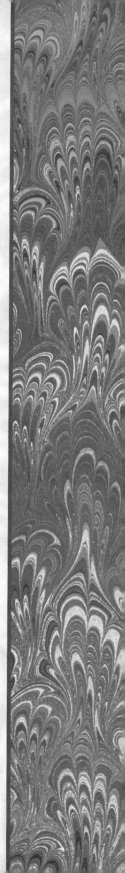

Introduction

When I Get To The End Of The Way.

Charlie D. Tillman.

1. The sands have been washed in the foot-prints Of the Stran-ger on
2. There are so man-y hills to climb up-ward, I oft-en am
3. He loves me too well to for-sake me, Or give me a
4. When the last fee-ble step has been ta-ken, And the gates of that

D. C.—And the toils of the road will seem noth-ing, When I get to the
Last Verse—Then the toils of the road, etc.

Gal-i-lee's shore— And the voice that sub-dued the rough bil-lows
long-ing for rest; But He who ap-points me my path-way,
tri-al too much; All His peo-ple have been dear-ly pur-chased,
cit-y ap-pear, And the beau-ti-ful songs of the an-gels

end of the way. And the toils of the road will seem noth-ing,
Then the toils of the road, etc.

FINE.

Will be heard in Ju-de-a no more. But the path of that
Knows just what is need-ful and best. I know in His
Tho' Sa-tan will try to claim such. By and by I shall
Fl at out on my lis-ten-ing ear; When all that now

When I get to the end of the way.

D. C.

lone Gal-i-le-an With joy I will fol-low to-day;
word He hath prom-ised That my strength "it shall be as my day;"
see Him and praise Him, In the cit-y of un-end-ing day;
seems so mys-te-rious Will be bright and as clear as the day;

My Mother's Favorite Song

The idea for this book originated this way: On the morning of July the sixth, in the year of our Lord nineteen hundred ninety-four, I woke up at daylight, enthusiastically humming a song – actually it was a hymn. My wife, who was gently wrapped in a somnambulistic state of peaceful slumber, was rendered somewhat out of sorts by this unwarranted interruption of her nocturnal bliss and reproached me severely for being so rudely awakened. She asked me quite abruptly and somewhat . . . I was going to say *angrily*, but my wife is *never* angry with me – anger is a fault, and my wife has few if any of those personality deficiencies that might be described by the term "fault" . . . perhaps I should say that she was "indignant" – "righteously indignant" would be even more appropriate.

She asked me if I had suffered a temporary impairment of my rational faculties – or words to that effect – I believe her exact words were, "Are you crazy?!" This startled me no end because I have grown quite accustomed to her referring to me as "Lord," as Sarah referred to Abraham. When I had sufficiently recovered my composure from this unprecedented and unwarranted attack, upon not only my "divine right" of headship but my intellectual prowess as well, I attempted to explain the situation – which was no simple task because I didn't understand it myself.

Judi and I had spent the night at the home of our daughter-in-law's parents in Nashville, Tennessee. I have no idea why I should have awakened with this particular song running through my mind. I had not heard it or thought about it for at least thirty years or more. I know of no event that would have triggered the memory. In fact, if you had asked me prior to that morning if there were such a song, I honestly believe I would have had difficulty remembering.

It was a song that we sang occasionally at church when I was a child, but that is not where I really learned it –

> I learned it from my mother.
> It was her
> *kitchen song.*

I don't remember ever hearing her sing it anywhere else. It was also her *troubled song.* When mother was troubled, she worked, and while she worked – canning, sewing, fixing dinner, cleaning, baking, or doing dishes – she sang, and the songs she sang gave meaning, hope, and purpose to her life.

Whenever she and Dad weren't getting along, when we were in financial trouble or there were problems at church, when she was lonely or her faith was weak – she sang this song.

Since that morning, I have tried to piece together all the words and the melody she sang the words to. Actually, she sang two songs that have the same thought in them. I have since found both of the melodies and the words. As I remember, these are the words to the first song:

> "When I come to the end of my journey,
> I will rest at the close of the day.
> And the toils of the road will seem nothing,
> When I've gone the last mile of the way.

> When I've gone the last mile of the way,
> I will rest at the close of the day.
> And I know there are joys that await me,
> When I've gone the last mile of the way."

The second song went like this:

> "The sands have been washed of the footprints
> Of the stranger on Galilee's shore.
> And the voice that subdued the rough billows
> Will be heard in Judea no more.
> But the path of that lone Galilean,
> With joy I will follow today;

> And the toils of the road will seem nothing,
>   When I get to the end of the way.
> And the toils of the road will seem nothing,
>   When I get to the end of the way."

I understand those songs, and I understand why she sang them. I am grateful to God for the providence that brought them to my mind at this point in my life.

The road of faith that I have trod has been a long and difficult one. I have been tried by the fire of constant frustration with human frailty, doubt, disappointment, pride, and the dreariness and drudgery of unrequited toil. A great, solemn sadness pervades my life. I know I am a pilgrim and a stranger – an alien person who has here no permanent dwelling place. My hope is no less because of that – in fact, it is all the greater. I am a person who has taken up his cross and is trying to follow Jesus, and even a very light cross is no fun. I carry the reminders of my battles – the scars on my soul that mark the events of my pilgrimage. I am looking for that city with foundations.

I would not say that my life is void of happiness, but my happiness is no longer the dizzying happiness of thoughtless youth – it is the happiness I find in doing my duty. I do not say that my life has no joy, but it is an aching joy and it goes far deeper than "blue skies and rainbows" and is far better expressed in this song:

> "I come to the garden alone,
>   While the dew is still on the roses;
> And the voice I hear, falling on my ear,
>   The Son of God discloses.
> And He walks with me, and He talks with me,
>   And He tells me I am his own;
> And the *joy* we share as we tarry there,
>   None other has ever known."

That song transports me into the very presence and heart of Jesus. In my conversations with Him, I experience the meaning of heartache, loneliness, pain, and sin. He tells me to bear my cross with patience, even patience with myself, and to let it teach me – as it taught him – the great lesson of

obedience.

Jesus knew from the beginning that he was to be "a man of sorrows and acquainted with grief," so he warned us that "in the world, you will have tribulation." Jesus went to the cross "for the *joy* that was set before him." In his final words, he proclaimed victory over the forces that sought to defeat him by his triumphant declaration – "It is finished." So my mother and I join with thousands of other redeemed in proclaiming our victory over the world by singing,

> "The toils of the road
> will seem nothing,
> When I get
> to the end of the way."

Introduction

♦

6

ONE

Marriage

I know of no life experience that offers more potential for growth in those critical areas of personality and character development than marriage. And yet, I know of nothing in my life that reminds me more of my mother's favorite song about "toils of the road." I do not mean at all that there is some unprecedented flaw in either my wife or my marriage that would cause me to say that. Neither do I wish to intimate that there is some fatal flaw in the institution of marriage itself, although honesty demands that I confess that I have wondered at times about the wisdom of God in this area. I only mean that most of the heartaches of my life have resulted directly from a decision two people made in a moment of weakness some thirty-two years ago.

I do not believe that I have had a bad marriage. In fact, I have had an uncommonly good one. I do not wish to say that I regret the decision – or any of the heartaches, for that matter. In fact, they have made my life richer – more fulfilling – and have given me a depth of experience and satisfaction that I believe is unusual. I wouldn't have lived my life differently for anything. I never expected it to be easy – or wanted it to be easy. I learned early on that easy things are worthless things and that if life was going to be lived to the fullest – if I was going to get the most out of it – if I was going to drink the cup to the bottom – I would have to take great risks. Marriage is one of those risks. And so – in a measure – nothing has brought me more lasting pleasure, more depth of joy than the "toils" of marriage.

Our present "failure" rate – we call it divorce – proves that married people don't have what it takes to stay married – which in turn proves that marriage is tough. Of course, the fact that most of those who divorce marry again soon after proves that it's not really marriage itself that they're opposed to, it's only that they expected it to be easy, and when they discover that it isn't, they quit and sell themselves to shallowness.

Anybody who has a good marriage has paid a terrible price for it.

I approach the topic of marriage with much trepidation. Most folks are very uptight on this subject. I have included some stories in this chapter that are intended to be humorous and at the same time revealing. There are also some that are totally serious. My reasons for the serious pieces will be obvious, I hope. The reason for the humorous pieces is that we need more laughter in our marriages. We are so intent on getting everything *right* that we fail to see or appreciate the fact that both marriage and sex are often hilarious. Sometimes, instead of going to counseling, we need to go to a Laurel and Hardy slapstick-type movie and laugh our insides out. There is at least as much truth, as much practical, useful, healing marriage therapy in one "I Love Lucy" show as there is in all of Freud, Yung, Rogers, and the whole field of psychology put together.

We need to accept the natural, predestined differences between men and women and stop trying to make us all the same. It seems to me that the women's rights movement has conceded that being like a man is better than being like a woman, and so they want to do what men do. They want to think, act, talk, sweat, chase, do business, dress, and curse like men.

The fact is that men and women don't think alike, react alike, reason alike, have the same timing, the same sense of importance or approach to life, and nothing is going to change that. Thank God! What a boring world it would be if we were all men or all women. The wonder of it all is that God created us different, and if we would just accept the differences and loosen up a little, we would find out that marriage works – because God made it to work.

Much of the humor of these stories plays on these differences. It is not my intent to belittle or ridicule. I simply have taken real-life events and situations from my own marriage and that of others and amplified or added some mythology to them. It is my prayer that the result will cause you to laugh and shake your head. Marriage is a walk through an enchanted forest – enjoy the mystery – don't take the fun out of it by trying to logically or scientifically understand it.

To All the Girls

Before I get to what I want to talk about, I have to make a confession. Confessions are not easy, no matter what anybody says. Everybody has quirks here and there in their personality – little rusty spots on their armor – and I can't write this story without disclosing a quirk of my own. So I might as well get it out in the open before you discover it. It is said that "honest confession is good for the soul." I know my *soul* will feel better after I tell you this; I only hope the rest of me will too. Once this secret is out, perhaps I'll be able to walk erect instead of slinking furtively around corners. Maybe I'll be able to look my fellow man in the eye instead of averting my gaze. I might even be able to go back to my old barber and finally stop eating at McDonald's and Wendy's.

This may be worth it.

Okay, here goes – *I like Willie Nelson.* That's it! Don't look so dumbfounded. I don't know what you were expecting, and I hope you're not disappointed. Actually, it's not Willie Nelson personally that I like – I like some of his music. I *listen* to Willie Nelson deliberately – yes, I have purchased his tapes. There. It's out. You may do with me as you wish. I cannot spend my life cringing and groveling like a whipped dog. Castigate me, ridicule me, give me the forty lashes, trample my name into the dirt, hound me to the ends of the earth, but the truth is out.

Willie sings this song with another guy – whose name I can't pronounce, much less spell. It's called, "To All the Girls." (I suppose I'd better add a disclaimer here: There may be, depending upon the listener, some questionable insinuations in that song. But I place it in my own historical context, and I get very nostalgic whenever I hear it. Since that song provided the inspiration for this essay, I wish to dedicate it

to all the girls.

First, to all the girls at Freed-Hardeman College who got up at two or three o'clock on Sunday morning and made themselves beautiful for a ride of two or three hundred miles to my preaching appointments. To all the girls who endured flat tires and mechanical breakdowns and who lived in constant fear of running out of gasoline because I couldn't buy any until *after* I got paid for preaching. To all the girls who talked to keep me awake – who went long hours without food because I had no money to buy any – who helped me get up sermons on the way to church – who gave me insights and ideas that made the people at the churches where I preached think my Bible instructors were geniuses.

To all the girls who sang alto or tenor in places where it had never been heard and who listened patiently and attentively to my bungled, garbled, juvenile sermons. To all the girls who patiently endured the ill-concealed matchmakers – those wily old ladies who tried to marry me off on every occasion – who washed the dishes and tended the babies at the homes we ate in, and who accommodated themselves in every conceivable way to every inconceivable circumstance. To all the girls who, on the way home, encouraged and uplifted and who, when deposited back at their dormitory after twenty hours of nonstop involvement, smiled and said that they had enjoyed the day – and made me believe it. To all those girls – may God be as good to you as you were to me.

Second, I wish to dedicate this essay

to one very special girl.

To the girl who, with a smile and a willing heart, became my wife. To the girl who, too soon, became a woman worn with care and disillusionment – who moved seventeen times in fifteen years because of the brethren's intolerance or ambivalence or her husband's stubbornness, pride, and stupidity – who tried to understand why she could not have a home like other wives, a place to build her nest, to care for and raise her babies, a place to fix and fuss over – it didn't have to be much, *just hers,* but it could not be – who tried to make every temporary stop a home, a special place, and succeeded beyond any reasonable expectation.

To the girl who never had a man to help get the kids ready for church, who sat attentively through a thousand sermons – many she was hearing for the fourth or fifth time – with a child on her lap and one on each side and a hundred pairs of eyes watching for a slip. To the girl – now a woman – who taught her children to read, who spent night after night alone – while her husband *saved the world* – who washed and ironed and cooked and even went to school and got a degree and worked so her babies would never have to do without when her husband said the wrong thing and got fired. To the girl who smiled through it all and never complained – who bore every added burden with courage and good will – who kept going when there was no reason – who bore with her husband's pride, stubbornness, depression, and disillusionment – and who believed that God is love in spite of it all.

When we speak of *giants of faith* and the courage of the prophets, we think always of men, but only God in heaven knows what this woman – and ten thousand others have borne for his sake.

Marriage

◆

12

To this girl –
this very special girl –
I dedicate my love
and my undying respect.
Surely her treasure is where
moth and rust cannot harm it.
To all the girls.

Saturday Morning

I still can't believe it really happened. I was steamed about it for weeks after. I – well – let me start from the beginning.

Saturday mornings are special. They are meant for early *nestling* activities. Now don't be embarrassed; we need to learn to laugh at ourselves; and sex is hilarious. What else in this world occupies so much of our conversation, interest, financial and social planning,

and takes so little of our time?

If we weren't so uptight about it – so concerned about getting it right – we would enjoy it more, maybe even do more of it!

Anyway, Saturday mornings were meant for late, great breakfasts – for walking around the neighborhood, getting and contributing to the local gossip – for running unimportant errands and for just being lazy in general. They seldom work out that way, but that's what they're for. The schedule for this particular Saturday was all fouled up, but I was determined to get it *unfouled,* so I worked it all out. I would get up at 7:00 – for my early "nestling" activities – leave at 7:40, get to the post office when it opened at 8:00, mail my packages, leave at 8:15, arrive at the appliance dealer at 8:30, get the part I needed for the washing machine, and be home by 9:00. I should finish the repair job by 9:30 and have the rest of my Saturday to while away in the appropriate fashion that I have described above.

It all started wonderfully. I got up – and I *almost* left on time; however, as I bounced energetically up the post office steps whistling "Yankee Doodle," I came face-to-face with a sign that read, "Closed on Saturdays." My shock and chagrin were indescribable. The good old, ever-lovin', dependable – rain, shine, sleet, and snow – post office was not open!

I was frosted.

Just shows what shape this country's in. Man, back in '47, when *I* worked for the post office, back in *the good old days* when men were men and women were . . . sweet potatoes – well, something different than what they are now – anyway, back then, the post office opened at 8:00 sharp, *every day* – except of course – Sundays; and we knew that nothing ought to be open on Sundays – except of course – churches and Big Daddy's Delightful Diner.

I shuffled back to the car, muttering under my breath – words too wonderful for language – my schedule shot, my whole morning thrown out of rhythm. I bought a copy of the local paper – the *Avalanche Journal* – to pass some time before the appliance store opened. Now you must understand that I lived in Lubbock, Texas, where the nearest thing to a hill is the overpass on the interstate highway. I read that title again – *Avalanche Journal* – how could anybody in Lubbock, Texas, know anything about avalanches? You've got to have mountains for avalanches – this place doesn't even have a hill. Nobody around here has ever seen anything *slide* – much less an avalanche – there's no place to slide *down* – no place to slide *to*. *Avalanche Journal* – the guy who named this paper must have been a blind poet who moved here from Colorado

after he went blind.

Finally, the appliance store opened. I ran in and got my part and drove home. By the time I arrived, I was in no mood to be trifled with. We didn't have a dog to kick, so I was looking for some new family atrocity as an excuse to vent my anger. As I walked in the house, my son asked me if I had gotten a new window pane for his bedroom. Of course I hadn't – I didn't even know it was broken. Here was the opportunity I was looking for. "I don't know how you managed to do something so stupid, but you are going to pay for it, young man." I said in an angry, threatening tone –

I was feeling better already.

"I didn't break it, honest Dad," he replied hurriedly.
"Where is your brother hiding?"
"He didn't do it either."
"Then who did?" My exasperation was rising to a dangerous level.
"Ask Mom."

Marriage

♦

14

I should have known better. There was something in his voice that said, *"Don't* ask Mom," but my frustration overcame my better judgement.

"Judi!!!" I yelled, "Where are you?"

She said, "Don't yell stupid, I'm right here, what do you want?"

"I want to know — and I want to know *right now* — who broke this window?"

I spoke in my most intimidating tone — a tone that is calculated to cause the children to run to their rooms and cower in mortal terror under their beds — a tone that is also calculated to make their mother cringe and grovel in submission and to speak with the utmost deference for my authority.

"I did," she said. She not only didn't grovel, but there was a definite lack of humility or even apology in her tone. In fact, what she said was, "Do you want to make an issue out of this, Buster? Because if you do, I am ready to take some of that, *'Blessed Assurance'* out of you."

Still angry, but with some restraint, I asked, "How did you do that?"

"If it's any of your business," she began in a very defensive tone that said that it most certainly was *not* any of my business, "it was one of those perfectly normal things that could have happened to anybody —

I was killing a fly."

She stopped there as though that was a perfectly sensible, adequate, and complete explanation. I knew I was treading on dangerous soil, but I plunged ahead. "I think I don't completely understand exactly how those two things go together," I said timidly.

"Well," she said, with disgust dripping from her voice, "I should have known that it was useless for a *woman* to try to explain anything to a *man*. I suppose I'll have to tell you the whole story."

Very meekly, I apologized for my stupidity and begged her to indulge me.

"Well, after you left, I decided to make a pumpkin pie. I had just taken it out of the oven and placed it on the counter to cool. When I went back to check on it, there was a fly walking around on it. That made my blood boil. I tried to shoo it away, but it wouldn't move, so I rolled up a newspaper and hit it. I missed the fly, but I splattered pumpkin pie all over the kitchen. That *really* made me mad. I chased the fly into Lincoln's bedroom, and it landed on the window. I couldn't hit it with the newspaper because it had pumpkin pie on it and I didn't want to mess up the window, so I took off my shoe and bashed his stupid, miserable brains out with the heel, which broke the stupid, miserable window. Now doesn't that make perfectly good sense?"

As I stood there looking at the broken window, I began to get tickled. The more I thought about my wife, seething with rage, bent upon destruction, hounding her quarry unmercifully — until in desperation, the helpless creature, gasping for breath, abandoned any hope of escape and landed on a window, only to be smashed by a shoe – the funnier it all seemed; and right then I needed a laugh.

I assured my wife that it made perfectly good sense. I applauded her determination and judgement and went to the hardware store to buy a new window.

I laughed for a week.

As I sit here at my computer, revising this story, I see that I first wrote it down over twenty years ago. Every time I tell the story it gets more and more funny. It is also true that the story has *grown* as the years have gone by, and no one is now able to determine the actual events of the original episode, and no one cares either – except my wife – who has learned to enjoy the story as much as anyone.

The moral of this story depends on who you are. If you're a fly, the moral is don't land on pumpkin pies or window panes. If you're a man, the moral is that women are fearsome things and neither their pies nor their logic are to be trifled with. If you're a woman, the moral is that men's egos are very fragile and that their bark is worse than their bite, so at least *act* a little submissive now and then. I think that the overall moral is that first – Saturday mornings were meant for special things and anybody who messes with the divine plan is placing his life, health, and eternal happiness in great danger; second – it's good to laugh – laughter will lengthen your life span, improve your marriage, increase your humility and your appreciation, and make your testimony for Jesus more believable.

𝔍𝔣

Going Home

> "Warren," she said, "he has come home to die:
> You needn't be afraid he'll leave you this time."
> *"Home?"* he mocked gently.
> "Yes, what else but home?

It all depends on what you mean by home.
Of course he's nothing to us, any more
Than was the hound that came a stranger to us
Out of the woods, worn out upon the trail."
"Home is the place where, when you have to go there,
They have to take you in."
"I should have called it
Something you somehow haven't to deserve."
—Robert Frost, *The Death of the Hired Man*

If you had asked him why he came back, he would have said that quite honestly, he didn't know. He had been born here and had graduated from high school here and married here. He had grown up in this town. He had played football here and, after four years of college, had returned to marry his high school sweetheart. He hadn't been back in years. It wasn't that he had no good memories. It was that

the latest and most dominant were bad.

Lately, he had just felt a great wrongness in his life. An undefined anxiety – depression – heaviness. He found himself sitting at his desk drumming his fingers and staring vacantly at reports wondering why they were important. Sometimes he turned the little sign on the front of his desk around – "Frank Thomas" it said. "Who is Frank Thomas?" he wondered. He gazed long moments out his office window at the windows in other office buildings, wondering who worked over there and what they were like. He wondered what they thought about and if they ever looked at his window and wondered about him. He also noticed, with some alarm, that he was having trouble making even the most simple decisions.

He found himself watching – with total detachment – the mad, chaotic scramble of five o'clock traffic that swirled around him as he drove methodically to his apartment. There was a time when he would have been honking his horn – cursing under his breath – tight lipped, teeth clenched, white knuckled – one foot on the brake, one on the accelerator – fighting it out with the rest of the snarling pack –

but not now.

He knew he was lonely, but this maddening, haunting feeling that nothing seemed to shake was more than loneliness – it was like the instinct that drives a wounded animal to its den. He had felt the need to *get somewhere* – someplace where he could find his center again, his foundation – his *home*. Yes, that was exactly what he wanted, and this town was the closest thing to home he had ever known.

It was that time that comes to every thoughtful person – that time that leads some to drink, some to drugs, some to work harder, some to power, some to affairs, some to church, some to diets, travel, poetry, mysticism, fitness centers, sporting events, TV, or cheap novels.

It drove him
home.

When he drove into town, he was very disappointed. Much was gone; much more had changed. He didn't recognize anyone. Now that he was here, he didn't know what to do. He had thought that just coming back would provide the reason – it didn't. He drove around a little – went by the high school, looking for old, familiar landmarks. He stopped in a restaurant for a cup of coffee and finally recognized an old acquaintance. They shook hands, exchanged pleasantries, bragged a little on what they had accomplished. "How's Susan?" Pete asked. It was an inevitable question, but it was the one he wanted to avoid most of all. "She's fine, I guess. I suppose you haven't heard that we're separated. I haven't seen her in nearly two years."

"Separated! No kidding! Gee, everybody thought you were Mr. and Mrs. ideal couple. Two years! Why don't you just get a divorce?"

He had wondered the same thing – many times. He wondered why she hadn't forced the issue – demanded one. He mumbled some nonsense about the financial difficulty of the settlement, and of course they couldn't agree about the kids – but there was something else, something more – something never put into words, but he knew what it was. Divorce was too *final – the end* – and neither of them had the courage or the heart to say that it was finally and forever over. That would close the book on too many things they wanted to keep.

Pete was in the real estate business, and finally Frank asked him if he remembered the house they had lived in. "Sure," Pete said. "In fact, I've got it listed." Without really thinking about it, Frank said, "Let's drive by, I'd like to see what they've done to the old place."

His mind flooded with memories as they drove down the familiar street – maybe he had been happier here than he thought. Pete had a key to the lockbox, and very shortly, Frank found himself wandering through the empty rooms. "This is it," he said to himself; "this is why I came back."

And he knew that was the truth.

The grass had not been cut in back. The previous owners had not cared properly for the grapes or the fruit trees; the bedrooms needed paint badly. "You know," he thought, "I always meant to pipe the water from the washing machine out to the trees, and I think Susan was right about putting a mantle over the fireplace. In fact, now that Scott is bigger, *we* could finish that back room, put in another bath, and have a bedroom to ourselves."

It began to dawn upon him – very slowly – what a good time he was having, how excited he was, that he was planning in terms of *we* instead of *I* – and that gave meaning to the future. But his excitement vanished as he realized that it was all a myth, a cruel unreality. It struck him forcefully that he didn't own this house, he didn't live in this town, he had no job here, and of course, Susan and the kids lived far away. But the idea wouldn't leave him, and he knew – just as a homing pigeon knows – that he was home and that *this was his one chance* and that

he had to try.

"How much are they asking, Pete?"

"Seventy-five thousand, but they'll take sixty-eight."

"I'll take it." Frank couldn't believe it was his voice that he heard. There was assurance in it. For the first time in a long time, *he had a plan* – he knew exactly what he was doing and why. "I'll call her," he thought, "I'll call her tonight." But he couldn't wait for tonight, so he called her at work. Normally he asked for "Susan," but today he asked for "Mrs. Frank Thomas." He heard the secretary whisper, "Susan, it's for you, some guy wants to speak to *Mrs. Frank Thomas.*" When she picked up the phone, her first words were, "Frank, I hope this is you, I've been thinking about you all day. Where are you?"

"Susan, I just bought the old house back. Could we get together and talk this weekend? It's important to me."

"I just happen to be free this weekend, and I don't know anybody I'd rather spend it with than you."

Are you looking out windows into other windows? Are you spending more and more time at "Happy Hour?" Are you looking for ways to get your mind off things?

Is there a "divine providence"
working in your life?
*Do you need
to call somebody?*

Adam and Eve

"And the Lord God fashioned into a woman
the rib which He had taken from the man,
and brought her to the man."
—Genesis 2:22

Marriage

♦

20

"I have something for you, Adam."

"Wow!" (his response translated roughly). "Where did you find that – it – I mean – *Wow!* I thought I'd already seen and named everything you'd made."

"I didn't *find* her, Adam; I *made* her. I made her for you."

"Is that what you were doing while I was asleep? Did you say *her?*"

"Yes, *her."*

"You mean, she's like me – except she's the *other kind?*"

"Yes."

"Thank you very much! She's . . . well, she's *great,* I mean she's *perfect."*

The Maker left them to themselves. And although He knew what would happen, it gave him real pleasure to watch it for the first time – *the way of a man with a maid.* It began, as it has always begun –

with talk.

"The Maker called you *Adam?"*

"Yes, that's my name."

"Am I to have a name?"

"Well, I suppose so. I've named everything else. Let's see, I've got it. *Eve!* That's it; I'll call you *Eve.* How do you like that?"

"It's not very creative – I think I like Adam better. Why can't I be Adam?"

"Well, that would be stupid. It wouldn't make sense if we both had the same name – besides, names mean things, and you *can't* be Adam because Adam means man and you aren't man – you're – boy, are you good looking! I seem to have lost my train of thought.

What was I saying?"

"You were saying something about the meaning of my name and why it couldn't be Adam. What is 'boy,' and what is 'train of thought'?"

"Oh yes, well, what I was saying is that you are woman, because you came out of me. You see, God, the Maker, took one of my ribs – look; see the scar? *Don't touch it!* Good grief, it's still sore – anyway – he formed you out of my rib, and that's why I named you Eve, because that's what your name means;

and 'boy' is another word for man – except it means young man; and 'train of thought' is a saying that will come into existence about ten thousand years from now when there are things called 'trains' – and please don't ask me to explain that, but it means to pursue a systematic pattern of thought."

"Oh. Seems silly to me. What are you so excited about, anyway? I just thought I liked the name Adam. Are your answers to questions always so long and complicated? I really don't care what you call me. And if 'boy' means young man, why did you call me that? I thought you said I wasn't man, and what does 'good grief' and 'make sense' mean?"

"'Make sense' is like *logical*, like one thing follows another, like if this is true then that is true; and 'boy' is used – oh forget it; and 'good grief' is a colloquialism, and don't you dare ask me what that means; and if you didn't care, then why make such a fuss? I've named sixteen zillion things – took me about a thousand days! You never saw such a line up of animals, and I named 'em – every last one I named! Thought sure I'd run out of words, but I named them all – from terns, tigers, and tyrannosauruses to parakeets, petrels, and penguins – man, I thought He had me on penguins – did you ever see a penguin? Funniest thing He ever made except camels, platypuses, and kangaroos. Now those kangaroos –"

"Adam, I think you lost your 'train of thought' again."

"What? Oh yes, what I was saying was – let me tell you, if you were *me* standing here looking at *you,* you'd lose your train of thought too."

"You were going to make some point about my making a fuss over my name."

"Well, yes, I was. I was going to say that I had named fourteen zillion things – "

"You said sixteen zillion last time."

"There you go again – see – fourteen zillion, sixteen zillion. It's just a figure of speech – "

"A what?"

"A figure of speech, you know, a figure of – man, speaking of figures – you've got one; I mean, you're *beautiful.* I've never seen anything quite like you – and I've seen a lot. Did you ever see an elephant or a hippopotamus? Man, they're something! And right when I was naming the hippopotamus – I only had 'hippo' out – two male leopards got into it over some female leopard, and I thought we were going to have a riot until another female leopard showed up and – "

"Adam, you were going to tell me about a figure of speech."

"Well, yes, I was, except I keep losing track of where I am and you keep interrupting. I've named twenty-five zil – fourteen zil – a whole gob of

animals – and not one single one ever argued about their name. They just said, 'Yes sir; thank you sir,' and they went right on."

"But I'm not an animal. Does a figure of speech *make sense?*"

"Yes, of course, and boy, you're sure not an animal – and you ask the darndest questions – and am I ever glad – that you're not an animal, I mean. You know, you're sensational; I mean, *you're a ten.* I don't know how He did it."

"Did what? And what's a ten?"

"Made something like you, and a ten is another figure of speech that means perfect. I mean, He's made some pretty fantastic stuff, but

you are the greatest!"

"You're not half bad yourself, Adam. In fact, you're by far the most attractive thing I've seen since I got here."

"You mean it? You really think I'm good looking? Have you seen the orangutans and the giraffes? Speaking of giraffes, the other day two of them got into the garden, and it infuriated me – I mean – they've got the whole world to eat in, and they got into *my* garden. I chased them about ten miles before I – "

"What's a mile? And what is a garden?"

"Well, a mile is a long way. It's from here to – well, about to that live oak over there by the river – and the garden, well, that's where we live."

"We?"

"Well, sure, you and I – I mean, that is if you want to. I don't mean to be pushy, but I sure would like for you to live with me – it would be great! And now that I've seen you, I think the Maker meant for us to live together; it wouldn't seem right not to, because – well, you know – the giraffes live together and the eagles – man, you can't separate them. In fact, it was only about three weeks ago one of them hurt its wing, and the other one wouldn't leave it for anything – brought it food and protected it and – "

"Adam."

"Yes."

"Adam, I would love to live with you in your garden or any other place you wish. There are many things I don't know, but I do know that *my place is with you,* and it always will be."

"You would? I mean, it is? Wow! And to think you chose me."

"Adam, what is 'chose'?"

And so it always was, and so it will ever be, the greatest of all God's miracles – that two things, when seen standing apart, appear so incorrigibly different and diametrically opposed but when placed together fit so wonderfully well. No one understands it, and the more we study it and try to "make

sense" out of it and force the two to be the same, the more trouble we have making it work. Perhaps it wasn't meant to be figured out –

only to be wondered at and appreciated.

Winter of Our Discontent

"Now is the winter of our discontent
made glorious summer by this son of York."
—Shakespeare, King Lear

Author's note: John Steinbeck wrote a marvelous, poignant novel with this same title. His work made a profound and lasting impression on me. When I finished the following story, I could not imagine a more accurate or descriptive title.

It was spring at last. Judi was pregnant – in fact – she was *extremely* pregnant – it was our first child. We lived in a very small apartment in Mount Clemens, Michigan. It was 1964. It had been *a long, hard winter.* All along the roadways were great mounds of soot-blackened, grimy, slowly melting snow, standing as bleak reminders of the cold and lonely months behind us. The departed snow left a newly naked and embarrassed landscape, covered with an uninviting array of dead, brown weeds and grass, sprinkled with scattered bits of blown, discarded trash that had been conveniently hidden until now. Spring didn't look like the *beginning* of something –

it looked like the end.

If I say that this happened in the winter of '64, "winter" sounds like an isolated entity – like saying "senior year." *A Michigan winter is not a single thing.* It is a multifaceted, amalgamation of things that get all mixed up and twisted together. The event that I am about to record was not a single event; it was the culmination of a thousand events, some so infinitely small that neither of us noticed or remembered them – but they happened – they had been happening since we began our courtship and marriage.

We only had one car, which I used in my work. I was busy in my job – I left early and came home late. I went places, met people, had lunch, hunted, fished, played golf. Judi was home alone every day, *and she was pregnant*. I emphasize her pregnancy because *no man has ever experienced it or understands it* (few have even tried – understanding it, I mean) and because pregnancy is such a unique thing – especially the first one. We knew very few people – she had no transportation and no place to go.

The winter had been made even longer by the fact that we had no money and therefore could not *buy* our way out of the oppressive isolation that had settled over us. There were no shopping trips, no movies, no evenings out.

We had been married long enough for the new and the curiosity to wear off, but not long enough to be comfortable with each other or our vanished, unrealistic expectations.

We had lost the world of our wishes –
but we had not replaced it
with one of our hopes.
It had been a very long winter!

Spring hadn't been much help – not in Michigan. Cold, damp winds blew strong over the brown, soggy fields – gray, overcast, threatening skies depressed – temperatures made promises that were never kept – and still no money.

One sunny, encouraging Friday morning as I left the house, I mentioned quite casually that if things went well at work and I got off early, we might drive up the river road to Charlevoix and have dinner.

"Oh, could we?" There was great expectation in her voice, but I wasn't paying attention.

Things went unexpectedly well at work, and by 11:30 I was finished. An unexpected sale had put some unexpected dollars in my pocket, and when my fishing buddy Larry called and told me that the perch were running in the Clinton River, my unexpected expectations were totally out of control.

I didn't deliberately break my word to Judi – in some ways that would have been more honorable.

I did something worse –
I forgot her.

I broke all speed records getting home – locked up all four wheels and skidded to a stop in a cloud of dust in the driveway – ran into the house and

yelled, "Hi, I'm home," as I yanked off my tie and unbuttoned my shirt, preparing to change into fishing clothes.

"What are you doing?"

It wasn't a challenge; it was a pleading question, but I didn't hear *the pleading* –

I just heard the question.

"I'm going fishing with Larry; the perch are running in the Clinton River."

I hadn't seen her yet, but now she came into the bedroom. She had her hair all done up and she was dressed in her only Sunday "pregnant" dress –

but I never noticed.

"Oh," she said. There was hurt and disappointment in the "Oh"–

but I didn't hear it.

"Could you fix me a thermos of tea and a couple of sandwiches?"

"Sure," she said. "How long will you be gone?" There was *longing* in the question, but I was totally occupied with my preparations.

"Oh, probably till dark – depends on how good it is."

She was standing just inside the door as I rushed past, fishing rods in one hand, lunch in the other.

"Have a good time," she said, and although it was sincere, there was pain in it; but the pain escaped me – at least it escaped my consciousness.

"I'm sure I will," I said. *"You have a good time too."*

"Sure," she said.

I put the rods in the trunk and the lunch on the seat. I started the motor and started to back up, but something was nagging at me. I went over a list of the things I would need, but that wasn't it. I had the eerie feeling that I had forgotten something, that something was missing, so I got out and went back inside to look.

She was standing right where I had left her – just inside the door – eyes wide open and huge tears rolling down both cheeks. She wasn't shaking or sobbing; she was just standing there – hands at her sides, eyes wide open, tears running down – looking at me.

"Honey, what's wrong?" I was so dumb – so lost in my own world, my own happiness, feelings, and pleasures, my own needs and wants – *that I didn't know anybody else had any.*

"You never have time for me."

She didn't yell, didn't even raise her voice; it would have been easier if she had. It was just a quiet statement of truth that left me convicted and heartsick. Everything just sort of went out of me – I felt lost, empty, and sick all at the same time. I just stood there – I had no words for the feeling that *the entire foundation of my life* had just been destroyed, taken right out from under me, leaving me dangling. Her words seemed to hang in the air –

"You never have time for me."

I didn't know that I was *supposed* to have time for her, or for anybody else for that matter – unless it served some selfish purpose. Again, I want you to see that I wasn't mean or vicious. I wasn't one to speak harshly or be abusive, I was simply and totally self-centered – so much so that –

I didn't even know it.

What does a man do with a crying wife? I went fishing – not with Larry, with Judi – but my heart wasn't in the fishing. I don't even remember if we caught anything. We sat on the riverbank, and we held hands and talked – but not much – I wasn't ready. We ate the sandwiches and drank the tea, and once, she took my hand and placed it on her extended tummy – "Feel that?" she said.

"Wow!" I said.

"That's your son kicking around in there."

It was the beginning – no it actually wasn't – beginnings are hard to pin down. It had begun long ago, somewhere in the dim recesses of my childhood. Perhaps it was the beginning of awareness – an awareness of other people, of what a marriage is supposed to be. I lay awake late that night – long after I heard the slow, steady breathing that meant she was asleep – with all kinds of new thoughts buzzing around in my head. I didn't know it, but *the winter of our discontent* was over. I don't know exactly when it ended, because I don't know exactly when it began – but it was becoming the spring of promise, because

I was becoming a man.

Read it slowly – very slowly – and with care –

> "When I was a child, I used to speak as a child,
> think as a child, reason as a child;
> *when I became a man,*
> I did away with childish things. . . .
> But now abide faith, hope, love,
> these three;
> but the greatest of these
> is love."
> —1 Corinthians 13:11, 13

Marriage

♦

26

The winter of our discontent had been created by my selfishness – by my refusal to put my egocentric childhood behind me and grow into the man that God intended me to be so that I could begin to learn the meaning of love. The first duty of a husband or wife is *to grow up – to put childhood aside –*

to become a man or woman –
and to think of others.

Sunday Morning and Snakes

I heard the following apocryphal story several years ago from a friend of mine and enjoyed it so much that I thought I would write it down and give it a permanent form. It is about a man and his wife who had planned their retirement very carefully. Not only had they set aside a sufficient amount of money, they had begun building their country retirement home long before they retired. They worked on the house on weekends and during vacations and finally finished it just in time for their long awaited retirement.

On the first Sunday after they moved in, they decided to forsake an old habit and not to go to church. Instead, they took a long morning walk. When they returned, they decided to shower and then go out for breakfast. While her husband was in the shower, she sat on the screened-in porch and read. As she was sitting there, a rather small but sinister looking snake crawled out from under the couch. She was horrified. She screamed, jumped up, and ran to the bathroom to get her husband.

Over the noise of the shower, the husband heard his wife babbling hysterically about a ten-foot rattlesnake, capable of killing a grizzly bear, being loose in their house. The husband, like most men, assumed that his wife was hallucinating and calmly assured her that he was master of the situation. Girding a towel about his loins and arming himself with a broomstick, he went forth like Sylvester Stallone to dispatch the unfortunate monster.

The snake, seeing the husband approaching with death in his eye, beat a hasty retreat back under the sofa. The husband, watching the tail disappear, was a little disconcerted, because he now knew that there really was a snake. He thought about calling 911, but it was a very small snake, and after placing his manhood on the line, he decided to proceed on his own. He got down on his knees and peered under the couch. He couldn't see the snake, so he decided to try poking the broomstick around to drive it out into the open. His wife was simultaneously entreating caution and urging action, and he was trying to reassure her.

All the noise awoke the family spaniel who now came running onto the porch barking excitedly, dodging and dancing around the husband, trying to poke his nose at whatever was under the couch. The husband was now trying desperately to calm both his wife and the dog, while still poking furiously under the couch, trying to drive the snake out. In the frenzy of excitement, the dog touched his cold, wet nose to the exposed backside of the stooped-over husband. The husband, assuming that the snake had outmaneuvered him and bitten him, jumped up, grabbed the spot where he assumed the dastardly infraction had been committed, emitted a strangled cry of horror, and fainted dead away.

The wife, unaware of the problem, assumed that the excitement had caused her husband to have a heart attack, sprang into action, and called 911. The paramedics arrived promptly, resuscitated the husband, and gave him an injection to calm him. Then they placed him on a stretcher with the intention of carrying him to the waiting ambulance.

As they picked him up, however, the snake, in a desperate attempt to gain his freedom, spotted the open door and made for it. The only thing in his path was the foot of one of the paramedics. When he crawled over it, the paramedic jumped and tripped over an end table. He dropped his end of the stretcher and fell on the husband, breaking his leg.

The moral of this story is that going to church on Sunday mornings can save you a lot of trouble.

They Know Not What They Do

"If 'twere done, when 'tis done,
Then 'twere well it was done quickly."
—William Shakespeare, *Macbeth*

In the play *Macbeth,* Lady Macbeth has been urging her recently victorious and immensely popular army-leader husband to sacrifice his misplaced loyalty to his king, kill him, and take his place. Macbeth, who is hesitant, argues that it is *never that simple;* but his wife insults his manhood, questions his courage, and insists that once the killing is done, life will be great, everyone will soon forget, and there will be no reprisals. The above quotation is Macbeth's response to her urging. He says that if killing the king really won't affect his tomorrows, then it's better to get it over with as soon as possible. But there is a significant hesitation in his response based on that most important of all words –

if!

They had been *playing with the idea* for some time, flirting with the possibilities. She carelessly, it seemed, brushed his shoulder with her hand when she passed his desk; he nearly always remarked on how attractive she looked. When the boss took the staff to lunch, they always sat together and chatted intimately about *completely innocent* things. Occasionally, when one of them stayed after work, the other stayed also, always with reasons good enough to satisfy even themselves. When one was asked to serve on a planning committee – the other volunteered. They always remembered each others birthday *but never their anniversaries.* They played cute little jokes on each other, always *completely innocent ones*, and occasionally bought each other nice gifts – on birthdays or Christmas or Valentines. They were aware –

and unaware.

They were both reasonably happy in their marriages; their family problems were the ordinary ones. Neither really began the game with a conscious decision to be unfaithful – they just enjoyed exciting possibilities. In fact, they would have been horrified, indignant, if anyone had even suggested that there was anything improper about their behavior.

The process reached the inevitable climax quite *accidentally.* Well, *almost* accidentally. He had gone to Chicago on business for about a week. She had a sister in Chicago. When he had been gone two days, her sister called saying that her niece had been severely injured in an accident. She told herself that she was going to see her niece – to help her sister – and it was true, except *it wasn't true* – not in that great eternal sense of truth,

and she knew it.

When she called him at his hotel, he was quite surprised – but excited. They agreed to meet in the lobby and have dinner together. They went to a nice restaurant, had a very expensive meal – and a drink or two – but neither of them ate much. They visited for awhile, but the conversation was tense. The playing was over – this was the real thing.

The essential problem was that neither of them saw beyond. They both believed it could be done – done quickly, quietly, joyously – and that then they could return – go back to what had been.

Nothing would be changed.
They would be no different and
nothing would be lost.

After all, the media constantly portrayed it that way – everybody has a great time and nobody gets hurt. And they were quite willing to believe it. Tomorrow would simply be another day of fun in the sun; they would do it, and they would be no different. But they were wrong!

Somehow the new day
did not erase
the previous night.

When Jesus, on the cross says, "Father forgive them, they *know not* what they do." He means exactly that. The leaders of the Jews believe that with his death, the threat to their security will die – that things will go back to the way they were before he came along, that they will leave the scene of the cross, go home, eat dinner, sleep through the night, and in the morning life will fall right back into its old familiar groove – that they will be no different.

They do not know that things
will never be the same.

They will never sleep secure or undisturbed again. The curse of their infamous deed will surface in every moment they spend alone. It will be just beyond speech – but very much in consciousness.

Even their children will not escape the curse. The blood of betrayal will seep into the very fabric of their families – staining, spotting, creating insurmountable barriers of isolation, contention – a never-ending feeling of wrongness that, like Lady Macbeth's hands, *will not wash.* Somehow they will never be able to face each other. Every time their eyes meet, they will auto-

matically look away. And even when they brazen it out, they will know that somehow they have lost some undefined thing of great value – something represented by words like honor, integrity, loyalty – even faith. The guilt will separate; they will never again know peace. They will ask *why* ten thousand times, but they will never hear the answer.

> "If 'twere done, when 'tis done,
> Then 'twere well it was done quickly."

> If you do it,
> will it ever really be *done?*

The Zipper

I first heard this story from an old friend named Harold Neal in Garland, Texas, about thirty years ago. He told it for the truth. I had forgotten the story until my good friend and brother, Charles Mickey, told it about two years ago. He did not tell it for the truth, which leads me to believe it is a preacher's story. I have no idea whether or not this event, or something like it, actually happened, and I suppose that is no longer important. It has so much of *probability* in it that it certainly could have happened, and what degree of *improbability* is in it will not prevent married couples from finding themselves in it somewhere.

Early one morning, a not newly, but recently married couple was getting ready for work. There was a tense and pronounced silence in the bedroom. He was mad because she had taken so long in the bathroom that he was now late. Her stay in the bathroom was deliberate because she was mad at him for not fixing the garbage disposal. Now she could have simply told him that, but women's minds just don't work that way – it's part of the marvel. He knew she was mad, but he didn't have a clue why.

He'd been married to this woman long enough to know that the surest way *not* to find out was to ask. He knew that if he asked what was wrong, she would either say: "What's wrong? Nothing is wrong! That's what's wrong! I wish something were wrong! What makes you think something is wrong?" or, "What's wrong? *You* have the nerve to ask *me* what's wrong? You know darn well what's wrong! Are you trying to start an argument, Buster? Because if you are, I'm more than ready!"

Of course there was the possibility that she'd say, "What's wrong? I'll tell you what's wrong – you're so dumb you don't know what's wrong – that's what's wrong."

Finally, he decided to take an indirect approach.

"Well," he said, "it sure takes *some people* a long time to fix their hair." (Did you ever notice how naturally we slip into the *third person* in these conversations?)

"Not nearly as long as it takes *some people* to fix the garbage disposal," came the terse reply. (Now he knew what the problem was, but he was angry and he couldn't resist the temptation to respond.)

"That may be true, but if I did fix it, at least when I finished I would have more to show for my efforts than you do." (Big mistake.)

"I won't comment about the results of *your efforts* in certain areas of our marriage, except to say that they have been somewhat less than satisfying and terribly unrewarding. So let me give you a piece of friendly advice – stick with the garbage disposal. I realize that it may tax your *mechanical ability,* but when you've proved that you can handle simple things, I'll help you move up to more complicated ones."

"Actually, my love, the disposal isn't broken – it's *clogged up* because *some person* doesn't have enough sense not to shove too much stuff down it at one time."

"Oh sure, just like *some people* – since they don't have the *mechanical ability* of a do-do bird – blame their failures on others. My *dad* could fix anything. And don't give me that, 'my love' business either."

"Your poor, hen-pecked father couldn't fix his false teeth, unless of course your mother told him how; and if *you* had the brains of a goose, the disposal wouldn't need fixing."

Just as he said this, she was zipping up her dress. He had made her so mad that she yanked the zipper as hard as she could, and it hung – right between her shoulder blades. She reached around her neck and pulled it up with all her might, and then she reached around behind her back and yanked it down; but because of the awkward position, she couldn't budge it. Her *pride* wouldn't let her ask her husband for help, but her *vanity* wouldn't let her go to work with her dress not zipped.

She looked in the mirror and saw her husband smiling – that smug, superior, condescending smile that absolutely infuriated her. He'd been watching the whole thing, knew exactly how she felt, and did not offer to help.

"Got a little *mechanical* problem?" he said.

"Yes, I do," she seethed. "Now wipe that stupid smirk off your face – you look like a baboon who just found a banana – come over here, and help me get this thing loose."

"I'm sure I don't have the *mechanical ability* to fix a broken zipper. Why don't you call your father?"

"You make me so mad! If he were closer, I would call him – believe me. But as *incompetent* as you are, you're all I've got – besides, it's not broken, it's just *stuck* – so it shouldn't tax your limited skills."

Her husband came over and released it quite easily, but he couldn't resist running it up and down about ten times just to show her how easy it was. When it got so hot that smoke was coming off the zipper and out her ears, he finally turned loose of it. She grabbed her purse and bolted out of the house, determined to get revenge.

All day, every time she thought about it – and she thought about it a lot – she got more and more angry and more determined to put him in his place.

That evening she got home a little later than usual. The garage door was closed and her opener wouldn't open it, so she had to park in the driveway and come in through the side garage door. As she made her way around the car to the kitchen door, she saw her husband's waist and legs sticking out from under the car – he was obviously trying to repair something. Here was her golden opportunity. She reached down, grabbed the zipper on his pants, and ran it up and down till it got so hot she couldn't hang on to it any longer. From under the car she heard one startled exclamation, a thump, and then silence.

She marched triumphantly into the house with that same smug, completely satisfied smile on her face that her husband had had that morning. To her absolute astonishment, her husband was standing at the refrigerator getting a drink.

"How did you get in here?" she exclaimed.

"By the usual method – I walked."

"Who's under the car?"

"Oh, that's Fred, he came over to help me fix that exhaust leak." (Fred was one of their deacon friends from church.)

Marriage

♦

33

"You won't believe what I just did," she said. And he didn't. They decided they had better go out to attempt an explanation to Fred – but when they called his name, Fred wouldn't come out from under the car. They finally grabbed his legs and dragged him out. Fred was unconscious. When she had grabbed his zipper, he had been so surprised and excited that he had raised up quickly and hit his head on the car frame.

The next week there was a note in the church bulletin that read: "If a certain person in this church asks you to come over and help him work on his car, be sure to wear pants that button up the front. If you don't understand this note – see Fred."

I know you're thinking that this kind of thing doesn't really happen, but I assure you that it does.

They Say, and Do Not Do

"The scribes and the Pharisees
sit in Moses' seat. Therefore
whatever they tell you to observe,
that observe and do,
but do not do according
to their works;
for they say,
and do not
do."
—Matthew 23:2–3

The singing that preceded the evening lecture had just begun. The floor of the field house was filled to capacity, so my friend and I were sitting in the bleachers. As we were singing the first song, a relatively young couple came in. They were both a little on the chunky side, and his dress was perhaps a bit too casual for the occasion. The only seats left were in the bleachers, and as usual, they were the most difficult to get to — right at the top.

For a chunky guy, he did real good getting there. Wearing tennis shoes helped a lot, and he jumped gingerly from one row to the next. He sat down, picked up a songbook, and looked expectantly toward the speaker's platform. His wife, dressed in a rather tight-fitting skirt and half-heels, was still trying awkwardly to negotiate the first step. Ultimately she did so, but she stumbled and almost lost her balance. She looked tentatively at the remaining steps and then imploringly to the top row where her husband sat,

completely oblivious to her plight.

The song leader announced the next selection and the husband turned — I suppose to say something to his wife — and for the first time noticed that she hadn't made it yet. He looked down in her direction and, in a highly audible, obviously irritated voice, said, *"Hurry up!"* He never moved to help her, never evinced the slightest concern for her safety or embarrassment, and when she finally arrived — with the helping hands of everyone she passed — he acted as though *she* had humiliated *him*.

He had his Bible, his note pad, and his pen. He sang with fervor, listened attentively, took copious notes, and nodded his head in concert with the points the speaker made. The sermon was on the theme of the call of Jesus to his disciples to *take up their cross and follow him*. The speaker emphasized that our Christian witness in the world was through the power of a changed life.

I am sure that this young man's moral life was a good one — he impressed me as one who would not smoke, drink, or curse — and I want to commend that as well as bringing his Bible, taking notes, and listening attentively — we would all do well to imitate those things. I simply want us to see that

the way he treated his wife was shameful —
immoral.

In effect, it was a denial of all of the good qualities he otherwise exhibited. I also want to point out that his good qualities were mechanical and external in nature — relatively easy to perform by habit — while his fault was a *sin of disposition* — a basic Christian character flaw that results from spiritual and moral frailty, which in turn results from a failure to experience grace.

May God forgive us all — me in particular — for every time we deny his Spirit and act inconsistently with what we profess orally. May God open our eyes to our hypocrisies so that we will not bring reproach to his name. May we also see that —

morality goes far beyond the sexual and physical.

Marriage

♦

Marriage

♦

36

It is a mind set – a way of thinking
that affects every aspect of our lives.

"The scribes and the Pharisees
sit in Moses' seat. Therefore
whatever they tell you to observe,
that observe and do,
but do not do according
to their works;
for they say,
and do not
do."
—Matthew 23:2–3

TWO

Forgiveness

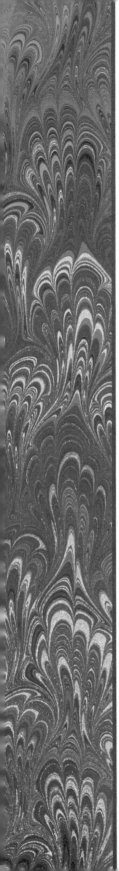

I don't know of anything we need and want more than forgiveness. I don't know of anything that is harder to do and that we are less willing to do than forgive. Forgiveness ought to be easy – but it isn't. It ought to come *naturally* – but it doesn't. Forgiveness releases people from their indebtedness to us – but sometimes we prefer to keep those obligations and use them as manipulative tools. Did you realize that you can lose your soul in everlasting condemnation for being unwilling to forgive? Read Matthew 6:12–15. That makes it pretty serious. Before you read the rest of this introduction, I want to ask you to read Luke 7:36–50. You won't get much out of this introduction if you don't.

There are three characters in this story – the sinful woman, Simon the Pharisee, and Jesus. A brief analysis of their spiritual awareness reveals much. Jesus knows who He is, who the woman is, and who Simon is. The woman knows who and what she is, and further, she knows who Jesus is and who Simon is. She is under no illusions about herself; therefore she has no pride – and that is the key to forgiveness and a right relationship with God. She is miles further down the road to sanctification than Simon. This story is not really about the woman; it is about Simon the Pharisee, because in this story it is Simon alone who doesn't know who anybody is –

especially himself.

Simon sees the woman as "that kind of woman." I have often wondered how he knew so much about her? Simon sees himself as vastly superior to her – because she is a *sinner* and he is not. He sees himself as vastly superior to Jesus – first, because Jesus lacks his acumen in determining her character and second, because Jesus is so lacking in personal pride that he allows this vile creature to touch him, and Simon's dignity and social position would never allow that –

at least not in public.

The story ends with the woman leaving Simon's house with her sins forgiven and at peace with God and herself. The story ends with Simon at home – with his sins and his pride intact, having no comprehension of the fact that he is totally lost and in danger of the fires of hell.

The woman, having received grace and forgiveness, is now in a position to grant it. Simon, feeling no need for either grace or forgiveness, would never think of asking for it or extending it.

There is much in Scripture about forgiveness; in fact, I guess you could say that *everything* in Scripture is either directly or indirectly about forgiveness. Jesus died on Calvary so that God could bestow on us absolute forgiveness. I know you already know this, but let me remind you that Jesus died for everyone. The reason Jesus died is that everyone needs forgiveness –

even Simon,

even you,

even me.

Nobody *deserves* God's forgiveness. If we deserved it, we wouldn't need it – because deserving undermines the very nature of forgiveness. That is also true of forgiveness between people. We must forgive people because they need it and because God has forgiven us. *Nobody ever deserves it* – it is ridiculous to tell someone that when they perform in a certain way, we'll forgive them, or to think that some actions or attitudes on our part will somehow make us deserving of forgiveness.

Forgiveness simply cannot be earned.

It is an act of grace,

and it must be received

as an act of grace.

That does not mean that there's nothing we can do and ought to do to make it easier and more satisfying – both to forgive and be forgiven. It does mean that no matter what we do, we can't demand it or earn it.

God provided the means of forgiveness on the cross. He did that because he *wanted* to forgive us. The forgiveness we extend to others must be extended on the same basis – because they need it and we want to forgive them.

Forgiveness is a blessing to both parties. It keeps us from bitterness, and it frees us from the burden of the accumulation of old wrongs. Only our pride stands between us and the blessing of forgiveness. We are either –

too proud to ask for it –

too proud to receive it –

or too proud to give it.

We must learn to forgive one another

as God has forgiven us.

The Great Gifts

Christmas is a time for giving – and receiving. It is also a time for *forgiving* – because that's what God did at Christmas – He forgave us. When we didn't even know we needed it – He forgave us through Jesus. Christmas is also a time that calls for *insight* and *understanding* because without those things, the real meaning will be lost in the noise and hustle. This is a story about Christmas – about giving and receiving – about insight and understanding – and about

forgiveness.

This is a Christmas story, and you must never lose sight of the central fact that without Christmas, without the spirit of humility and goodwill generated by our awareness of His coming, *this story could not have happened*. You must be both a child and an adult to understand this story.

In 1949 I was in the seventh grade at Mary Lyon Junior High in Royal Oak, Michigan. My parents were having a difficult time financially, which was nothing new, but I found myself needing money occasionally, which *was* something new for me – I mean, I had never needed money before. I wouldn't have known what to spend it on, but now I knew because – I had discovered girls.

I decided to get a paper route. I got a route delivering the *Detroit Free Press*. I picked up my papers at 5:30 A.M. and delivered them until about 7:15. I hated getting up – in the winter months especially – because it was totally dark the whole time, bitterly cold, and I couldn't ride my bike because of the snow and ice. But I earned the princely sum of eight dollars per week – when I could collect from my customers, that is –

which was almost never.

Of course my customers weren't up when I delivered my papers – which always made me wonder – I mean, why does a person want a paper at 5:30 in the morning when they don't get up until 7:30. Anyway, in order to collect, I had to try to catch them in the evening. One of the places I delivered to was an apartment building of several stories. Mostly single people lived there, and they were rarely at home.

The Christmas of 1949 was a *particularly* bad time financially and relationally at home – I didn't know how very bad it was 'till much later. My mom and dad weren't getting along at all, and we had taken in boarders to supplement our income. Some of them were alcoholics. Occasionally, we'd find one asleep in the bathtub, and not only did they keep us up at night with their shouting, they didn't pay their rent. This made matters worse between my folks because my dad would feel sorry for them and wouldn't insist that they either pay or move out, which made my mother furious – she said she wished he would feel sorry for her sometimes.

At Christmas time, we didn't have a tree. My dad had as much pride as anybody, I suppose, so he wouldn't just say that we couldn't afford one. When I mentioned it, my mother said that we weren't going to have one this year, that we couldn't afford one, and even if we could – *it was stupid to clutter up your house with a dead tree.* She was very cross and spoke sharply, which was unusual for her, so I didn't bring it up any more. I wanted a tree badly, though, and I thought – in my naive way – that if we had one, everybody would feel better.

About three days before Christmas I was out collecting for my paper route. It was fairly late – long after dark – it was snowing and very cold. I went to the apartment building to try to catch a customer who hadn't paid me for nearly two months – she owed me seven dollars. Much to my surprise, she was home. She invited me in, and not only did she pay me, she gave me a dollar tip! It was a windfall for me – I now had *eight whole dollars.*

What happened next was providential because I had absolutely no plan or intention of doing what I did. On the way home, I walked past a Christmas tree lot, and the idea hit me. The selection wasn't very good because it was so close to the holiday, but there was this one real nice tree. It had been a very expensive tree and no one had bought it; now it was so close to Christmas that the man was afraid no one would. He wanted ten dollars for it, but when I – in my gullible innocence – told him I only had eight, he said he might sell it for that. I really didn't want to spend the whole eight dollars on the tree, but it was so pretty that I finally agreed.

I dragged it all the way home – about a mile, I think – and I tried hard not to damage it or break off any limbs. The snow helped to cushion it, and it was still in pretty good shape when I got home. You can't imagine how proud and excited I was. I propped it up against the railing on our front porch and went in. My heart was bursting as I announced that I had a surprise. I got Mom and Dad to come to the front door, and then I switched on the porch light. There was our Christmas tree, with the snow glistening on its branches – our beautiful Christmas tree.

I had saved the day.

"Where did you get that tree?" my mother exclaimed. But it wasn't the kind of exclamation that indicates pleasure.

Forgiveness

♦

42

"I bought it up on Main Street. Isn't it just the most perfect tree you ever saw?" I said, trying to maintain my enthusiasm.

"Where did you get the money?" Her tone was accusing, and it began to dawn on me that this wasn't going to turn out as I had planned.

"From my paper route." I explained about the customer who had paid me.

"And you spent the *whole eight dollars* on this tree?" she exclaimed.

She went into a tirade about how stupid it was to spend my money on a dumb tree that would be thrown out and burned in a few days. She told me how irresponsible I was and how I was just like my dad with all those foolish, romantic, noble notions about fairy tales and happy endings and that it was about time I grew up and learned some sense about the realities of life and how to take care of money and spend it on things that were needed and not on silly things. She said that I was going to end up in the poorhouse because I believed in stupid things like Christmas trees, things that didn't amount to anything.

I just stood there. My mother had never talked to me like that before, and I just couldn't believe what I was hearing. I felt awful, and I began to cry. I didn't want to cry, but she was so angry, and her words were just pouring out in a stream that she couldn't seem to stop. Finally, she reached out and snapped off the porch light. "Leave it there," she said. "Leave that tree there 'till it rots, so every time we see it, we'll all be reminded of how stupid the men in this family are." Then she stormed up the stairs to her bedroom, and we didn't see her until the next day.

My dad tried hard to patch things up. He said that Mom wasn't feeling too good and made all kinds of excuses for her. He said that I shouldn't take what she said too seriously. He said it was just a bad time and that she would be better tomorrow –

but he was wrong –
she wasn't better.

He and I brought the tree in, and we made a stand for it. He got out the box of ornaments, and we decorated it as best we could; but men aren't too good at things like that, and besides, it wasn't the same without Mom. There were a few presents under it by Christmas day – although I can't remember a single one of them – but Mom wouldn't have anything to do with it. It was the worst Christmas I ever had. The happiest day of that season was the day after Christmas when Dad said he thought it would be best if we took the tree down. We *never* took our tree down until after New Year's day, but I didn't argue; I was glad to take it down and get it out of my sight. We

Forgiveness

♦

43

burned it in the backyard. Mom never said any more about it – good or bad – but it was a scar on my soul,

and I never forgot.

Judi and I married in August of 1963, and Dad died on October 10 of that year. Over the next seven years, we lived in many places. Mom sort of divided up the year – either living with my sister Jary or with us. In 1971 we were living in Wichita, Kansas – Lincoln was about seven, Brendan was three, and Kristen was a baby. Mom was staying with us during the holidays. On Christmas Eve I stayed up very late. Mom, Judi, and the kids had long since gone to bed with visions of sugar plums dancing in their heads. I was sitting in the living room staring into the blinking lights on our tree and reading Matthew's account of the birth of Jesus. I looked at all of the presents and relived all the Christmases of my past. I was totally alone with my thoughts, alternating between joy and melancholy, and I got to thinking about my paper route, that tree, what my mother had said to me, and how dad had tried to make things better.

I heard a noise in the kitchen and discovered that it was Mom. She couldn't sleep either and had got up to make herself a cup of hot tea – which was her remedy for just about everything. As she waited for the water to boil, she walked into the living room and discovered me there. She didn't say much for a while – she just sat and gazed at the tree, the blinking lights, and all the presents – many of which were from her to our children. She saw my open Bible and asked me what I was reading. When I told her, she asked if I would read it to her, and I did.

"This is how the birth of Jesus Christ came about."

"Read it to me out of the King James," she said. This was no time to argue the merits of translations, and besides, I like to read out of the King James, myself, sometimes. I went and got my King James and read,

"Now the birth of Jesus Christ was on this wise."

I saw her nod of affirmation at the familiar words. "That's better," she said – *and it was, you know.*

"And they will call His name Immanuel –
which means – God with us."

When the kettle began to whistle, she went and made her tea. She came back, and we started to visit. I told her how happy I was that she was with us for Christmas and how I wished that Dad could have lived to see his grandchildren and to enjoy this time because he always loved Christmas so. It got very quiet for a moment, and then she said, "Do you remember that

Forgiveness

♦

44

time on Twelve Mile Road when you bought that tree with your paper route money?"

"Yes," I said, "I've just been thinking about it." She hesitated for a long moment, as though she were on the verge of something that was bottled up so deeply inside her soul that it might take surgery to get it out. Finally, great tears started down her face, and she cried,

"Oh son, please forgive me.

"That time and that Christmas have been a burden on my heart for twenty-five years. I wish your dad were here so I could tell him how sorry I am for what I said. Your dad was a good man, and it hurts me to know that he went to his grave without ever hearing me say that I was sorry. Nothing will ever make what I said right, but you need to know that your dad never did have any money sense (which was all too true). We were fighting all the time — though not in front of you — we were two months behind on our house payments, we had no money for groceries, your dad was talking about going back to Arkansas, and that tree was the last straw. I took it all out on you. It doesn't make what I did right, but I hoped that someday, when you were older, you would understand. I've wanted to say something for ever so long, and I'm so glad it's finally out."

Well, we both cried a little and held each other, and I forgave her — *it wasn't hard, you know.* Then we talked for a long time, and I *did* understand; I saw what I had never seen, and the bitterness and sadness that had gathered up in me for all those years gradually washed away.

It was marvelously simple.

The great gifts of this season — or any season — can't be put under the tree; you can't wear them or eat them or drive them or play with them. We spend so much time on the *lesser gifts* — toys, sweaters, jewelry, the mint, anise, and dill of Christmas — and so little on *the great gifts* — the understanding, grace, peace, and *forgiveness.* It's no wonder that the holiday leaves us empty, because when it's over, the only reminders we have are the dirty dishes and the January bills.

The great gifts are like *the one gift* — the gift that began it all back there in Bethlehem of Judea. You can't buy them, and they're not on anybody's shopping list. They come as He came — quietly, freely, unexpectedly — and if you're not careful, you miss them entirely because the *want* list keeps you at the mall where the holiday sales, tinsel, background music, and glitter keep you from seeing the star over Bethlehem or hearing the angel's song.

Forgiveness

♦

"How silently, how silently, the wondrous gift is given!
So God imparts to human hearts the blessing of His heav'n.
No ear may hear His coming, but in this world of sin,
Where meek souls will,
receive Him still,
The dear Christ
enters in."
—"O Little Town of Bethlehem"

Forgiveness Is Good News

One of the classic contradictions that I face as a minister – especially in my counseling work – is created by the contact I have with two diametrically opposed classes of people. The first class is made up of those who have successfully rationalized and justified their sins. They have convinced themselves that they are good, decent, moral, upright citizens because they keep their grass mowed, their cars washed, support the Girl Scouts and Little League, and attend PTA. It is inconceivable to them that God could have any less of an opinion of them than they have of themselves, and so they feel little if any need for salvation or forgiveness. Disillusioning them is not only unpleasant, it is often impossible.

The second is their antithesis. These people are so overwhelmed by futility created by a growing sense of lostness – and what it means to be lost – so painfully aware of their sinfulness and culpability – that they despair over both God's ability and willingness to forgive them. "You just don't understand what I've done – what a wretched, miserable, low-life sinner I am," they say. There is far more hope for this second group than the first. Conviction of sin is evidence of the acceptance of the work of the Holy Spirit. My task with them is not only far more pleasant – because the gospel really is *good news* to them – it is far more successful.

I tell them that the gospel was not preached immediately following the flood when the people were new and true and few. It was preached in the course of an ongoing history. It was shouted in the noisy streets of the major centers of commerce to soldiers, lawyers, sorcerers, prostitutes, politicians, tradesmen, and merchants – to people who were exceedingly wicked. It was whispered in the quiet walkways of small towns and villages to slaves, grape growers, farmers, shepherds, fishermen, housewives, and church goers – to people

who were no less wicked,
but less spectacularly so.

Perhaps Paul's reminder to the Corinthian Christians that they had once been fornicators, idolaters, adulterers, homosexuals, thieves, drunkards, and swindlers gives us some indication of the types of folks who responded to the gospel.

The people who heard the gospel were adults – adults with a heritage – environmental, social, historical, and personal. That heritage was different in every community, nation, and individual, and yet the gospel had a neutralizing effect on all who responded. *The gospel did not snatch them from the realities of their past; it made the past inconsequential* – so Paul could simply wipe out ten million sins by saying –

"but you were washed."

Those folks had to find a way to live honestly with their past and a new way to live in the present. The gospel provided that way.

The gospel was intended to save the people of the first century. God did not have to wait two or three hundred years until some new generation could *get everything right* before He could save a few. Neither was the gospel to be preached to some select group who had providentially not messed up their lives to the point that salvation was at best *impractical* or at worst *impossible.* My first point is that the gospel has power to save – to save today, to save immediately, to bring assurance, forgiveness, sonship, and peace with God – none of which are predicated upon a person's ability or determination to begin immediately to go back and "make right" their history of sin.

That simply cannot be done.

My second point is so simple that I am almost embarrassed to write it. God really *wants* to save us. He genuinely loves us, and up to the point of violating our ability to choose, He has done everything possible to make redemption feasible for every person who seeks after it. This vital truth brings a whole new attitude toward God's teachings. God seeks our good, our happiness. He did not set up a diabolical scheme that promised hope and happiness and then create conditions so difficult or complex that no one would ever be able to attain it.

Anyone who really wants to be forgiven *can* be – the gospel has the power to do it. I am familiar with our Lord's statement that "The gate is small and the way is narrow that leads to life," and I am prepared to accept that statement at face value. I would only say that we need to examine *why* that is so. It is not because the type or accumulation of our sins is so massive and complex that redemption and forgiveness are impossible due to some deficiency in the cleansing power of the blood of Jesus. It is not because God's plan requires us to perform the Herculean task of *correcting* all of our past mistakes. It is because our pride is so great that we will not acknowledge our wretchedness, lostness, and helplessness; neither will we accept His grace.

> It is because
> our love affair with sin
> is so great
> that we will not
> give it up.

Evaluations

Several years ago I received a letter from the principal of the high school where I used to teach. When I taught there, he wasn't the principal – he was a teacher – he has since been *demoted* from the ranks of the *useful* to the *useless*. It is altogether too bad because he was a fine teacher, and I feel sorry for him. He wrote to say that a former student of mine had come to his office recently on a very painful mission and that the student had requested that he contact me concerning the subject of his visit. I never cease to be amazed at the providential workings of God.

This is the story:

Often, one of the most disconcerting aspects of teaching is *student evaluations.* They take place twice every year, somewhere near the end of each semester. The students are handed a form with questions on it, and they are asked to respond. The questions are of this nature:

1. The teacher was prepared: Sometimes. Rarely. Always.
2. The teacher graded fairly: Sometimes. Rarely. Always.
3. The work assignments were reasonable: Sometimes. Rarely. Always.
4. I received the grades I deserved: Sometimes. Rarely. Always.
5. The class was stimulating and enjoyable: Sometimes. Rarely. Always.

Students circle the most appropriate response and add comments if they wish. Most teachers try to act as if they don't care, and I suppose it's true that some don't –

but the good ones do –
they care a lot.

Good teachers await evaluation day with trepidation and anxiety because these student expressions are a critical factor in determining how successful they have been in some important areas. Student evaluations tell – more than anything else – if they *like you* and if they *respect you.* Both of those things – whether we want to admit it or not – have much to do with how *much* they learned and

how *well* they learned.

I have had my share of anxiety and some of it was *fully justified.* Students can be brutal. Some of them took a shot at me – and scored heavily. It's their one chance to *get even* – to settle old scores – and there will always be those who take full advantage. Sometimes you know it's coming – and you tell yourself that being *ripped* by that student is an honor; but even then it hurts, because it's a sure sign of failure – even though it may not be your fault.

I had a brilliant student once – his name was John. In my teaching career, spanning some twenty years, I have only had about eight or ten *brilliant* ones, so I remember them. Unlike many folks, I use the word *brilliant* very selectively so that the noun, adjective, or adverb form

retains some meaning.

What I'm saying is that some folks – particularly parents, politicians, and principals – apply the word *brilliant* to every kid they see. The consequence is that it means absolutely nothing. John was so far ahead of his classmates in every area that it was almost impossible to keep him busy, much less motivated. I tried very hard and felt that I had done reasonably well; but even

Forgiveness

♦

more than that, I thought I had established a solid personal relationship with him.

I thought we liked each other.

Not too long before evaluation time, I gave John a low grade on an essay test – at least it was low for him – I think it was a C. He was incensed – he *never* got a C. He told me that I had given much better grades to students who had done poorly compared to him. I explained that I expected much more from him than I did from some of the others and that since he had obviously put little effort into his paper, I had rewarded him accordingly. He said that I had no *right* to treat him differently – that it was *unfair.* I told him that I had *every right* to do so – that it was my *duty* and that he had given every indication that he *wanted* to be treated differently. And as for *fairness,* I wasn't too concerned with it, and if he expected to be treated *fairly* in the world, he was in for

a big surprise!

On the teacher evaluation form, he killed me – gave me the poorest marks possible, wrote derogatory comments, and even signed his name – which wasn't required. It really hurt me. I was a long time recovering, and even then, it left a sensitive scar on my soul that twinged

every time evaluations were due.

We never talked about it. He seemed determined to avoid me after that and never signed up for another of my classes. I felt that it would be inappropriate for me to approach him. A year later he graduated with the highest possible honors and went to college on an academic scholarship. He came back once or twice for some of the annual school events, and I would see him from a distance, and then I moved far away.

Seven years passed.

The principal told me that John had just walked into his office one day, completely unannounced, and told him the story of the evaluation. He said that it had burdened his heart during his entire college career and that it simply would not leave him. He said that every time he returned home, it was difficult for him to come back to his old school – so filled with happy memories – except for one that *plagued him* and kept him from enjoying the rest. He said that he had done a mean, despicable thing in a moment of anger – and now he wished to undo it, because he wouldn't sleep well or be at peace until it was off his mind and my record. He said that it probably wouldn't make any difference after so long – except to him and to me. He said that I had served him well – had told him the truth – which few people had done – and that he had learned a lot over the last seven years that had given him a different view on many things.

The evaluation was retrieved, and he wrote a new one. The young man left the principal's office greatly relieved, and I received the principal's letter with much gratitude.

Would you like to retrieve an evaluation you have written – perhaps in a moment of anger – and write a new one? Are there some shadows hanging over your life that you would like to clear away so that you may sleep peacefully? Have you resented someone for telling you the truth? In a lifetime of many happy memories are there a few bad ones that keep you from enjoying the others?

What keeps you from doing it? Is your pride so great that a lifetime of regret is worth more than a moment of humility?

May God forgive you.

Is it possible that you have learned some things since you made that evaluation – things that have changed your perspective? Maybe it was a *spoken* evaluation – or even a *mental* one. How much peace and joy could you bring to someone's life and to your own by retrieving it?

Don't think about it –
that will get you nowhere –
do it!
For the love of God –
do it!
For Jesus' sake –
do it!
For your dear family's sake and
for your own soul's sake –
do it!
Do it now!
Pick up the phone,
get some paper and pen and –
do it!

"Oh," you say, "I couldn't do that. You don't understand; it is much too complicated."

Is it that you cannot,
or is it that you
will not?

Forgiveness

♦

51

Forgiven

I have never seen it, and the story may be apocryphal, but I am told there is a grave in or near New York City with a marker that bears a singular inscription. It is one word –

Forgiven!

I am intrigued by the story, and my imagination is carried away with possible explanations for this mysterious reminder. The actual story may be far less interesting than those created by my fancy.

Who put it there, I ask? I am told the grave is very old. What was forgiven? Was it murder, adultery, betrayal? Surely it must have been some great wrong or series of wrongs to warrant such a foreboding – yet victorious – farewell. What kept him unforgiven 'till death? Was it because there was no penitence? Or perhaps the crime was so great that it separated the forgiver and the forgiven – either physically or emotionally – and no opportunity ever presented itself. The forgiver may have had such a hardened heart against the trespasser that only death brought the softening that allowed for it. Perhaps forgiveness was tendered, but the offender felt such a depth of guilt that it could not be accepted. The possibilities add to the mystery.

Looking at my life, taking it all in, I find so much that needs forgiveness. I think that when my time comes, I would like all those who knew me and loved me – and maybe especially those whom I offended and who perhaps didn't love me as much as either of us would have liked – to sort of get together and put a marker over me that said –

Forgiven.

I would like that. I'm sure we would all be better for it.

Oh yes, I know it would be so much better to do it while we are all alive, but I am not so naive as to hope that our *pride* will always allow for that. Sometimes the wrongs run too deep, the pain does not subside, and the sense of betrayal cannot be forgotten. Our Father knows the limitations of human forgiveness, and it is by His grace that death brings the final release.

If it were for no other reason,
death would be such a blessing to us.

And the burdens that are laid down in death are not only those of the deceased. No, at every funeral, all of us who pass by emit a sigh of relief and place gently in the coffin all the wrongs we have felt, and our tears wash forever away the burdens of the years as we write –

Forgiven
upon the memory in our heart.

Of course it is our Father who erects the final marker – who sets in place the stone and writes His final epitaph over those who are called to Him. Does He not stamp *Forgiven* on the life of all that are His? Is that not His final assessment?

By the power of the blood of My Son,
I declare this person –
Forgiven.

The Neighborhood Moochers

About two months ago, I was talking to a close relative of mine who still lives in the same area of Michigan where I was raised; he goes to church where my parents and I went. He asked me if I remembered a lady named Norma who had lived right down the street from them. It took me a moment to respond, because I remembered her *all too well,* but I finally managed a weak affirmation. He said that she had died a week or two earlier. I was sorry to hear it. Norma played a very important role in my growing up. She didn't plan to, God just providentially used her for that purpose. I suppose that since both she and my parents are gone, I ought to tell this story for my children and for yours. Although it is very embarrassing to me, I can tell it with a good heart and no one can be hurt by it but me.

When I was twelve, our family finances got so bad that we moved into a cabin in an old trailer park at the corner of Twelve Mile Road and Crooks Road. Originally these cabins had been built as the precursors of motels –

as a place for travelers to spend the night. As the town had spread out around them and travelers no longer came that way, the cabins fell into disuse, so the owners decided to rent them out by the month. My dad operated a Standard Oil gas station right across the street, so it was a convenient place for us to live.

I soon made friends with another boy in the trailer park named Don. In most ways, we had little in common. We were drawn together by our age, physical proximity, our mutual poverty, and our love for baseball.

We were baseball fanatics. We played at every opportunity, and when we couldn't find a game, we played catch in the trailer park. When dark came, we would play catch near the office lights of the trailer park until the residents got tired of the noise of the ball splatting in our gloves and drove us off. Then we would go and peruse our baseball cards. We had hundreds of them. We knew the names, positions, batting averages, and ERAs of every Detroit Tiger player.

When the neighborhood kids played, it was sort of understood that we would take turns supplying a ball. Don and I never did supply because we never had a decent ball, and our friends constantly reminded us of the fact. They called us the

neighborhood moochers.

When we showed up to play, they would say, *"Here come the neighborhood moochers."* For those of you who may not know the word *moocher* – it's another way of calling a person a *bum* or *beggar.*

Don and I would go to the high school field and spend long hours on Saturday looking for stray balls. The ones we found were always in sorry condition. The stitches were frayed or loose, and the covers were torn. We tried to hide *a multitude of sins* with black electrical tape, but the results were very dissatisfying.

We began to talk about how great it would be to see the looks on our friends' faces if we showed up with a brand new ball – especially a *Reach.* That was the kind the Tigers played with. They had them at Montgomery Ward, but they were $2.75 and might as well have been $100. But we couldn't get it out of our minds or our conversation. We didn't like to be called *bums* or *moochers* by our friends. We would walk to Royal Oak and go to Montgomery Ward to look at the baseballs. We would pick up the display model and lovingly caress the smooth, white, horsehide cover, finger the flawless red stitching, admire the dark blue "Reach" printed on the side and imagine ourselves hitting home runs and throwing blazing fast balls.

Forgiveness

♦

It would not have occurred to me to steal one –
at least not seriously.

My home life and religious training had created inhibitions far too deep for that. *But Don was not religious,* and the only reservations he had were limited to the possibilities of getting caught. He mentioned it often. I would not consider it. Then he made a suggestion that allowed me to rationalize my reserves. He said that he would actually steal the ball, I would only divert the sales clerk. I thought that I could do that, so I went along –

but I knew better.

Forgiveness

♦

55

I did my job. I diverted the sales clerk by pretending to be interested in some article far away from the baseballs. Don had on a jacket, and he slipped the ball underneath his jacket and under his armpit and walked out of the store. In a couple of minutes, I followed. As I made my way up the stairs, I heard a familiar female voice call my name. I turned, and there stood Norma, a lady who went to church with us.

She asked me to come back down and talk to her. I didn't want to, but I went. She asked me what I was doing at the store. I was so flustered and nervous that I couldn't say anything. She told me that she was a store detective and that she had seen Don take the baseball and knew that I had helped him. I tried at first to explain the harmlessness of my involvement, but it was no use – I was just as guilty as Don, and

we both knew it.

There are no words to adequately describe all the feelings that poured over me in a moment of time – what this would mean to my family, the church, my friends. She told me to go and get Don and to bring him and the ball back.

He was standing outside, flushed with excitement because we had *gotten away with it.* When I told him we hadn't, he wanted to run. He said no one could catch us, but

I knew there was no place
for me to run to.

I told him we had to go back. He wouldn't go – but he gave me the ball and said I could go back if I wanted to, and he took off.

Like a sheep to the slaughter, I went back. I told Norma that Don had run away. She said that she didn't care about him, but she just couldn't understand how I could do such a thing. *I didn't understand it either.* I really didn't, because I didn't know much about sin and how it creeps up on a person, how it takes advantage of every weakness and exploits every desire until we find a way of doing it that doesn't seem so bad. We talked for a long time, and I cried – she did too. I wondered what she was going to do with me.

When we finished talking, she just sat sort of hunched over with her chin resting in her hand. She looked at me for a long time – like she was having trouble making up her mind. She finally straightened up and sighed, a great, big, long one – like she had been holding her breath for about ten minutes – which let me know she had made up her mind. She reached out and took me by my chin, and she held my face right up to hers and made me look straight into her eyes, and she said,

"Johnny, you go home,
and don't you ever let me catch you
in this store without your parents,
ever again.
This will stay
between the two of us."

I don't remember ever going back into Montgomery Ward ever again –

not even with my parents.

If they went there to shop, I made some excuse to stay outside, and I still don't shop at Montgomery Ward without looking over my shoulder for Norma. When I think of *forgiveness,* of the inexpressible delight there is in pardon, I think of that experience.

Now I have grown older and much more discreet about stealing baseballs. My justifications and rationalizations are much more elaborate. But it always ends up the same way. I hear a familiar voice calling my name, and that rush of confusion, guilt, and shame comes over me, because I know I am caught once again. I hear that voice say, "What are you doing in this store?" And at first I try to explain the harmlessness of my involvement. I give all of the standard excuses, but it's no good –

we *both* know.

"Did you think you could get away with that?
When are you going to learn?
I saw you do it."

And then we talk, and I cry – so does He – and I wonder what He's going to do with me. It's not jail this time, not a criminal record, it's not my reputation or the church, or even my family that I'm worried about – no, this is the big one – *I could go to hell for this!* He sits hunched over in his chair, his head resting in his hand, and he looks at me as though he's trying to make up his mind. Finally, he straightens up and lets out a sigh – a big one – and I know He's made up His mind. He reaches out and takes me by the chin, and He makes me look straight into his eyes and he says –

"Johnny, I forgive you;
go home.
And don't you ever
let me catch you in this store again –
unless *I'm* with you."

Forgiveness

♦

THREE

Kindness

Have you ever noticed how much of the recorded life of Jesus was spent doing kind things? It occurs to me that His first miracle, turning the water to wine at Cana of Galilee, was generated out of kindness. He had no ulterior motives. It was not a deed done to prove anything or to place people under obligation; He did it simply and naturally because He had the power to do it, He was concerned for people's feelings, and He wanted to save His host from embarrassment.

We live in a culture where kindness is often deprecated as weakness. It does not fit the image of success that we wish to portray. Those who practice kindness are labeled as suckers and are thought of as being out of touch with reality.

Jesus spent a great deal of his time simply showing concern for others. His compassion for the multitudes, scattered like sheep with no shepherd, was born out of kindness. When he looked into the eyes and heart of an angry, exasperated, and troubled housewife, his words, "Martha, Martha, you are troubled about many things," are not words spoken harshly or in rebuke. They are words of kindness that reflect his understanding and concern for her concern.

In no area do we fail more to be like Jesus than in our relationships with each other. As you travel your road, remember that the only way any of us is going to make it "to the end of the way" is if we help one another. Remember kindness. Only God knows how much division, anger, divorce, strife, and ill will could be avoided if we but practice the simple art of

kindness.

ALABAMA CHRISTIAN
ACADEMY
MRS SMITH
GRADE 1
1989 1990

The World Is at War

I visited an elementary school today. I hadn't been in one for a long time. I had been asked to speak to the first through fifth grades — which is a frightening thing. What does an adult say to children? I decided I could talk to them about *kindness*. When I walked in, they were coming from their classrooms to the area where I would address them.

I thought they were much different than I was when I was small. Their dress, their hair, their speech — what they talked about was different. Then I remembered that when I was their age — *the world was at war.* We overheard our parents talking in hushed, serious tones about war news — the possibility of an attack upon our mainland — what would happen if the British were forced to surrender.

The son of the people up the street had been killed — a boy who had played ball with me, who was as familiar and as real to me as our lilac bushes. They said that he had died in some far-off mysterious place called the Philippines. Our teacher showed it to us on the map. It was just a tiny speck of a place in the middle of the ocean — and I wondered how Ervin had got there from our street and how it was possible for him to be dead — and what that word meant. When I asked if he had died because he was sick, they told me that he was shot by a Japanese person, and I wondered why a Japanese would do that — was he mad at Ervin? The war affected even us small ones.

I was glad for these kids that their world was not at war — that the frightening shadow of impending national disaster did not hang over them and darken their thoughts. But then it occurred to me — right there — that I was wrong: *we are at war.* It is a war that poses a far greater threat to the well being of our children than Hitler's S.S. troops ever posed. It is a conflict that is more sinister than fascism or communism, because it is less ominous in appearance and *makes war upon the will* — upon eternal principles and moral foundations — not simply our bodies. It is a war that rages every day, closer and closer to the center of our vitality, our homes, and our families. It is a war against

the enemy within —
the god of self.

I was shaken from this reverie by a little kid who was standing in front of me, looking straight up, asking me something. As he looked me over, I looked him over, and I noticed immediately that one of his tennis shoes was untied and that his zipper was about half open. His hair needed combing, but there was nothing wrong with his smile, in spite of the tooth that was missing.

He looked me over real good, starting at my boots and proceeding to my receding hairline (actually my hairline used to recede; now it doesn't exist).

"Hey Mister, how come you got boots on?" It wasn't impertinence, just friendly curiosity.

"Because I come from Texas, and I like boots," I said.

"I don't wear boots, they're for *old* people. I wear Reeboks."

"Well, good for you," I said, a little perturbed. "I used to wear Reeboks, but now I wear Nikes."

"Oh," he said, obviously impressed. "What's your name?"

"John. What's yours?"

"Well, my name's Richard, but nobody ever calls me that except when they're mad."

"What do they call you?"

"R. J. My middle name's Jerome, so they call me R. J. What are you doing here? Are you somebody's dad?"

"Well, yes I am, but not in this school. I wish I was somebody's dad in this school. I came to speak to you this morning."

"Oh! I sure hope you talk so I can understand you. I didn't understand a word the last two men said."

He turned to take a seat, and I smiled when I noticed that when he had stuffed his shirt down in his pants, he had wadded it inside his underwear. You could see the "Fruit of the Loom" label on his underwear because they were wrong-side-out. "God bless you, R. J.," I murmured under my breath. "I pray to God that I do talk so you can understand me, and I hope that what I have to say

will be worth remembering."

My first impression, when I saw them all sitting there in front of me, eagerly awaiting what I had to say, was how small they were. My second impression was that I wondered how long it would be before they lost their eagerness and innocence −

a long time, I hoped.

Maybe they haven't changed too much after all. Given any kind of chance − and treated with *kindness* − they will grow into decent human beings and be able to turn their world into a respectable place where

kindness is a virtue
and not a weakness.

Kindness

♦

64

I wonder if we will give them that chance. Or will we go on sacrificing them on the altars of divorce and broken homes to satiate that monster that lives within us – that monster called

self actualization?

⚜

Wasted Time

When I think of Jim, I think of some classic lines from an old Jim Croce song –

"Yea, he big and dumb as a man can come,
But he stronger than a country hoss,
And when the bad folks all get together at night
You know, they all call Big Jim, 'Boss.'"

Jim was big, very big, and he was tough, but he wasn't mean. He would never sucker-punch a guy, and he didn't go looking for trouble – he didn't have to –

it came to him.

He was painfully slow of mind. He sat in the back corner of my ninth-grade English classroom – sullen, resentful, silent. He never answered a question, never turned in a paper, never took a test, never opened his book, and only when I occasionally departed from the lesson to tell a story did I ever notice a flicker of interest.

Jim loved stories.

He would have his head down on his desk – to all appearances either asleep or bored out of his mind – but when a story began, his head came up, and his eyes never left me. He wasn't hard to like, and after the first few weeks – when his well deserved suspicion toward educators had subsided – he would sort of wander into my room during lunch and after school. The first time he came in, I was quite surprised, and I asked, "Did you forget something, Jim?"

"Oh – no," he said. I waited, expecting him to say why he was there. He said nothing; he just shuffled his feet nervously and stared into space.

"Was there something you needed Jim?"

"No, I just wondered what you were doing."

"I'm grading papers and doing lesson plans."

"Oh – you mind if I watch?"

"Not at all. Would you like to have a seat?"

"Oh – no. You mind if I just stand here by the desk?"

"No, not at all. But if you'd like, you can drag up a chair."

And so the pattern was set. Jim came in regularly and sat by my desk and watched as I prepared for the next day. He rarely said anything. Sometimes we would talk about sports or girls or school things. I couldn't help but wonder at the loneliness, emptiness, and confusion in his life that drove him to spend his afternoons in this way. Occasionally, he would ask why I had marked something wrong or what we were going to do the next day in class. I tried finding things for him to do – like cleaning the chalkboards, arranging the desks, or emptying the trash cans. He was so eager to help – to make some contribution, to involve himself in the educational process – that it was heartbreaking.

> I got interested in Jim.
> I wondered if I could
> teach him something.

I went to the curriculum lab at the University of Michigan and located some stories with second- and third-grade-level vocabulary and teen-level plots and interest. I brought the books to my classroom. I told Jim that I wanted to determine if the books were appropriate for his grade level and that I would take it as a favor if he would read them and give me his opinion. He read them during class. *Reading was hard work for Jim.* I watched him, sitting in his corner, laboring over the pages, scowling, lips moving, mouthing words, sometimes spelling them out. Sometimes he got so involved in a story that he would laugh out loud at what amused him or mutter his angry disapproval at what he didn't like. If any of his classmates said anything about his reactions, one look from Jim would freeze them into silence.

Every now and then, during some lull, he would approach my desk rather casually, place the book before me, and point to a word.

"What word is that, Mr. Smith?"

"Why that's *thought*, Jim."

Kindness

♦

66

"Are you sure? It don't look like *thought.*"

"Yes, Jim, I'm sure. You see, some words aren't spelled like they sound. *Thought* is one of them. I know that t-h-o-u-g-h-t doesn't look right; you just have to memorize it."

One snowy day, I had much work to do after school. Most of the kids had long since gone home. Jim came in. We spoke – the normal type stuff. He didn't stand by my desk or drag up a chair; he went to his seat in the corner. He was silent, but I knew something was bothering him. I went on with my paper grading and lesson preparation. After a while, Jim asked if he might read one of the books I had bought for him. I took one out and gave it to him. He stood by my desk, slowly thumbing the pages.

"You bought these just for me, didn't you?" I don't know if he had figured it out or if someone had told him.

"Yes Jim, I bought them just for you."

"Why?"

"Because I thought you might enjoy them and learn to read better."

"Don't waste your time on me. I ain't worth it. I can't learn nothin'."

"I haven't *wasted my time,* Jim, and you can learn. Maybe not like some of the other kids, but you can learn, and I believe you're worth it. I bought the books because I like you and I wanted you to know that I think you're important."

I know that I have wasted much time. I could waste even more, grieving over lost years and wasted opportunities, but I wasn't wasting my time on Jim. I don't believe that Jesus ever thought His time was wasted – not even on Judas Iscariot or Simon the Pharisee.

Any time spent in His name,
any gift extended in love –
because He has loved us –
any act of kindness done –
because He has been so kind to me –
is never wasted.

Getting an A

Jim's wood shop teacher was named Simons. He was a fine man who gave much of himself to his students. *He had little to work with*. The school district had no funds to repair and maintain the few woodworking machines he had, much less to update them with modern equipment. They were reluctant to purchase the supplies necessary to complete even the simplest project. They argued that the kids would either steal them or use them for purposes other than that for which they were intended – and there was some validity to their arguments. The students had no money to buy their own, so Mr. Simons was left with no equipment, no wood, and thirty or forty tough kids to teach.

The shop room was in the basement of the building. It was a large, gloomy, dismal, damp, half-lit, coal-bin of an affair. Mr. Simons found some five-gallon buckets of army surplus paint on sale for practically nothing and decided that he would challenge the boys with renovating the shop room itself. It was a grand idea, and the boys took to it. They replaced lights, fixed gaping holes in the ceilings, wire-brushed the cement walls, filled in cracks, mopped the floors, and then began the glorious task of painting. Jim absolutely delighted in it. He had found his niche – something he could do. He came in before school to paint and stayed after school. He worked during his lunch hour and would have come on Saturdays if anyone would have let him in.

It was his only successful school experience.

At the end of the first marking period, Mr. Simons gave Jim an A. It was an act of kindness, and Jim needed kindness. He was the happiest kid imaginable. The beaming look on his face, the pride in his voice when he brought his card to me – pointing to the grade – produced both laughter and tears. How could anything so simple produce such joy? An A – the only one he had ever had in nine years of school and the only one he was ever likely to get. He showed it to every teacher, and we all rejoiced with him.

The next morning before class, I witnessed the following scene in the hallway. It was early; few students had arrived. My room was just a short way down and across the hall from the school office. I heard some rather loud voices coming from the office area and stepped to my door to investigate.

Mr. Simons, his back to the lockers, was being confronted by a very large woman who towered over him. She had her left hand firmly planted on his shoulder, pinning him to the wall; her right hand was waving a report card, rather threateningly, before his nose. Her voice was harsh and strong. It was Jim's mother.

"Don't you never give my son no A in this school. My son is too stupid to get an A," she shouted.

I was in total sympathy with Mr. Simons. He was absolutely helpless, embarrassed. A crowd was gathering, and he wanted to avoid any further agitation.

"Mrs.____, Jim deserved an A in my class, and I gave it to him. If you don't like it, you take that card and put whatever grade you want on it."

It was a brilliant thing to say.

When Jim came to class, he was more sullen and withdrawn than ever. Hopelessness was written all over him. What an incredible change from the Jim who had been so enthusiastic about his first A. My heart ached for him. He would never live down the scene his mother had created. He couldn't fight everybody, and his classmates hounded him unmercifully. I tried to spare him; I pleaded with the kids, but it did little good.

Could you find a way to give someone an A today? Maybe just because they need it and because it is in your power to give it.

It wouldn't cost you much,
and the return is the best
this world affords.

The Difference

It's funny how one memory leads to another. As I was writing the two previous stories, I was reminded of another teaching experience with Jim. The school I taught in was very old. It had fourteen-foot ceilings and huge windows. The kids who attended this ghetto school were tough, and they were extremely poor. Maybe that's how they got so tough. Christmas has always been my favorite holiday, and I determined that this year I was going to try to make it special for my kids.

I got permission from my principal, and I bought a Christmas tree. It was a blue spruce. It was twelve feet tall, and it must have been eight or ten feet in circumference. I got two of the boys, Jim and Chris, to help me drag it in and build a stand for it. We put it right in the middle of our classroom. For two or three days, *school* was going to take a back seat. I asked the kids to bring one ornament from home – approximately 120 in all. I was surprised at the variety. Some were homemade, but many were new and cheap – obviously something that they had purchased for the occasion – which meant they probably didn't have any at home.

Kindness

♦

70

Even at this time of year, they were ready to fight at the drop of a hat. If somebody put their ornament where somebody else wanted theirs, they would fight. If somebody knocked one off, there was sure to be a fight. If somebody didn't bring one – or brought two – there was a fight. It was a frustrating time for me, because I wanted Christmas to bring them together – to teach them kindness –

like it's supposed to.

When the tree was finished, I spent one whole school day, each period, trying to explain about Christmas – what it meant to me and what I thought it ought to be like. I told them that it was against school policy to read the Bible in class, but if they had no objections, I was going to do it anyway. When they found out it was contrary to school policy

they insisted that it must be read.

On Wednesday I read the gospel accounts of Jesus' birth, and I also began reading *A Christmas Carol,* by Charles Dickens. I could sense that they liked it, *although they dared not show it.* On Thursday I continued reading Dickens each period until my voice was nearly gone. Many of them were moved. I could tell it. In Jim's class, one of the girls began to cry when it appeared that Tiny Tim was going to die – not loudly, but someone noticed and ridiculed her.

"Hey, look, Brenda's crying."

"I am not," she sobbed, "and I'll smash your face if you say I am."

Jim stood up and grabbed the boy who had spoken by the shirt collar. He jerked him out of his seat and held him with his feet about six inches off the floor.

"You shut your filthy big mouth. Let her cry if she wants to. I might cry myself, and if I do, you'd better start crying, too, or I'll give you something real personal to cry about. Now, I'm gonna hear the rest of this story, and I mean to hear it without no stops." (He meant interruptions.)

The story went on, and there were no interruptions. I believe they came to love Tiny Tim and Bob Crachitt for the same reason they had loved the story of Jesus' birth. He was poor and they were poor, and he was oppressed – the underdog – and they saw themselves as oppressed, as always being the underdogs – *and they were.* For all their toughness, Jesus and Tiny Tim melted them. They had never had the chance to be children, and when Tiny Tim recovered and Scrooge was humbled, they laughed and clapped their hands and were very pleased.

I believe it made them kinder, gentler with each other. And why shouldn't it? It has done so for me and for a million others. We were not so different – them and me – a few dollars, some social graces, verbal skills, and age.

Kindness

♦

71

> The real difference
> was Jesus.

On Sensitivity

She was a part-time clerk, hired for the Christmas rush. She was nineteen – maybe – a college freshman home for the holidays. She was trying to earn a few dollars to buy some gifts and maybe have a little left to take back to school. She was small, unsure of herself, unfamiliar with the computerized cash register, and very vulnerable. She didn't know where layaway was, or the catalog department. Her department manager was gone on break, and she was surrounded by a growing circle of impatient, demanding, querulous people who all wanted a piece of her simultaneously.

The person confronting her was a rather tall, large, angular woman dressed in a stylish –

> but old-stylish manner.

"You advertised this item on sale; I'd like to know where it is." The tone was accusing and caustic.

The clerk – eyes bent to the floor, gnawing her lower lip – replied, "Honestly Ma'am, I don't know. If you'll just wait for the department head to return, I'm sure he can help you."

The angular lady, sensing her superiority over the subdued clerk got a little louder. "I have no time to wait on department heads! When *you* advertise an item, *you* should have it. Why don't *you* know where it is? *You* work here, don't *you?*"

The clerk, visibly shaken, nearing tears, said, "Yes, Ma'am, but I just started here yesterday, and they moved me to this department this morning, and I just don't know – and if you'd just be patient – I – "

"Patient!" The angular woman interrupted. *"Patient!"* She repeated. "My dear little *know-nothing.* I marvel at your generation of *sniveling, quiver-lipped, spineless, apologizers!* When I was your age, Miss, I had two children. I hoed, picked, cooked, cleaned, washed, mended, fixed – and you can't even tell me where the mixer bowls are!"

Feeling guilty for having watched so long, I mustered my best smile and stepped forward, right between the clerk and the angular lady.

"Hi," I said.

I was really trying to sound cheerful and reassuring. Much to my chagrin, the little clerk looked into my beaming face, filled with holiday goodwill, and she dissolved into tears. The angular lady harrumped and stormed off with a parting, "Well, I never!"

The rest of the crowd – some sheepishly, some indignantly – melted away when it became obvious that their needs were not going to be met. I was left alone with a sobbing salesclerk.

"Why can't they be more kind?" she sobbed. "Why can't they understand? I try so hard to be pleasant and kind, and they just step on me."

I reflect on that scene, and it occurs to me that the angular lady was probably telling the truth about herself. I'll bet she really did all of those things – and the world is a better place because of people like her – but it didn't give her the right to shatter the delicate framework of this girl's personality. It's probably true that kids are more fragile today. Their environment has made them so. Both their mental and emotional constitutions lack the decisiveness, discipline, and sturdiness of earlier generations. They break more easily; they give in more quickly; they lack that sense of personal identity that gives both direction and assurance. It does occur to me that what the angular lady – and much of the crowd who supported her – was missing was

humility

and the kindness and sensitivity that seems always to accompany it.

Must we always purchase our victories,

affirm our superiority,

at the expense of

someone else's dignity?

The holidays present so many opportunities to teach lasting lessons and create sustaining memories that, if they had no other value, that alone would justify their existence. In all of the preparation, traveling, shopping, bargain hunting, wrapping, card sending, office partying, and insanity that surrounds the Christmas season, don't rush past what's important. Let's be sure that the kindness — the *peace on earth and goodwill toward men* — that we extend during this holiday includes the paper boy, postal clerks, Salvation Army bell ringers, other drivers, and

sales clerks.

Kindness

♦

73

The Good Samaritan

I want to tell you a story about the Good Samaritan and kindness. That story is rather short. The preliminary to that story is much longer than the story about kindness. If you want to skip this part, go ahead; but I warn you that you will not appreciate the part about the Good Samaritan if you do.

Lubbock, Texas, doesn't have much of a reputation for rainfall — actually,

Lubbock, Texas, doesn't have much of a reputation!

I think the original settlers of West Texas were condemned murderers who chose to live there rather than be hanged. Many of them later regretted their decision and hung one another. Their children simply don't know any better and assume that most other places are either equally bad or

nowhere near as good.

The average annual precipitation is about nine inches — *in a wet year* — and that's not so bad except that invariably it all comes between 10:00 and 10:30 A.M. on the seventeenth of October. Actually, I guess you could say that it rains more often, but *it never hits the ground,* so it doesn't count. The reason it doesn't hit the ground is that the wind blows so hard in West Texas that it rains horizontally — you get to see the rain go by — and if you're tall enough, you get to *feel* it — although *feeling* it is very dangerous, because several people have lost their lives by having their bodies riddled with wind-driven rain. Eventually, the rain falls in Louisiana where the wind is slowed by the hills and trees, which are the first obstacles it meets.

When I lived in West Texas, I was a preacher — and no place ever needed preaching worse — and no place was ever so hard to preach in. The reason is that the whole Christian system rests on the concept of the resurrection, of life after death, and the judgment of God. But in West Texas, ideas of heaven and hell don't have much meaning. They simply can't conceive of heaven as Scripture describes it. In the Bible it's a place with rivers, trees, and walls. Folks in West Texas have never seen rivers and trees, and the idea of walls, or being closed in or not able to see, gives them claustrophobia. In West Texas *you can see* — you can see a rattlesnake coiled up on a rock forty miles away. And you can tell if it's a western diamondback, a coon tail, or a mojave green.

West Texans sit on their back porches — although just why they have back porches is a mystery — you can see the same thing from the front porch or the side porch or the basement, for that matter. They sit there with out-of-state visitors and say with wonder, "Just look at *that!*" And the guests stare intently toward the horizon — which is broken only by a solitary, leaning fence post from which dangles an even more solitary piece of broken barbed wire. "That *what?*" says the puzzled guest. "Why *that!*" says the exasperated West Texan, moving his arm in a broad sweeping gesture to which he adds another emphatic, *"That!"* The poor guest stares until his eyes water, searching for the "that," but "that" can only be seen by a practiced eye, an eye that has been trained for many years and, over those years, has come to believe that there really is a "that" to be seen. Now I hope you can understand why a West Texan shakes his head in dismay when a preacher tries to motivate his audience to righteous living by holding out the promise of heaven, because

he doesn't want to go there.

It's even worse when it comes to hell. West Texans have no trouble visualizing hell, and the more a preacher describes it in biblical terms, the more a West Texan will smile and nod his head in agreement. The problem is that after living in West Texas,

hell sounds pretty inviting –

in fact –

it sounds like a nicer version of home.

Threatening a West Texan with hell is like threatening a dieting person with

a box of chocolates.

Kindness

75

The first year I lived in Lubbock, Texas, on the seventeenth of October, at approximately 9:45 A.M. – totally unaware of the impending disaster – I was about to leave my office with the intent of running some errands. They never tell the secret of the rain to newcomers, because it's one of the *local initiation rites.* I must say, however, that my secretary tried to warn me –

in her own way.

As I was going out the door she said,

"You do know what *date* this is, don't you?"

"Certainly," I said, "It's Tuesday."

"No," she said – with that trace of annoyance in her voice that says some people are just too stupid to be helped – "I don't mean what *day,* I mean what *date!*"

"No," I said. "I don't know what date it is; is it important?"

She leaned across her desk and whispered in a tone indicating that she was about to reveal a great secret. "I should hope to tell you it's important," she said.

"Oh really," I said, trying to figure out if I had missed an important date – like my anniversary or the opening day of pheasant season or maybe even Easter.

"It's October *seventeenth!*"

"So what am I supposed to know about October seventeenth?" I asked with some interest.

"Well," she said, obviously disgusted with my obtuseness, "if you don't know, you just can't expect people to tell you everything – but don't say you weren't warned." And with that, she clammed up. I mean it; I couldn't get another word out of her.

That's why I was out running some errands when the deluge hit. It came totally without warning. I did notice that the wind speed had increased to eighty-two mph and that there were *two* clouds in the sky. When the first drops hit my windshield, I stopped and got out. I thought someone was throwing apples at my car. No, it was raining. It was raining the biggest drops of water I had ever seen. Maybe God had made a mistake – either that or the fire department had opened the top of every fire hydrant in town.

Within moments, the streets were flooded. Because there is no place for water to run *to* in Lubbock, the streets just fill up, and then the playa lakes fill up, then the yards fill up, and then the houses fill up, and when the water is seven feet deep, the *cap rock* (the subterranean rock formation that West Texas sits on) *tilts* – and all the water runs off the edge and down to the Brazos river, to Post and then to Snyder and eventually to the Rio Grande.

I used to hear people describe torrential downpours by saying, "It was like pouring clabbered milk out of a jug." I have never had the pleasure or the experience of doing that – pouring clabbered milk out of a jug, I mean – and I'm not absolutely sure what "clabbered milk" is, but it doesn't sound too pleasant, and I will gladly forego any opportunity to do so which might present itself – but I always thought it was a neat saying, and I think that this particular rainfall would deserve that description –

"It was like pouring clabbered milk out of a jug."

There is a low place in Lubbock, Texas, on Avenue P (low is a relative term, especially in Lubbock, Texas) where water collects, and on this day, the water was very deep. The low spot is designated by a *historical marker* – because, dearly beloved, it's a historical spot. The marker explains that this spot was originally a *Buffalo Wallow* (a hollowed out place caused by millions of buffalo taking a mud bath there), and it has been carefully preserved for posterity.

You must understand the mind-set of West Texas people in order to understand what happened next. *First,* you must understand that they only see rain once a year, and when it comes it sort of unnerves them. *Second,* you must understand that living in West Texas over a period of years does something to a person's mind – it creates an adversary relationship with the elements. In West Texas –

the weather is your enemy.

West Texans have suffered so much at the hands of the weather gods that they are defiant. When the weather presents some new outrage, they grit their teeth, shake their fists at the sky, and go a little insane. You can't let the weather beat you – if you do, you have to leave West Texas.

I sincerely hope that you have enjoyed and appreciated this little preliminary to my story, and I'm also sure that you are wondering about what all of this has to do with the Good Samaritan. Don't lose heart, there is a connection, and I'm getting to it right now.

As I approached the Buffalo Wallow on Avenue P, I was driving my four-wheel drive Ford Bronco, so the historic low spot didn't present a problem for me. There was already one car, about a quarter of the way through the wallow, stalled in about sixteen inches of water. There were two cars in front of me. The first ignored the stalled car and went around it, proceeding valiantly, but died just past it. The lady driving the second car stuck her arm out the window, shook her clenched fist at the water, veered to the left around the two stalled cars, accelerated madly, and made a heroic effort. I thought her momentum might carry her through, but her car disappeared under a wall of water and then succumbed to the elements.

As I drove cautiously around the stalled vehicles, I noticed that the lady in the last car was very elderly. I quickly pulled in behind her with some chivalrous notion of helping her out of her predicament. Much to my surprise, just as I pulled up behind her, she got out with her dress hiked up, her shoes in her hand, and a newspaper over her head. When she opened the car door, the water – at least two feet deep – filled her car to that level. The rapidly rushing, muddy water was swirling angrily around her legs and I feared for her. It was raining sheets. I rolled down my window and shouted, "Can I help you?"

"Not from there," she responded rather crisply.

It had not occurred to me that I might actually have to get out in this weather. A little taken back, I quickly removed my shoes and socks, rolled up my trousers, and went to her assistance. Taking her by the arm, we began the slow, unsteady process of going to the curb. *I was quickly reminded of how long it had been since I had gone barefooted.* Every pebble felt like a chunk of glass. I had visions of severe lacerations, contusions, stitches, and transfusions. I jumped and danced and emitted various unheroic noises to indicate pain. That old woman never quivered. She must have had leprosy of the foot or else calluses a half-inch thick.

"Are you all right, Sonny?" She said with genuine concern in her voice.

"Yes ma'am, I'm fine, E-E-E-O-O-I-W-C-H." (That's a free translation of the original tongue.)

We made it to the sidewalk, and she assured me that her house was right around the corner and that she would make it home just fine. I was much relieved to hear it. The thought of getting further from my car in my bare feet brought tears to my eyes.

Being a good Samaritan can get a little sticky. I like the idea – but I would much prefer to do it under more convenient circumstances. I don't want to lose time – get my hands dirty – my clothes messed up – spend any money – or get personally involved.

Finding chances to be a good Samaritan
with that criteria –
severely limits my opportunities.

I honestly am much more sympathetic with the priest and the Levite who "passed by on the other side" than I have ever been before. It was obvious that to render assistance was simply going to involve

too much hassle.

Being a Good Samaritan
isn't all it's cracked up to be.
Preaching about kindness is all right –
but *doing* it is a different story.

Kindness

♦

FOUR

Providence

Providence is one of the ever present aspects of God's grace that helps us bear life's toils. Nothing brings more despair into our lives than the fatalistic notion that "what will be will be" – that there is absolutely nothing that can change, stop, or prevent the wheels of unrelenting time and circumstance. Nothing makes the cross of life harder to bear than the idea that my life is a leaf cast adrift on the current of a great river, borne irresistibly toward a predetermined and unalterable end.

Providence is the supernatural intervention of God in the affairs of this world to bring about his will in our lives. When things happen that we cannot rationally or logically explain, we normally call it "luck," "chance," "fate," "fortune," "coincidence," or even "Mother Nature." We don't know what any of those terms mean, but they give us the comfort of having a name for something that is beyond our comprehension – much like saying that an unexplained illness is due to a virus. They are pagan, superstitious terms that express our unwitting belief that there are powers "out there" that cause things to happen "here" in ways that are outside our experience.

A personal faith in providence will bring patience, comfort, hope, and purpose to our lives as we experience the grief and pain this world has to offer. Believing in God's personal and practical willingness to intervene in my life, believing that the circumstances of my existence are not merely the "slings and arrows of outrageous fortune," believing that God not only answers prayer, but that he constantly works to bring about his gracious will – not only gives us strength to bear our burdens but gives our burdens meaning and purpose as well.

Faith in God's providential working creates order in a world that seems totally chaotic.

Providence

My grandmother Carlsen was short. Her face was guant, with a decid-edly unhealthy, yellowish pallor. Her cheekbones were high and protruding, and she wore steel-rimmed glasses. Her dresses were straight, shapeless, non-descript affairs, and I cannot remember her ever dressing up. Her hair was gray and thin, and it was always pulled straight back into a tight ball at the back of her head. She had several teeth missing, and the remaining ones were yellow and crooked, which caused her to chew in a peculiar fashion. She was a little stooped, and one of her shoulders hung lower than the other, so she always looked a little lopsided – sort of slanted. I don't remember ever hear-ing her laugh

or seeing her happy.

She lived in downtown Detroit on Seventeenth Street, not far from Michigan Avenue. The appearance of her house was much like her. The foundation had decayed, and the entire structure slanted, tilting dangerously to one side. Inside, it was always damp, chilly, and dark. She never opened the blinds, and only one light ever burned. It hung down by its frayed yel-low cord from the cracked plaster ceiling over the kitchen table, where we always sat. It was a bare light bulb, with no shade or covering.

When you entered the house, you were in the living room, if such it could be called, for no one ever really *lived* there. It was stacked high with an odd assortment of old furniture – at least I always supposed it was furni-ture. Whatever it was, it was covered by an even more odd assortment of old sheets and cloths, and it gave off an unhealthy, musty odor. The dust lay thick upon the rotting, disintegrating cloths, and it got on your clothes and skin when you walked the narrow, winding path from the front door to the kitchen. There was something about that dust that was almost sinister. It seemed that only with several hard scrubbings would it come off.

I did not like to go there.

It was a forbidding, old place in a forbidding, old neighborhood. The children who lived there were unfriendly and suspicious. The slanting floors, the semi-darkness, even my grandmother herself, gave off an eerie unpleas-antness that made me long for my rural home.

My grandmother drank. I knew little about it for a long time and under-stood less. As I grew older, it came to my attention that she drank a lot. My mother went to visit her once or twice a month. I'm sure she went with a heavy heart. She took me with her for support and for an excuse to leave. She knew she would be upbraided for her lack of devotion and that she would have to listen to my grandmother retell the story of all the wrongs she had suffered at the hands of her family.

Unfortunately, it was all too true. She had been wronged. She had been abused, cheated, and lied to by those nearest her. They had taken advantage of her age and her weakness for drink and had stolen from her. She was bitter, cynical, and thoroughly miserable, and she sought constantly to bring my mother into that web of misery that was the only source of purpose she had in her old age.

As we rode the bus to my grandmother's house, which would take hours, and as we returned, my mother would talk to me about her childhood and about my grandmother in better days. She told the stories in such a way that it helped me understand all that my grandmother had been through and the things that had made her this way. I grew to feel very sorry for my grandmother, and I learned how

circumstances can change people.

Those stories made lasting impressions on me. I remember most of them to this very day. Mother would almost always begin by telling me about how she came to this country from Canada as a little girl, about the naturalization process, then about her life on the streets of Detroit in the early 1900s. She told of being placed in a foster home when her parents could not keep her, of going to work for AT&T as a long-distance operator, of loose, wild living, and then of meeting my dad, of marriage, and of my sister being born. And then, in great detail, she would tell the story of her faith. She obeyed the gospel the very first time she heard it, under the preaching of Jewel Norman.

As she told the story of her life, it was always in view of a great, guiding providence. Even a child could understand that she believed that God had been intimately and practically involved in her history and that only by his grace had she been born into his family. Because she believed that so firmly, it came to me that I also was under his providential care, and it gave me a peace – even as a child – and a confidence

that greatly altered my life.

I urge you, not only to tell your history to your children, but to tell it in such a way that *God's providence* is evident. Help them see how they fit into that providence. It will provide the basis for the kind of relationship that will sustain them

when the bad times come.

Providence

♦

84

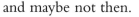

Making a Believer

The guys I fished with always said I was *lucky.* I protested that there was no such thing – especially where fish were concerned. I was firmly convinced that my ability to always catch the biggest and the most fish was due solely to my casting skill, my perseverance, and an uncanny, inborn, genetic sensitivity to what the fish were dining on, on any particular day. Roger was a doubter. Like Thomas, he would not believe without some good, hard, incontrovertible, eye-witness-type evidence –

and maybe not then.

We were fishing at Lakeville, north of Rochester, which is the name of a lake and its adjacent town. It was our third or fourth trip of the spring, and each time I had caught the most and the largest. Roger was steeped in unbelief, absolutely hardened in his

luck theory.

One of our favorite spots was a beautiful, lily-pad-covered, tree-lined cove, where an ancient willow grew. The long, slender, branches of this towering tree arched high and then curved gracefully, forty feet out, over and down to the water. It was an ideal place for lurking bass. There was a sort of natural opening between the branches of the tree on the east side. It wasn't very large, but through it, you could see right to the base of the tree. It was a real challenge. I told Roger that I was going to throw my plastic worm right through that opening, hit the base of the tree, and then slowly drag the lure into the water, allowing it to sink down into the roots. I was sure there was a five pound bass hiding there.

He laughed.

It was a very tricky cast, and I knew my reputation was *on the line.* I took careful aim, gauged the wind and the distance, and flipped the worm in a high, arching curve. My direction was perfect, my *distance,* however, was something less than that. I became so intrigued watching that worm sail through the air that I forgot to thumb the line. I was shocked when the worm disappeared over the top of the willow and plopped into the water on the other side.

"Perfect," I said –
Roger exploded with laughter.

I immediately tried to retrieve my worm, but the line was hopelessly tangled in the tree limbs. As I worked frantically to extricate the snarled line, we could hear the plastic worm bouncing and splashing on the surface on the other side of the tree. Roger was about to die laughing; he set his pole aside and lay down in the bottom of the boat, holding his stomach while tears streamed down both cheeks. But when a huge bass exploded on the surface and devoured my plastic worm, he sat up and nearly choked.

It was obvious what was going to happen, so I just relaxed. The strong, but supple, branches of the willow tree played the fish perfectly. I waited until it was exhausted – then moved the boat around to the other side, netted the fish, unhooked him, took out my scales, weighed it at five pounds, four ounces, and slipped it into the live well. I cut the worm and sinker off, went back to the other side of the tree, easily pulled the line back through the tree, and moved across the cove to begin fishing again. Roger sat in dumb amazement during this entire operation.

I thought old Roger was going to die of apoplexy, have a coronary, or bust something as he tried to come up with a rational explanation for what was now obviously superior fishing acumen. In order to make it easier for him and to show that I was not excessively proud, I carefully explained that just as I released the cast, I realized that it was a little later in the day than I had first calculated and that consequently the bass would be feeding on the shady side of the tree – what he had witnessed was simply the result of a last minute change of plan. I confessed that I had made *one mistake.* I had honestly thought that the fish would weigh no more than four pounds, ten ounces.

It grieves me to say that Roger lacked the simple honesty of Thomas, who, when faced with the physical reality of the resurrection, had the intellectual integrity to acknowledge what was obviously true and cast doubt aside. Roger, faced even with this *indisputable evidence* of my skill, remained a skeptic and quit fishing. He said that no intelligent person could possibly enjoy a sport where an orangutan would be more likely to succeed than a man.

I wonder what he meant by that?

Our vocabularies often betray our unbelief about God's active and practical intervention in our lives. Consider the nature of the typical words used to explain both our successes and failures – *planning, intelligence, perception, savvy, courage, luck, intuition, coincidence, chance, fate.* Is there not a certain arrogance, paganism, and pride in these words? How large a role does God play in the affairs of men?

The story of Joseph occupies much of the book of Genesis. It is an *incredible* story – a story that has more fairy godmothers, glass slippers, magic mirrors, and bean stalks than anything conceived or told since that time. It is a story that gives credit for every unbelievable *coincidence,* every preposterous bit of *luck* that comes Joseph's way as the specific, *providential intervention* and intent of God.

Are we to believe that the story of Joseph is an isolated case, told only to make its readers wish that they could be so *lucky?*

Are we to believe that God has ceased his active involvement now that his creatures have achieved the sophistication necessary to guide themselves? Or is the story told to give hope and assurance of the *providential* working of God in the lives of all of his people?

> "A man can receive nothing,
> unless it has been given him
> from heaven."
> —John 3:27

I wonder if we believe that?

Providence and Grace

He was a baseball player – a pretty good one, I guess – although I never saw him play – but not good enough for division one colleges and certainly not good enough to be a professional. But for our school, he was good enough to get a full scholarship. He was short, muscular, and good looking in a small-town, slender, clean-cut sort of way. He came to the small, church-

Providence

♦

88

sponsored college where I taught because of the scholarship and because he was a Christian – not a particularly *good* one – but he knew the terminology and most of the basic doctrines. He was also a student in my literature class – and he was a very *poor* one. I learned that he was a senior and that he had put off taking his last required English class until his last semester because he

hated English.

I wouldn't say that he didn't try at all, but his efforts were feeble – as was his interest – and he was further hampered by marginal reading and writing skills. He wasn't dumb exactly; he was intellectually lazy, totally undisciplined, and – worst of all – he had no imagination. He had made it through high school on his good manners, his athletic ability, and his pleasant personality. He was the perfect example of the mindless dullness that characterizes so many children who have been

raised on television.

He came to class regularly and on time. He never took notes, never showed any interest, never participated. He didn't sleep exactly – that is, he never actually closed his eyes. But it was easy to tell that his lights weren't on. He never answered a question, never ventured an opinion – I honestly don't think

he ever had one.

I don't remember when it happened, but at some point late in the semester, I caught him watching me, and *his lights were on.* It was like he had been suddenly awakened from a long and satisfying sleep with the notion that something of great importance – like dinner – had just slipped right by him and he wondered what he had missed.

The week before finals, I analyze all of my students' grades and inform them of where they stand. I tell them what they have to do on the final exam in order to either improve or decline. Those who are in danger of failing, I call into my office. It was the first conversation I had ever had with him. I told him he had to make a seventy on the final to pass the class – anything less would fail him.

He said that he knew he had done poorly and that he was sincerely sorry – not just about his grade, but because he had realized toward the end that there was much about literature that was worth learning and *he had missed it.* He also told me that if he failed my class, he would not graduate. He said he had a job lined up, but if he didn't get his degree, he would be disqualified. I gave him some study hints, and he left.

During the final, he actually perspired. He was tense, tight as a fiddle string. I could tell that he had really studied, because I watched him change his answers often. He took the entire three hours that was allotted for the test, and he was the last person to leave the room. When he handed the test to me, it was like he was holding out his life.

After the final, I went to my office to grade the tests. I wasn't too surprised when he knocked on my door about an hour later. He asked if I had graded his paper, and I said no. He asked if he could wait, and I said yes. I dug through the stack, found his paper, and began to grade it. He stood by my desk – his apprehension filled the room. He winced visibly every time my red pen left a mark. He was awake now, and life was real. He was watching his future slip away in lines of red ink. When I finished, I added his score. He didn't make it! He did better than I expected – a sixty-two – but

Providence

♦

89

a sixty-two is not seventy.

"I'm sorry," I said; and I was.

"Is it like baseball?" he asked. "When you're out, you're out, and it doesn't matter how close you came to being safe?"

"Pretty much," I said.

"I really tried Mr. Smith; I gave it my very best. Does that count for anything?"

"It ought to make you feel better, and that counts for something, but it doesn't change the score. You need to admit that you have not tried this semester. You can't just practice hard the day before the game and expect to win."

You need to understand that I have very fixed notions about grading, and I still believe those notions are correct. My philosophy is, if the numbers don't really mean anything, why fool with them? He sat down by my desk and put his head in his hands. I knew what was going on in his brain –

I have been there.

He was visibly shaken, and he asked if we could visit. I said yes, but cautioned him that I did not change scores. He needed to talk, and talk he did. He talked about his hometown, his folks, his high school, his hopes. I learned a lot about him. I've heard lots of sob stories; in fact, I've heard all of them. They don't have much effect on me; but I came to believe in this young man – not so much in what he was saying – but in *him*. I had a feeling about this kid, a sort of creepy kind of feeling, and feelings like that should never be ignored.

Rules are necessary things, and I believe in them, but *the Sabbath was made for man – not man for the Sabbath* – which means that people and circumstances are always more important than rules. I made up my mind.

"Tim," I said, "I'm going to pass you. I am not going to change your score. I'm going to pass you because I have the power to do it. Make no mistake, *you deserve to fail;* in fact, you *have failed.* That is a fact I cannot change. What I am doing is an act of *grace.* I don't know if you will appreciate or understand what I'm saying, but I hope that someday you'll realize that what I'm doing for you today is what God does for you and me every day."

Big tears welled up in his eyes. I think it had been a very long time since he had cried – or since he had felt like it. He tried to thank me – but what can you say to an act of pure grace? He was terribly embarrassed, but it did him good. I stood up, gave him a big hug, told him I loved him, and pushed him out the door so I could finish grading my papers.

The next Sunday, he showed up at the church where I preached. I was impressed and grateful for the interest, even though I knew it might simply be a payback in order to ease his conscience. The next Sunday he was back again, and he came Wednesday night for Bible study too. About two months later, he had a girl with him, whom he very proudly introduced to me as Amy.

A few weeks later he called and asked if I would eat lunch with him. As we visited, he said he had a lot of questions about the Bible and so did Amy. He wondered if I would study with them. For the next three weeks, we studied twice a week – sometimes for two hours – and one night, after intense investigation and soul searching, he said he was ready to make a step of faith and commit his life to God. I think Amy had made up her mind the week before. I called a few of the church members, and we met at the building. We sang a few songs, prayed, and then Tim and Amy confessed their lostness, their unworthiness, and accepted God's grace by being born again in baptism.

Years have passed. Now they live in Mississippi. He has a good job, has gained thirty pounds and two children. He and Amy love each other, their children, and God. They go to church regularly and are faithful to each other. Every now and then they call to say *Hi* and *We love you.* Every time I hang up the phone, the wonder of it all sweeps over me.

What I mean is – I gave the kid a lousy D instead of an F. How earth shattering can that be? I mean, what human being would ever devise a plan to totally change the entire history of people's lives and their children's and grandchildren's by making a mark on a piece of paper that looks like this *D* instead of like this *F?* And people tell me that miracles have ceased and that stories like Philip and the Eunuch don't happen anymore – and that God's providential working ceased about A.D. 100.

The more a person is aware of the grace of God at work in their lives in a daily, providential way – the more they're willing to extend it

to others.

There I Am

We didn't mean for it to be a special Saturday. In fact, we had planned to do entirely different things than we ended up doing. Judi had to do some work at school and some grocery shopping, Kristen had spent Friday night at a friend's house and wouldn't be home until late afternoon, Lincoln had been out very late on a date and wouldn't get up till noon, and Debbie was going to the store with Judi. I had intended to take Brendan with me to cut firewood, but we decided to go rabbit hunting instead.

We woke up at daylight to a steady drizzle of cold rain. The rain would certainly have kept us from woodcutting – because that is "work." But it didn't keep us from rabbit hunting – because that is "fun." For four hours, we relentlessly pursued our quarry among the rocks, cactus, snake weed, creosote brush, and occasional small junipers of the Hualapai mountains. We arrived home dead tired, soaked to the skin, and chilled to the bone; and we had ten rabbits to clean.

By the time we finished cleaning the rabbits, Judi and Debbie had come home, as had Kristen. Lincoln finally decided to join the land of the living. There is nothing so delicious as a hot shower and dry clothes after being cold and wet for a long time – in fact – I have been known to get cold and wet just to enjoy that pleasure. To make it even better, Judi sat us down to a steaming bowl of hot rabbit stew and freshly baked cranberry muffins – it just doesn't get any better.

After eating, I went out to sit on the back porch and watch it rain on the mountains. The view was mostly obliterated by low hanging, heavy, gray clouds that drifted in and out; but occasionally the clouds would lift and present a misty prospect of majestic peaks. The air was heavy with the pungent, bittersweet smell of desert sage and creosote. There is no smell like the desert during and after a rain.

I hadn't been out there too long when Judi came out with a cup of hot chocolate and joined me. Pretty soon, Debbie drifted out and was eventually followed by the other three. We sat in lawn chairs and chaise longues. The wind swept in off the mountains and it turned cold, so we pulled our chairs into a circle and covered our feet and legs with community blankets. It was warm and snug there. We could have gone in, but it was better on the porch.

Our proximity to each other, the rain, the cold, the smells, the comfortable warmth in our stomachs — all conspired to produce a feeling of camaraderie, and we began to talk. Old times, new times, friends past and present, places now and then — all blended and mingled into a harmony produced by the commonalty of our family. We sat like that for a long time, held together by a mutual reluctance to break the spell because we knew we could never create another moment *just like this one.* It was approaching dark when we finally went in.

Such moments are a mystery. They come unbidden, unplanned — they come *providentially.* It seems that every now and then God decides to take matters into his own hands because we're too dumb or too busy to do it ourselves. We try to create special times artificially by spending lots of money — by making elaborate plans. But they do not happen that way; they happen by his providential grace — by his direct intervention in our lives. There are no special moments — no hearts as one — without him. Truly, where two or three are gathered together in his name,

he is in their midst.

Unspotted from the World

"Pure and undefiled religion
before God and the Father is this:
to visit orphans and widows
in their affliction,
and to keep oneself
unspotted from the world."
—James 1:27

The first time I met him was at church, and it was quite by accident, that is, if you have no faith in *providence*. You couldn't help but notice him. He had the nicest head of thick, curly, dark brown hair you've ever seen and a radiant, white, even-toothed smile that warmed your heart. After services, he introduced himself as Frank, and then he introduced his friends. He laughed and said that they had intended to go to another church on the same street as ours but had gotten their directions confused, somehow, and after being seated in our assembly, they were too embarrassed to get up and walk out. He had several questions about the sermon.

I visited with him for awhile, but his questions weren't easy to answer and one led to another. As luck would have it – that is, if you don't believe in *providence* – Judi had prepared a huge turkey dinner for some folks who had a last-minute emergency and had to change their plans. Since they couldn't come, I invited Frank and his friends over for dinner. We had a great time. We spent the entire afternoon visiting and studying. He was back in my office on Monday. Within a week, he and some of his friends accepted Jesus in baptism.

He was so hungry to learn. He showed up at my office at odd hours with questions and troublesome passages. He wasn't trying to trap me or prove anything. He really wanted to know the answers. I found out that although his home was in the area, he was living in a conscientious-objector camp near Palo Alto. He was the first conscientious objector I had ever known personally. Since he had only been a Christian a few days, his objections to military service were not based on biblical principles but on personal convictions. His responses to my questions about his feelings in this area impressed me greatly. They were thoughtful and showed a depth of perspective and courage. I learned a lot from Frank.

From the very first, there was something unique about him. He took his decision to be a disciple of Jesus so seriously and yet he was so happy. It always seemed that a little bit of sunshine followed Frank everywhere he went. His guardian angel must have known he was *special,* because he didn't allow Frank to step in or on anything. His bountiful good nature unsettled even the most irascible and suspicious mentalities – and there were several of those at church. He wore his hair quite long, and his dress was a little *too* casual for some folks. But his grooming style wasn't his *flag,* he wasn't trying to make a reputation or prove anything; he just didn't care about clothes. If I asked him to dress up for something, he didn't mind or take it as an affront, although he sometimes lacked the means.

And you know what? He didn't own a car. He didn't seem to need one. He had a very old motorcycle, but it seldom ran. Most of the time, he rode a ten-speed or walked. I just couldn't get over it. He was twenty years old, outrageously good looking, very much alive – he could sing and play the guitar like nobody I had ever heard before –

and he didn't own a car!

One time he came to see me, and I wasn't home. Judi told him I would probably be there in a little while, so he decided to wait. That was another thing about Frank – he was never in a hurry. This next scene is imprinted on my mind.

When I approached my house, I could see this large group of about ten to fifteen neighborhood children all sitting in a circle in my front yard, with Frank in the middle. When I pulled into the driveway, not a child moved – not even my own. As I walked over to the group, I could hear Frank's animated voice reading a children's Bible story. The children sat quietly, attentively, until he finished.

I didn't even recognize some of them. I don't know how he got them together or by what magic he held them, but I know there was something so honest, so simple, so pure in his love that the children – children are especially sensitive to honesty and purity – recognized it and responded. He was a type of Pied Piper, and it was a blessing to bask for a while in his innocence and devotion.

I learned a lot from Frank. God sent him to help me believe again in the transforming power of the gospel. Frank dissipated some of the cynicism and hardness that had crept into my heart over the years of folks lying to me, disappointing me, betraying me. He was a special, providential gift – from God to me. When I think of what it means to be *unspotted from the world,* I always think of Frank, and I wonder if he has remained so. I wonder if the complacency, the selfishness, the love affair with sin and materialism – which has even invaded the church – has somehow touched him and narrowed his eyes. I wonder if the children still gather around him.

Providence

"Dear Lord,
In your great providence,
send me another Frank
to remind me
that there are still some
who are
unspotted from the world."

Something Is Wrong

It all began because he forget to turn his car radio on. Those who believe in that sort of thing would call it *providential,* but he did not believe in that sort of thing and would have dismissed it as *circumstantial.*

His wife Carol had turned the radio off the evening before because it was news time and her life was depressing enough without the news. Vic always listened to the radio. It was a thirty-minute commute to work, and he passed the time by tapping his fingers on the steering wheel, mouthing a few words and occasionally even trying to imitate the lead singer. But today – at 6:15 A.M. – he simply forgot to turn it on and consequently fell into an unaccustomed pattern of subconscious thought. Out of that jumbled maze of conflicting future plans and dissatisfaction with past and present ones, a synthesis began to arise. Like a giant air bubble escaping from deep beneath the floor of the ocean where it has lain trapped for centuries, a thought rose with ever increasing speed and burst upon the surface of his consciousness –

something is wrong.

The words were clear, unmistakable. But then they dissipated, leaving only a nagging irritation, like when you don't feel good, but you aren't exactly sick. He reached over quickly and snapped on the stereo – a reflexive defense against such unwelcome intrusions – and the thought was lost in the familiar rhythms and lyrics. Well, not exactly lost, but it didn't bother him for many days.

The next time it happened was due to another rare "circumstantial" occurrence. It was the kind of thing that doesn't happen often, but when it does, it is perfectly believable, and the story is told and retold. Only a *very* religious person would have called it providence, and he wasn't even mildly religious. This time, he and Carol had gone to some friends' house for dinner. They lived a little less than a mile away. They were late arriving, and in the hurry and confusion of carrying in the salad and some rolls Carol had made, Vic *accidentally* hit his automatic door locks and locked both his keys and Carol's purse in the car. Their friends had one car in the shop and the other loaned out to a teenage son. Since his house was so close, he decided just to walk home and get his extra set of keys.

A mile is a lot farther than you think when you're alone and it's quiet. There really isn't much to do but think, and he hadn't gone far when the process began. He recognized it, and made several evasive mental moves to block its progress. He walked faster – he concentrated on logistic problems at work – he planned a vacation – but always, behind every maneuver, the process accelerated toward its conclusion. He wished desperately for his telephone, television, radio, even a book or secretary, but nothing came to his aid. He couldn't hold it down. It absolutely burst into consciousness –

Something is Wrong!

And of course something was; in fact, nearly everything was. His job was dissatisfying, yet very demanding. He owed large amounts of money, which kept him tied to a situation he wished to quit. His marriage was superficial and more convenient than necessary. He had little interest in his children, and they had even less in him. Nothing seemed to taste good anymore, and his laughter was mechanical and heavy. And one other thing – underneath it all – were those eternal *whys?* His response to the nagging questions had been evasion and philosophy – both of which lack depth and left him empty and dissatisfied.

He was frantic.

Like the first escaping bubble, so the next thought rose unbidden from so deep within that he could not have identified the place, and the source was totally beyond his reckoning. "Oh God," he murmured audibly, "help me."

And He did.

By *God,* he didn't mean that well-defined, infinite, fully revealed, divine personality known and understood by those whose faith has matured by patiently studying and meditating upon the creation and the Holy Scrip-

tures. He only knew that his problems and questions were greater than him-self, and so he used a colloquialism that he had learned both from his child-hood and his culture. But that great, eternal Spirit, which in the beginning moved upon the face of the waters and which hovers, ever near us, waiting for even the slightest opening, dispatched a messenger to respond.

The message was conveyed to a fellow employee in his department – an underling actually, a rather unobtrusive man whom he knew only slightly but whom he had always regarded with some degree of sympathetic disdain because of his lack of drive and business acumen. This employee put a note on his desk two days later, inviting him to a men's Bible study and discus-sion group at his home. Normally, Vic would have smiled condescendingly and discarded the note. But this time he put it in his pocket, and when the evening came, he went. He was never the same –

and he was glad.

Jesus Cares

I was returning from speaking at a lectureship in a small West Texas town. It was late; I was tired. I was driving alone across what appeared to be end-less flatness. I was depressed. I felt . . . well . . . *inadequate.* Do you ever feel inadequate? Things were just piling up – things that I was responsible for but had no authority over. By authority, I mean that I did not originate them; and although I was involved in the ongoing process of resolution, I had no control over the factors that would result in their termination.

Feeling inadequate was not new to me; neither was it inappropriate. I *am* inadequate – terribly so – and I am not in control. But even within the boundaries of that realization, I expect – and others certainly expect – at least a minimal level of competency – the superficial ability to press the but-tons that will keep the show going.

As is usual at this stage of my depression, a survival mechanism flipped a switch in my brain, which in turn lit up a red-lettered, digital display that read – *count your blessings.* But this time, that little display made me mad. At that moment, I wasn't interested in counting my blessings. It's not that I don't have them; it's just that no matter what level of blessing or achievement I have, it only serves as the foundation from which I attempt to leap to the next level.

When someone – who perceives himself as having fewer blessings than I – tells me, with some degree of recrimination, to count my blessings, he only means that he has already counted them (but not his own) and found that although he has room to complain, I certainly do not. When someone who has more blessings tells me, with a note of condescension, to count my blessings, he only means that I should be content with less than he has. And so at every level, we see that blessings are those things that *others* have. What I have are either what I deserve or need, and nobody counts those or is grateful for them.

By the time I had worked my way through that mental muddle, I had covered about thirty miles. I paused in my deliberations long enough to check my rear view mirror, to turn up the beeper on my radar detector, and to look about me. No perceivable change in the landscape was apparent, and so I lapsed back into the depression that had darkened my thoughts.

The miles crawled by endlessly. Just before I got to O'Donell, I tried the radio for a diversion. Some song about old dogs, children, and watermelon wine being the only things in the world worth a dime came wailing at my ears – greater depression. I tried listening to the tape of the lecture I had just given – massive trauma. And then, as I rounded a slight curve, my headlights illuminated a sign on the side of the road. It was hanging from an old, mesquite fence post. I couldn't make out all of the letters, but I knew what it said:

Jes—
Car—

It was old, faded, and hanging precariously. I had passed the sign before, but had never noticed it. Some pilgrim had taken the time and gone to the trouble to post this reminder, and tonight, of all the dark nights in the year, I had seen it.

I hit the brakes, made a U-turn, and went back. I parked my car where my headlights would light the area and made my way—suit, white shirt, tie, dress shoes and all—through the "bar" ditch, to the old fence. I straightened the sign, secured it as best I could with some baling wire, and went back to the car – feeling that I was not quite as useless as I had imagined and knowing that

I was in control of some things.

I went on up the highway a short distance, made another U-turn, and drove slowly back by the sign – *my* sign. I could see it plainly now and so could any other sojourner traveling this way.

Jesus
Cares

He really does, you know. And sometimes, when we really need it, his caring makes all the difference.

Providence

FIVE

Loneliness

I used to dread loneliness – almost more than anything. I had no idea why it came – or why it left, for that matter. It just sort of slipped up on me – stealthily, gently, and slowly. I have noticed that it comes more frequently with age and is of a different quality. I also have discovered why it comes. I used to think it was the same thing as depression, but it isn't – at least it isn't anymore. I can be lonely without being depressed, although I don't believe I am ever depressed without being lonely.

When my wife says, "What's the matter? Are you depressed?" I can immediately say, "No, it's not that; I think I'm just lonely." And when she says, "Why?" or "Lonely for what?" I say, "I'm not exactly sure, but it has something to do with home."

My sense of loneliness will only grow from this point on, but I don't dread it anymore. As my love for my life and for this earth grows less and less – as I learn that there is no lasting satisfaction, appeal, or joy in the things of this earth – as eternity gets closer and more real, as more and more of my loved ones steal silently away, I know that nothing here is ever going to fill that undefined vacuum in my life that I call loneliness. It isn't morbid; it doesn't rob me of either my joy or my determination to live every day to its fullest. It's a sign of maturity, of growth in God.

There are many things that lessen the emptiness that goes with loneliness, and this chapter is designed to bring a positive and spiritual outlook to your life. Sharing these good years with my wife; watching my children grow and begin their families; meditating on God's Word, praying, communing with God, and singing songs of praise; visiting old scenes and anticipating new ones; accepting the challenge every day to make a difference in someone's life; utilizing every experience and lesson God has taught me to help some struggling pilgrim on his way – all of these give me strength to live with my loneliness without wallowing in despair.

Loneliness helps me understand the apostle Paul's statement about his "desire to depart and be with Jesus." I also understand what he said right after that, too – the part about God not being finished with him here and as long as he was here he was going to live usefully and productively. May God help us all to be so determined.

Look at the Birds

When I lived in San Antonio, Texas, I could not find a job. It was a humiliating time for me, because I had never been in that position before. My wife had secured a teaching position, which was very helpful financially but increased my sense of failure immeasurably. It was a time of much introspection, soul searching, and personal loneliness for me. It was also a time when I discovered that I had not made as much progress in my quest to know God as I thought I had – in fact –

I had taken a few steps backward.

Through the kindness and generosity of many dear people who loved me practically and with good hearts, I was helped to start a firewood business. I bought chain saws, a truck, and the necessary tools – was given a place to cut wood near Seguin – and I began. I had never operated a chain saw before in my life. It's amazing how quickly you can learn something when the need is upon you. I left the house at 3:30 A.M. and often did not return until long after dark. Because my need was great, I priced my wood modestly, and I sold all I could cut. I was totally alone all day.

The sheer, unrelenting, brute labor was good for me. I do not mean that I thought it was good for me at the time – I mean, *looking back,* it was good for me. At the time I felt very sorry for myself. I thought I was the only person in the world who had to work for a living. Because I worked alone, my bitterness and resentment were increased by my isolation.

One very cold and overcast day, I was particularly depressed. I was tired, broke, far behind in filling my orders, and frustrated with the cruel misfortunes of life, which seemed to mock me. Here I was with a college education, cutting firewood. At one point my chain was dulled when it struck a small rock that had lodged at the joint of a limb on the hickory tree I was cutting. I had just sharpened it – a very arduous and time-consuming task – and in my already depressed and harried condition, it was the last straw. I sat down on the stump of the tree I had just cut and my eyes began to fill with tears. Miles from any person, totally alone, I sat and cried.

Eventually, I cried it out. And when I began to be restored, I noticed a very small bird, a wren I think, perched on a limb almost within touching distance. It seemed totally unafraid and watched me with what I judged to be friendly curiosity. I spoke to it. I know that sounds dumb – totally irrational – but I did. I was so alone that I needed to speak to something, and the bird was the only thing around. "Hi," I said. It jumped quickly to a higher limb, but not farther away. It bounced and jerked so cheerfully and lightly that it made me laugh – a soft, gentle, inside kind of laugh. "What are you so happy about? Do you ever get lonely or depressed?" I didn't expect an answer, but when it cocked its head to one side and looked at me with such an intelligent curiosity, I listened intently just for a moment in spite of myself. When I was a child I might have expected an answer – and got it too – but not now; I am far too old and wise for that.

The little bird was company, and he lifted my spirits. As I watched him (or her), I remembered Jesus saying,

> *"Look at the birds –*
> *are you not worth more than they?"*

That passage kept running through my mind, like I was supposed to learn something from it. It was like I was hearing it for the first time,

> "Look at the birds" – Jesus said –
> *"Look!*
> *Look!*
> *Look at the birds!"*

I began to realize that I never had, you know. I had *seen* birds – I had *hunted* birds – I had *shot* birds – I had *cleaned* birds, *cut up* birds, *cooked* birds, *eaten* birds – I had even *fed* birds – but I had never *looked* at them.

> "God help me," I thought –
> "and God forgive me
> for not looking at the birds."

I have argued doctrine until the smallest gnat was not only strained out but dissected. I have pondered the grace/works tension until I nearly snapped. I have worried and wearied myself over women's role in the church and questions about authority until I was wretched – because I thought God wanted me to – and He does. But I had never *looked at the birds,* because I thought that passage was symbolic or figurative or maybe unimportant. I had not learned the *weightier matters* of the law that bring balance, restore harmony, and cure loneliness.

If I had spent more time looking at the birds, I would have been a better person, I would have known far more about loving God, my brethren, my enemies, my family – even myself – and I would have been less lonely. Wrestling with millennialism and questions about the Holy Spirit is all right, I suppose, but it does not speak to the real issues of life. I do not at all mean that I should not wrestle with those things. I do mean that a person can cure his loneliness and learn more about his relationship to God by *looking at the birds* than he will by arguing doctrine.

Loneliness

♦

May God help us all
to take him seriously
when He tells us
to
look at the birds.

❧

Loneliness

"Perceiving then
that they were about to come
and take Him by force
to make Him king,
Jesus withdrew again
to the hills
by Himself."
—John 6:15

It is such different thing – to be alone and to be lonely. When I am lonely, no amount of people, friends, activity, or excitement can erase that feeling – because my loneliness comes from the hollowness inside me. I am lonely because of a longing, a yearning for something, someone, some undefinable peace or state that I am never quite able to identify and therefore cannot attain. I am never lonely because I choose to be, although I am often alone by choice.

The apostle John says that Jesus withdrew *again*. Apparently, Jesus was in the habit of deliberately separating Himself from others. It seems odd to me that our Lord should have felt the need to be alone. Perhaps I am not alone enough. When I am alone, I am often joined by myriads of those whom I have not seen for years and may not see for many more – and some are there that I shall not see again on this side. It is also a special time of communing with God and with myself, of reliving old scenes, a time of introspection, of direction analysis, a glad time – a sad time – it's good to be alone like that, and people who have been alone like that

always know each other.

To be too much alone is not good, because it often leads me to think too much about myself and to concentrate too much on negative things, the past, and personal problems. To be alone because I despise the hypocrisy and shallowness that I experience in human fellowship and am expected to display is not healthy either, for I must exist as a social person in order to fulfill my ministry and the calling of God.

Loneliness is such a sad affair – this line from an old Carpenter's song expresses an important truth. It is important because that which is sad should not always be avoided as though it were negative. To be sad because one is lonely may bring the realization of how desperately I need that void in my soul filled by the love and companionship of other human beings. It may also lead me to the realization that there is a yearning lingering within me that will never be satisfied by other humans or by anything to be found on this earth, but only by our Lord Jesus Himself.

I stood beside the dark waters of a Michigan lake one cold November dusk; and I watched the summer geese, wailing their parting cries, begin their journey to their predestined place; and I looked at barren October trees and felt the awesome, impending, silent power of approaching winter – and I was lonely, frightened by my feelings, and alone. As the darkness – both within and without – crept over me, I walked slowly, even reluctantly away, leaving that precious feeling, too deep for words, behind me. When I reached the top of the hill that overlooked home, I saw the flicker of kitchen lights, and I knew that supper was waiting, and a smile. My footsteps quickened, and I looked upward and said, *"Thank you,"* and hurried on.

People who have been alone like that
always know each other.

Loneliness

♦

108

I Will Lift Up My Eyes

"I lift up my eyes to the hills—
where does my help come from?
My help comes from the Lord,
the Maker of heaven and earth.
He will not let your foot slip—
he who watches over you
will not slumber."
—Psalm 121:1–3

If Psalm 120 sets the mood for Psalm 121, the psalmist is depressed. In our half superhuman, half mythological notions of Old Testament heroes, we seldom imagine them as feeling as we do. But the men and women of old sometimes felt lonely, depressed, melancholy, and frustrated, and their inability to deal with their problems on their own made them even more conscious of their helplessness. Have you ever felt like that? Have you ever looked in every direction for help, consolation, and hope, only to find more reason for despair. The author of Psalm 121 knew where to look for help –

he looked up!

Looking up makes us aware of possibilities, of space, distance, light, and eternity. This writer knew that his help would not come from the mountains, but from the God who made the mountains.

Satan constantly pulls our eyes down by attracting our attention to our surroundings – to bad news, traffic, red lights, smog, drugs, political corruption, family breakup, suicide, crime, sickness, disaster, hatred – the never ending deluge of negativism dumped upon us by every aspect of our media. I do *not* say that those things are not real – I *do* say that they are not the *only* realities, and I *do* say that they are not the *greatest* realities.

Paul admonishes his readers to "set your mind on things above, where Christ is seated at the right hand of God." Looking up, lifting up our eyes, gives us perspective on this life and brings us hope and peace in times of trouble. This psalmist now knows where his help comes from.

Do you?

May God help us, when things are dark, to look up. May the vast and limitless possibilities of space and eternity remind us of the greatness of the love of the one who not only created space but who created in us the longing to live forever. May that longing bring renewed hope and power to live this day for Him.

> "If then you have been raised up with Christ,
> keep seeking the things above,
> where Christ is,
> seated at the right hand of God.
> Set your mind on things above,
> not on earthly things."
> —Colossians 3:1–2

Sharing Silence

One of the things that often makes pain bearable is the consolation that comes from sharing our pain with those who have born similar pains. Knowing that others have experienced and endured brings relief to us, because hope – a light at the end of a dark tunnel – becomes a possibility.

When we are in pain, our tendency is to *talk it through* – to search for words and inflection that express accurately our feelings and give vent to our frustrations, anger, and hurt. When our listeners express understanding – the feelings are softened and tend to diminish.

But some feelings are too deep for words. They lie so close to our souls – our innermost beings – that human speech will never express them. Many aspects of love are that way. There is an old Negro spiritual that is built around a prophetic statement about Jesus from Isaiah 53 that says, "He was oppressed and afflicted, yet he did not open his mouth." The slaves sang –

> "They crucified my Lord,
> and He never said
> a mumbling word."

And why did He not? Was it not because His grief could not be stated – because the weight of the sins of mankind could not be expressed – because

His love for God and for God's creation could only be uttered in His silent acquiescence to the trial and crucifixion.

It is the blight of our time that we must always talk. It is a part of the "noise syndrome" that afflicts us. Noise is so much a part of our lives that we are nervous, apprehensive, often incapacitated without it. That is why they play background music in shopping malls, grocery stores, and restaurants – it is why we leave our radios or televisions running day and night – *because we cannot stand to be alone with ourselves.*

This is a story about a couple who had been married twenty-six years – twenty-six *good* years. It is a true story – it is true in the sense that it is based on an actual event – but it is true in an even deeper sense, and those who read and understand will nod their heads and say –

"Yes,

that is a

true story."

They were much in love when they married, and that love had deepened and broadened with passing years and tears. For five years they had been frustrated in their desire for children, but in that frustration and bewilderment, they had found a new need for each other. When Jimmy was born, all their hopes, dreams, and ambitions were realized.

He was not a healthy baby. The first year of his life was spent in and out of the hospital, and there were many sleepless nights, many tears, much anxiety, and no small amount of prayer. After that year, Jimmy seemed to decide that if he must stay here, he might as well have a real go at it. His health improved marvelously, and he became a perfect rounder – the neighborhood nuisance and favorite. By the time he was old enough for school, he was a robust, intelligent, outgoing young fellow.

But he never did have any brothers or sisters.

All of his mother's and father's love and attention were showered upon him. They grieved much privately for the other children who had never come to them, but they were thankful for Jimmy. He was a good athlete, a good student – never outstanding – but good enough to make them proud. He was also a thoughtful boy, with a deep, spiritual side, and this – more than all the rest – pleased them.

In his sophomore year of college, returning home for Thanksgiving, the car Jimmy was riding in was struck by a train, and all five occupants were killed instantly. As the word spread through the community, those who knew this couple came to visit. They fixed meals, they prayed with them, embraced them, shared their own losses, encouraged, and strengthened them in every possible way. They did all the things that are so important and seem so meaningless because we want to do something significant –

and we cannot.

The entire community mourned the loss of Jimmy and his four companions. The funeral came and went. The bodies were laid to rest. The tables cleared, the relatives went back home, the friends quit bringing meals and calling, and life returned to *normal*. For the first time in twenty years, they were alone again – in fact, they were more alone than they had ever been, because the aloneness was deepened by the loss of this part of their history. They asked all of the normal, historical questions – they said all of the normal, historical "What ifs?" And in the end, they had to be satisfied with the normal, historical not knowing –

they had to trust.

Now they sit alone in their living room in the late afternoon. They do not sit side by side – but they are very much together in their aloneness. The walls of the room are covered with Jimmy's memorabilia. As they sit, she looks at a picture of Jimmy on his first day at school, and her mind is flooded with Jimmy as a boy. She sees him trotting off to school, his Superman lunch pail bouncing in his hand, his curly head and laughing face turning back at the end of the driveway to wave goodbye; and she almost cries aloud for him to return and get his cap, but he disappears around the corner.

He sits looking at a different picture – a picture of Jimmy in his football uniform receiving an award for "outstanding attitude" – and he remembers his pride and then his shock when Jimmy had stepped to the microphone and asked him to come to the platform. When he arrived, Jimmy had put his arm around him and said, "This is my father, the finest father any boy ever had." And when he tried to speak, he had cried – it was embarrassing – but the whole stadium had stood and cheered in appreciation.

Sitting across from each other, lost in their own thoughts, their eyes meet and silent tears speak what words cannot say. But through the tears there comes a smile and an assurance, and he moves slowly across the room and takes her hand.

There are no words spoken – none to be spoken. To try to say it would lessen it. What they have, their priceless gift, is for them alone, for they alone have shared in paying the price that earns them the right to grieve – not for loss or for failure – but for completeness.

They are joined only by His presence.
For where two are truly together,
He is always there.

Loneliness

♦

112

What they share,
they share together.
Alone in
silence.

Tired of Living, Scared of Dying

The Broadway musical *Showboat* is one of the few Hollywood-type musical entertainments that still has the power to move me. The moment I always wait for is when the black slave sits on the bale of cotton and sings *Ol' Man River*. The last time I heard it, it was splendidly done and I was filled with the pathos it always evokes in me. It is a graphic song – a song that has survived, at least in part, because it touches on one of life's great themes. It is a tale of sorrow, longing, defeat, and hopelessness. It contains one line that speaks to the frustration of all who know they are slaves.

> "I gets weary – and sick of tryin',
> I'm tired of livin' – and scared of dyin'."

I feel that way often. I grow so weary with the burden of my life – a burden that no set of physical circumstances can ever truly lift – only postpone.

> I long for a sustained peace –
> a freedom from care.

There are some even more famous lines from a greater author that speak the same frustration. Familiarity has robbed them of their depth, and they are often quoted by those who learned the *words* in high school but have never learned their *meaning*. I have taken the liberty of changing a few terms into more modern vernacular.

> "To die, to sleep—
> No more—and by a sleep to say we end
> The heartache, and the thousand natural shocks
> That flesh is heir to! 'Tis a consummation

Devoutly to be wished. To die, to sleep—
To sleep—perchance to dream: yes, there's the problem,
For in that sleep of death what dreams may come. . . .

Who would bear life's burdens,
To grunt and sweat under a weary life,
But that the dread of something after death,
The unknown country, from whose borders
No traveler returns, puzzles the will,
And makes us rather bear those troubles we have,
Than fly to others that we know not of?"
—William Shakespeare, *Hamlet*

Loneliness

Read it again, slowly, carefully. Does not Hamlet say that *he is tired of living and scared of dying* – and is not that sentiment repeated in a million hearts a day in New York, in Hong Kong, in Istanbul, in Moscow, and in Little Rock – in the hearts of housewives, farmers, pharmacists, bankers, lawyers, and street cleaners? It is found in all great literature – in Melville, Dickens, Milton, Dostoyevski, Hawthorne, Fitzgerald, and Hemingway. Like the eternal struggle between good and evil, the theme of overcoming the unrelenting weariness of life produced by the aging process is woven into all great literature. We call it – *the tragic flaw.* And every thoughtful, sensitive, spiritual person has felt it at one time or another.

Henry David Thoreau, in one of his more lucid moments said,

"Most men lead lives of quiet desperation."

He was right, you know. We wouldn't dare admit it, not even to ourselves, but it is written all over our frantic lives.

Even the greatest literature of all – the Word of God – often displays its heroes in the throes of this dilemma. Solomon graphically and without reservation expressed that he was tired of living:

"'Meaningless! Meaningless!'
says the Teacher.
'Utterly meaningless! Everything is meaningless.'"
—Ecclesiastes 1:2

"When I surveyed all
that my hands had done
and what I had toiled to achieve,
everything was meaningless,
a chasing after the wind."
—Ecclesiastes 2:11

What do we do when we get weary and sick of trying – when we're tired of living and scared of dying – when *to be* – or *not to be* – really is the question? What will sustain us in that stark moment of absolute reality, when we come face to face with the fact that we too are nothing but slaves in the most practical sense imaginable?

At some point in our lives, we all face the frustration of being defeated – of realizing that in spite of our best efforts, life has deceived us by holding out youth and success and making us believe in them. That is when we must turn to the only foundation that will support us. Solomon found in the end that the secret to successful living was pretty simple. When you're tired of living and scared of dying, you should remember to –

> "Fear God
> and keep his commandments,
> for this is the whole duty
> of man."
> —Ecclesiastes 12:13

What Matters?

I went to the school today. I wanted to talk to the academic dean, but he wasn't there. The school year is over, the students are gone, the buildings are empty. I sat on a concrete bench in the courtyard, and an overpowering feeling of sadness, loneliness, futility, and despair engulfed me.

The parking lot is empty – they are all gone. Just yesterday they were here – their voices, their talk of boyfriends, girlfriends, cafeteria food, finals, summer plans, futures – those voices brought life. I am alone here – silently, sadly, reflectively alone. I would not mind, *except for the memories.* I feel old, very old and tired. All that I put into this year –

> did it matter?
> They are gone –

they have forgotten me.
What was it for?

The trees are green and silent; they cannot store laughter. It does not matter to them. The swings are still, and they do not care that yesterday's lovers have forsaken them – they have no memories. I wonder where they are. Do they imagine this place without them? Some have gone forever. Will we meet again? How meaningless this place is without them –

their beds are empty.

Loneliness

♦

116

This is a good time for me – a time to be treasured and not peremptorily dismissed, because in this moment I am free from the grip of daily cares and materialistic ambitions. I am free to see

what matters,
and
what does not.

This is the glorious thought that comes to me unbidden from within, and this I affirm: *It matters* that I knew them, that our lives touched, and that we were enlarged by that touch. *It matters* that that touch had significance only because of Jesus. It was His life, springing up in us, that flowed between us and gave meaning beyond human caring. It created a sympathy that will never leave us.

Family matters, and we were – are – family; *the church matters,* and we were – are – church; *love matters,* and we did – do – love; and hope, *yes, hope matters,* and we hoped – we hoped beyond transience.

And what is at the heart
of all that matters?
Jesus!
Jesus makes us family,
Jesus gives us hope.
Jesus taught us love.

Jesus is the life of the church – the glue that holds all together. And what do I hope that is not centered in – that is not secured by – the anchor of Jesus? "We love, because He first loved us," and it's true, you know.

"Jesus, Jesus, how I trust Him!
How I've proved Him, o'er and o'er!
Jesus, Jesus, precious Jesus!
O for grace to trust Him more!"
—Louisa M. R. Stead, "Tis So Sweet to Trust in Jesus"

And I proved Him today once again. Sitting right here on this concrete bench, I proved Him. Out of loneliness and hopelessness, Jesus brought life and hope. Out of the anguish of the feeling that nothing matters, He created purpose and joy. Jesus taught me that some things matter –

With Him,
everything matters –
without Him,
nothing matters.

Alone

I am alone.
Oh, there are people in the area,
but I am in my office.
My door is closed –
I am alone –

as alone as if I were soaring above the clouds with only the wind and stars to tell my loneliness to.

My son left this morning to return to college. At this moment he is driving the thousand miles that will separate us for the next few months. He too is alone, but his mind is filled with anticipation of his friends and the words to the music he listens to as he drives, and so – he is not aware of being alone, *and where there is no awareness – there is no loneliness.* I think of him – each moment,

farther away.

We tried to make plans to get together for spring break, but the distance is so great and the dates may not coincide. "Summer isn't too far away," we said hopefully, but there is no profitable work here, so he plans to work produce in the San Joaquin Valley in California. The work pays very well, and he certainly needs the money. I may not see him again until next fall.

I am *very* alone just now.

The phone rang a moment ago. It surprised me because I had told my secretary to hold my calls for awhile.

"I think you had better take this call," she said. "It's long distance, and it sounds serious."

"Oh no," I thought, "my worst fears come true. Oh God, please let him be alive, don't let this be a *message of death.*"

But it was.

It was a message of death.

But not my son's. Someone else's son. Someone else's husband, father, brother – an old friend. One whom I had expected to hold again – not at any certain time,

but certainly again.

I will not hold him again – not at spring break, not when school is out, not next fall. I shall not hold him again in this life – nor sing nor pray nor tell old stories. The eternal footman has made his call, and there is no postponing that summons.

I received the message *alone.*

No one here knows my old friend. His death means nothing to them. I cannot share the loss.

I grieve *alone.*

And yet – I am not alone! I am aware of His words – "I will be with you always," and I am reminded of that peace that can only come to those who place all their burdens – their very lives – ever so gently in His hands and rest in Jesus.

I look to the day
when I shall never again
say goodbye –
and never,
never be
alone.

Loneliness

◆

118

&

SIX

Grace

When I was growing up, I never heard much about grace at church – I mean, in sermons or classes. I slowly figured out that it was important and that we needed it, but we were sort of embarrassed by it. Now that we've discovered it, we're trying to make up for lost time and make the most of it. It has become an issue. Can we have too much grace? Will grace fix anything? Does grace mean that everybody is saved? Does grace mean that we don't have to do anything? See there, you thought grace was easy, and I think that God meant for it to be, but we've decided that you have to argue about it and work at it in order to have it.

We even catagorize some congregations as being "grace oriented" – whatever that means. I suppose that's okay, but it leaves other churches in a terrible fix. If they're not "grace oriented," then what are they oriented?

Nothing crucifies the self more than grace. And nothing is more painful than self-crucifixion. Nothing strikes a more savage blow against our basic pride and sense of self-worth than grace. Being able to accept grace is very hard, because it makes such intense demands. On my road to God, nothing I have encountered has baffled and frustrated me more than grace. It is the most nonsensical, illogical, unpredictable, unreasonable thing in all of God's arsenal of weapons that are designed to defeat the enemy within all of us –

ourselves.

You can't earn grace, but it's never cheap. You can't deserve it, but you can't get it unless you give up everything you have. You have to want it, but you can't do anything to get it. Once you have it, you must be constantly giving it away in order to keep it. If you lose it, no amount of effort will reveal it – it will find you. Grace is tricky. If you presume too much upon it, it makes you indolent and careless. If you treat it too lightly, it makes you legalistic and proud and leads to frustration. Make no mistake, living under grace is hard – because we don't understand it.

The following parables were written to teach you some things about grace. I hope when you're finished, you will believe in it, accept it, and trust God for it.

Trixie

We used to have a dog; her name was Trixie. We called her *Trixie the Won-derdog* — because we *wondered* about her. She was *supposed* to be a bird dog — a pointer, specifically. I say *supposed* to be because she was born to two dogs who were full-blooded pointers and she *looked* like a pointer, but something got messed up somewhere in the gene-transmitting process, and she turned out to be just a dog. She loved to run — and she loved to chase and point things — all kinds of things — robins or rabbits — turtles or turkeys — sand-pipers or Saint Bernards — gophers or grasshoppers — or anything else that moved, for that matter — she wasn't partial to game birds. But you see, a pointer is supposed to be partial — I mean, it's an attribute — and she didn't have it, so she became a *yard dog*. Lots of people have them, but usually they're not pointers. A yard dog is — well — it's a yard dog. They do a lot of lying in the sun, and mostly they just sort of stay in the yard — that's why we call them that —

yard dogs, I mean.

I got Trixie from a good friend of mine named Fred Jones — *Fred and me ain't quite so close anymore* — since I got Trixie, I mean. He told me that Trixie just needed some training — and he was right — the only problem was that *Trixie didn't take to training.* She had very definite notions about the direction of her life. I never really figured out if she was exceptionally stubborn, exceptionally stupid, or exceptionally smart, and I don't guess it matters much, because whatever she was, it worked for her. As long as she was in the yard, she was the most meek, obedient, subservient critter God ever made — turn her loose in an open field, and she was a tyrant who defied anybody to tell her what to do.

I had to tell you all of that to help you understand what happened. You see, we decided to move. We were moving a long way and to a place where we wouldn't have anywhere for Trixie, which didn't bother me too much. I called a few of my friends to see which one of them was just dying to take Trixie off of my hands. I discovered two things right off. First, I had fewer friends than I thought — second, Trixie's reputation had spread far and wide — they laughed at me. The time to move got very close, and I had not yet solved the "Trixie problem."

In a moment of sheer desperation, I called the animal shelter — which is a nice term for dog pound. They said they would take her, keep her a few days, and if nobody wanted her, they would *put her to sleep* — which is a nice way of saying they would

murder her —
all for only ten bucks.

Grace

♦

124

Well, I did it. I didn't think I could, but I was desperate, so I did. I called her out of the yard and led her to the car. She was really excited, because getting in the car always meant we were going hunting. She lay on the floor on the passenger side and licked my fingers as we drove — she also got her hair and saliva all over everything.

When we arrived, she followed me in, but she knew something was wrong. She was totally subdued; she sat quietly as I signed some papers and paid the ten dollars. An attendant came and took her leash from me to lead her away. I patted her on the head. "Good-bye Trix," I called after her. As an afterthought, I added, "Be a good dog" — which was really dumb, I know. She went reluctantly, tail between her legs, looking back accusingly over her shoulder at me. I watched her 'till she was out of sight. I had a lump in my throat as big as a cantaloupe and excess water around my eyes as I hurried out to the car.

The day passed slowly — I couldn't get her off my mind — but the deed was done, and I was glad to have it behind me.

Late that afternoon, I saw an old and dear friend fishing at one of the small ponds in town. I hadn't seen him recently, so I decided to stop and visit for awhile. We talked of many things, and I related to him my ordeal of the morning. I know you're way ahead of me, but he identified with my feelings and told me he would have been glad to take Trixie. I said I hoped he was sincere, because if he was, I was going back after her. He said he was, so early the next morning, I was back at the animal shelter. I guess it happens a lot. It was like they were expecting me. They charged me $10.50 to get her back, which I gladly paid, and they brought her to me. She acted as if she were very pleased to see me.

I took her to Jimmy's place — a large, fenced yard in a rural setting — and turned her loose.

She didn't even notice when I left.

This is a story about *salvation by grace,* about a dog who was *meant to be, born to be* something — *but was not.* A dog who stubbornly refused to change with admonition, training, instruction — even punishment. A dog who was sentenced to die —

and deserved it —

a dog who broke the heart of the owner who loved her and grieved over her. A dog who was brought back from the very jaws of death and given another chance.

You and I were born with a purpose. We were born to be something because we were made in the image of God. God has many expectations for us – He wants us to live according to His nature and His instructions. Our life here is a perpetual training ground. We, like Trixie, constantly disappoint Him, exasperate Him; we rebel against His training and instruction because we have our own plans for the direction of our lives. We all deserve to be taken to the animal shelter. But God graciously continues to buy us back, to give us another chance.

It needs to be said – it really does –

that *there is an animal shelter,*
and that dogs *do go there,*
and their owners do not always
come back for them.

One day God's patience will run out, and there will be no more chances –

even grace
has its limitations.

The Pinson Mounds

It was Friday night. I had been to Jackson, Tennessee, with my date and was now returning to the college we attended in Henderson. As we approached the thriving metropolis of Pinson – a city of seventy-five souls, known worldwide for the *Pinson Mounds* (nothing to do with candy bars) – the car started pulling radically to the left, which could only mean one thing – another flat tire. Incidentally, the Pinson Mounds are some rather nondescript small hills – heaps of earth – theoretically created by some aboriginal tribesmen during the sabre-toothed tiger era – with either burial, ceremonial, or religious connotations. I swerved quickly into a little roadside pullout sheltered by oak trees.

Now, the pullout wasn't such a bad place, especially in view of who I was with, and I was never one to cast aside lightly what had obviously been made available to me providentially. But eventually, I knew I was going to have to do something. Joan was very understanding, but she had to be back in the dormitory by 10:30, or we would both have to stand trial before the D.C. – *Discipline Committee* – to explain our whereabouts on the night in question. I had already had the dubious honor, if not pleasure, of receiving a personal invitation to appear before this venerated and august group of sages on several previous occasions and had no desire for a *return engagement.*

Across the street from the pullout was a one-stall, combination repair shop, junk dealer, post office, hardware, gas station, *you-name-it-we-got-it* place. It had closed before dark, but the owner/proprietor's house was next door. It was my only hope. There were no lights on, and it was obvious that they were in bed. I knocked timidly at first, but getting no response and being rather desperate, I banged loudly. This aroused the dog, who, from the sound he made, must have resembled King Kong, but he was chained. I began to hear the angry mutterings and rumblings of someone who obviously had a deep resentment toward this unwarranted disruption of his nocturnal bliss.

A light went on, the door opened slightly, and then he appeared. His hair was disheveled, his pants, hastily thrown on over long-handled underwear – which also served as his night-time attire – hung by one suspender. He was barefoot, his eyes were half-open, and when he opened the door, he had a most unpleasant expression on his face.

"Good evening sir," I said in my most cheerful, polite, and deferential tone.

"Good *morning* you mean," he said – neither cheerfully, politely, nor deferentially. "It's got to be after midnight – Whadayawant?"

"I'm very sorry to inconvenience you, sir, but you see, I have a problem."

"Don't give me that *inconvenience* rubbish – everybody's got problems, Sonny – even me," he said as he looked sourly and suspiciously at me.

"Oh really?" I said. "I'm sorry to hear that, but you see, I have a flat tire."

"Come back tomorrow." He started to close the door.

"But I can't do that," desperation was edging into my voice. "I'm from Freed-Hardeman, over in Henderson, and my girl has to be in the dorm by 10:30, and if I don't get her there, we'll be in big trouble." I tried to slide my foot forward so he couldn't close the door.

Grace

♦

126

"Put your spare tire on."

"Well sir, that's another problem. I don't *exactly* have a spare tire."

He emitted a long sigh of resignation and hopelessness, the kind of sigh that every parent learns all too quickly.

"Where's your car, Sonny?"

"Right over there behind those oaks," I said, as I pointed across the road.

"Okay. You go get the tire off and bring it over, and I'll fix it."

"Yes sir," I said enthusiastically. "But – well – actually, you see, I don't *exactly* have a jack either."

"Don't *exactly* have a jack? Son, either you have a jack or you don't have a jack. What *exactly* do you have? Do you have one *approximately?* Oh, forget it. There's one in that shed there beside the shop. Don't let Old Walt scare you; he's chained up. He sounds real fierce, but he's never *exactly* hurt anybody – seriously."

"Say, thanks a lot. You – uh – you wouldn't happen to have a lug wrench would you?"

"Oh Lord, why me?" he muttered under his breath. "Yea, there should be one in there with the jack," he said out loud. "Anything else you don't *exactly* have?"

"No sir," I said confidently, "that ought to just about do it."

It turned out that the jack was just about a foot from the end of Old Walt's chain, which looked very fragile. Old Walt was a bit much. He looked like a cross between a grizzly bear and a mountain lion, and he acted like he hadn't eaten in six weeks. He absolutely terrified me – lunging so hard against the end of his chain that he actually dragged his house, to which the chain was attached, behind him. His snarl began somewhere in the pit of his stomach, and by the time it came ripping, hissing, rattling, and roaring out his throat, it sounded like an avalanche. His eyes looked like laser beams, he had foam around his mouth, saliva dripped from his jaws, and when he snapped and ground his huge teeth, sparks flew. Old Walt was the original and archetypal *Junk Yard Dog.* I found a piece of rope, lassoed the jack, and dragged it close enough to me that I could grab it and run.

As I took the lug nuts off, I placed them in the hubcap for safe keeping. It was totally dark where the car was, and I had been too ashamed to ask for a flashlight, which I didn't *exactly* have either. The rim was rusted tightly to the drum, and I had to kick it with all my might to break it loose. When it finally flew off, it hit the edge of the hubcap and scattered the lug nuts in every direction, mostly under the car. I could only find one because the ground was about three inches deep in oak leaves. To make matters worse, I also discovered that I could *see through* my tire. It was absolutely ruined, and

Grace

♦

so was the inner tube. When I crossed the road again, tire in hand, I was simply wretched. My benefactor was in the garage.

"I don't think this tire is any good," I said apologetically. "You don't *happen* to have one do you?"

"I don't *happen* to have nothin', Sonny. What I got here I got *on purpose,* and I do have one." He rummaged around and eventually found a pretty decent tire.

"I could let you have this one for five bucks."

"Do you have one any less expensive? I don't *exactly* have five dollars," I said.

"How *much* less expensive? Maybe I could let it go for three," he said.

"I don't *exactly* have three either."

"Well, how much *exactly* do you have?" he said with exasperation.

"Well, if you put it in *exact* terms, I reached in my front pocket and counted out the change, "I have thirty-five cents," I said hopefully.

At that very moment, Joan appeared. She had grown tired of waiting and had come to see if I was making any progress.

Joan was very, very pretty.

"Who in the world is this?" he said, with a whistle and obvious admiration in his voice.

"Oh, this is Joan; she's my date."

He looked appreciatively at Joan.

"You sure must be some *talker,* Sonny. She sure didn't go with you for your *looks,* your *money,* your *brains,* or your *car."*

A pretty girl does wonders to men. His whole attitude changed in Joan's presence. He became gracious, kind, even cheerful – he forgot his inconvenience. He *gave* me the tire, found a tube, patched it, found some spare lug nuts, and helped me put it on. He even invited me to stop by and visit with him on my next trip to Jackson –

if I brought Joan.

He smiled when I told him I would try to repay him some day. "Oh," he said, "That's okay. Forget it. I'll get more than my money's worth telling this story over the next twenty-five years. But nobody will believe it."

It wasn't until I got back to my room that I began to realize that I had just learned something about *salvation by grace.* I had learned what it means to be totally helpless, to have *absolutely nothing* in your hands but your need, and to receive a *gift* that is offered to you cheerfully and at personal cost, a gift that you can never repay.

Grace Reigns

He heard the harsh grating of their boots on the stone corridors long before they arrived, and he wondered if some new prisoner was being brought to stagnate in the dark, damp, recesses of this accursed dungeon. The steps stopped outside his cell. What did they want of him? He had been there over a year, and no one but the person who brought his food had ever stopped before. A year – it seemed an eternity – no light, no conversation, no hope. That year had aged him – physically – emotionally – spiritually – he was not the man he had been when they had brought him, kicking and cursing, to this cell.

It had seemed so glorious – leading a rebellion against the oppression of the government. Everyone had been sympathetic. His small group of activists had been sure that the masses would join them if they took the lead. The conflict had been brief. They were hopelessly outnumbered, and they were no match for trained soldiers. The masses, for whom they had fought, either ran or stood silently by as the rebel leaders were captured, arrested, and tried.

He had done a lot of thinking since then; he certainly had had time for it. His future, once bright, now held nothing. He knew that he would grow old alone. He would never marry, never have friends or children. His dark, handsome face would quickly grow thin and sallow here where the sun never shone and the food was meager and lacking in nourishment. He often wondered about his parents and his brothers and sisters and of course –

he wondered about Ruth.

He cursed his foolish decision – a decision that had cost him everything! He thought daily of how he would do things differently if he just had the chance – just one *chance* – but there would be no chance for him. *Confined until death* – that was his sentence. No reprieve, no parole, no pardon!

In his desperation, he had even started praying! It was almost involuntary. He had heard about God all his life – it was for God that he had fought – not specifically, he admitted – but his religion was certainly part of the motivation behind the hatred he had for the foreign swine that were bleeding his country. It was a prayer born of desperation, not of hope. He knew that if he didn't get *that kind of help* – there was no help. He didn't think it would work, not even God could get him out of this place, and why should He anyway? He hadn't prayed since he was a child, and he felt quite foolish doing it. He was glad no one was there to see him as he knelt by his cot – just as he had when he was a child beside his mother – and offered up a simple petition –

"Oh God, if you know where I am, help me!"

Thoughts of his mother and his childhood flooded through him, and the tears came again, softly and quietly. That was something else that had changed during the year he had spent here – he had learned to cry. That was when he heard the footsteps. He knew they were soldiers by the hard and rhythmic sound of nailed boots on the stone. The regular keepers wore only sandals.

The key grated in the massive lock, and the door to his cell screeched as it swung open. "All right, come on; they want you upstairs." They grabbed him roughly and pushed him ahead of them. His mind was whirling. It could only mean one thing – they had decided to make a public example of him. He would be beaten and executed. He had seen these executions before, and he trembled.

After several flights of steps, the light grew, and he shielded his eyes – long accustomed to darkness – screening them from the intense brightness. The courtyard was in chaos – people were running and shouting. He guessed that the rabble had gathered to witness the entertainment and excitement that an execution offered.

As the guards shoved him out into the open courtyard, he finally understood what the mob was chanting.

"Barabbas, Barabbas,
release to us Barabbas!"

One of the soldiers shoved him forward, "All right," he said, "go on." He simply couldn't believe it. "But I don't understand; you mean I'm free to go? I can just leave?" The captain of the guards said, "I don't understand it either. They just told me that you had been pardoned – yes, you're free to go."

It is easy to pay lip service to grace – to talk about grace – to build *grace sand castles*. But unless it touches our experience – until we feel its power – it has little practical effect upon us. Until we can speak of grace in terms of how we are changed by it – in the same way that we would talk about the economy or pollution – it is little more than a theological conversation piece.

When we begin to speak of God's grace in this practical and providential way, many folks – even church-going ones – may look at us as though they think we are religious fanatics. They would not say that we are talking nonsense – but they feel that whatever it is we are talking about is over their heads and –

> the longer they live without it,
> the more positive they are
> that they do not need it.

Humility and Grace

As with most stories, there are some historical things you will have to understand before you can appreciate why the event I wish to record had such a profound impact on me. I was raised in a family that prided itself on its *independence* and that looked with disdain on those *shiftless* and *no account* folks who took *charity* or accepted anything from anybody that they had not earned. From my earliest remembrances it was grilled into me that I was to "pay my own way." My folks had gone through the great depression, and they had both stood in the work lines rather than accept government relief.

As I came into manhood, I accepted my family's philosophy completely, and I also looked down on anyone who accepted welfare and even more so those who took food stamps and became part of the burgeoning welfare state as recipients of the *public dole.* I taught my children to work – to work physically and to take satisfaction in their labor and to never be dependent on others – to go without if necessary, and to never, never accept

charity.

In 1968 I was a student at the University of Michigan. Judi and I had been married for five years, and we had two children – aged four and one. Judi was working as a substitute teacher, and I was employed by General Motors National Parts in Flint, Michigan. I worked the afternoon shift from

2:30 to 11:30 P.M. I had scheduled my classes in the mornings. Three days a week I had a 7:30 and a 9:30 class, and two days a week I had a 9:00 class. The only time I had for study was after I got home from work at about midnight. I arrived home, ate, and hit the books until 3:00 or 4:00 A.M. On Saturdays I went to the library and researched and wrote papers. My work, class, and study schedule allowed no time for family matters. Judi was substitute teaching, taking care of two small children, cooking, cleaning, typing my papers, and doing laundry. We were broke, exhausted, and irritable – to the point that we began to wonder if our marriage would survive.

When I got close to graduating, I had a choice to make – either I could spread out my last eighteen hours over two semesters or try to finish in one. The problem was that if I decided to finish in one, I would have to quit my job. We figured our budget down to the last penny, and although any slight ripple would bring disaster, we decided we would try it rather than risk losing our marriage. Judi got a permanent substitute job for six weeks, and my mom volunteered to come and stay with us so the children wouldn't have to have a baby-sitter. That influenced us to make a leap of faith. I quit my job with General Motors, signed up for eighteen hours, and the great race began.

We didn't make it.

I think we knew we wouldn't when we started – we just told ourselves we would because we wanted to believe it so badly. Things happened – nothing spectacular or unusual – we had car repairs, unanticipated medical bills, the utilities were higher than we had figured – none of it serious, but enough to upset our delicate finances. We began to sell things to make ends meet – we sold our second car, which really strained us because we had to work out how to get me to school and Judi to work. Then I sold my golf clubs. It may not sound like much of a sacrifice, but at one time I had been planning to become a professional golfer, and I had a special set of custom clubs made just for me. They were quite expensive, and I was very proud of them.

You know, when you're first starting out in marriage, you don't have much, and it's surprising how little you have to sell – I mean, things that would have value to someone else. When the golf clubs were gone, I only had one thing left of value that I could do without – my shotgun. I had had it for several years, and I was determined not to part with it. It might sound like a small sacrifice to someone who isn't into that sort of thing – but it was important to me. We held out for a long time, but I knew it was coming. When I was faced with the choice of either borrowing money from someone or selling my shotgun, the choice was easy. I called my friend Bruce

Welch in Indiana and asked him if he would buy it. He offered to lend me the money until I got back to work, but I just couldn't do it that way. He bought the shotgun on the condition that I could buy it back at some future date. (Twenty years later, he gave it back to me.)

It was the last thing of value that we owned.

Judi's permanent subbing job ran out, and she had to go day by day. Some days they called and some days they didn't. A pall of gloom settled over us, but we were close to the end. In mid-November I got a teaching offer from a principal named Morgan Robertson at Utley Junior High, starting the first of January. The money from the shotgun paid December's rent and bought enough groceries to last through Christmas. What Judi would make subbing would pay our utilities – there wouldn't be much Christmas – but we could survive.

I finished my degree and graduated late in December. I started teaching early in January, and we began finding a thousand ways to spend our first paycheck. I knew that the school district issued checks every two weeks, and since I had started at the end of a pay period, it would be two weeks before I would get a check. We marked the days.

I'll never forget that Friday.

After school I went to the office with the other teachers to get my check from my mailbox. I was really excited because I was going to take Judi out for dinner to celebrate. I was going to be *the man of the house* again – the *breadwinner*. I had broken out in a sweat by the time I put my hand in my mailbox. There were several pieces of mail in there – *but no check*. My heart was pounding erratically, and a hundred possibilities – all negative – crossed my mind. I carefully went through everything to make sure I hadn't missed it. *I hadn't missed it* – it wasn't there. "Well," I thought, "maybe the secretary has held it for me."

I went to her desk and asked if she knew what had happened to my check. I think she must have seen the concern and panic on my face. "Oh, Mr. Smith," she said. "I'm so sorry. Didn't they explain that when you hire in at mid-year, it takes two weeks for all your paper work to clear the district office and your name to be entered on the payroll computer? Your first check will come through two weeks from now."

I just couldn't believe it. I was stunned, speechless. I turned and wandered aimlessly out of the office, not knowing what I was going to do – what I was going to tell my wife, who was looking forward to her first night out in six months – my kids, who were old enough to know that today was a *big day* in their lives – that we were going to have pizza and hamburgers. I know

Grace

♦

133

it doesn't sound like much – but it was. When you haven't had it for a long time, it's important.

I was crushed and confused, and I had nowhere to turn, no last ditch maneuver, no hidden piggy bank for the last extremity – I had used up all of my last extremities. I drove home. I had never in my life been less anxious to get there. I parked the car in the driveway and walked to the back door. Judi was waiting for me. I could see her through the glass in the door as she rushed to greet me; she was already dressed in her very best, with her hair done and all – she was so excited and happy.

She knew something was wrong the minute she saw my face – before I ever opened the door – her face fell and her expectant smile turned to tears – she started crying before I even told her what had happened. I don't blame her; I mean, what do you expect when you've been working and going without and making do with almost nothing at all and a big hope comes and then it dies –

what else do you do but cry?

It's not so much the thing itself – it's the disappointment created by the expectation – that's what gets you. The size of the disappointment is in direct proportion to the size of the expectation. It's sort of like running a race – you know how far you have to run, so you create a mental threshold for it, and you hold yourself as the miles go by, and you conserve just enough energy to make it just as far as you have to go – *and no farther* – but if you get to what you believe is the finish line and find out that you've miscalculated the distance, you have no heart to go on. I opened the door and she hugged me and we both cried because –

we had no heart to go on.

I tried to explain what happened, and she understood – but it didn't help. I know that if you're sitting in your living room right now in a nice comfortable chair with a glass of iced tea and a sandwich, you're thinking, "So what's the big deal? It's only two more weeks." But for us – two weeks was a lifetime.

"What are we going to do?" she said. When you're the man of the house, you're supposed to know the answer to that – it's your job – it's what you promise her when you marry her – that you'll take care of her and she won't have to worry about those things because you'll take care of it.

"I don't know," I said –
and I didn't.

The first thing I did was to go upstairs to our bedroom to think for a minute and to pray. I asked God what He was doing to me; hadn't we suffered enough? I was angry and miserable, because up until now *I had been able to handle it.* Of course, that was the whole problem – but I couldn't see it. I don't know what I expected Him to do, actually. I didn't want Him to do anything except *show me how I could continue to handle it.*

I sat on the edge of the bed and prayed and thought. Then I thought about Ira – I don't know why, but I did. Looking back, it occurs to me that maybe that's one way God answers prayers. At the moment, we don't even see it because it seems so normal and simple – that's how it seemed to me – *normal and simple.* Maybe I could still pull the rabbit out of the hat, even if it would be a little awkward.

I had a good friend named Ira Willis who lived just around the corner from us. When I thought about Ira, I knew what I had to do – I mean, it was as clear as could be – it was something I had never done before – but now was the time. I called Ira to see if he was home. He was. I told him I needed to talk to him for a minute and that I would be right there. I told Judi where I was going. I said that I wouldn't be gone long but not to change her clothes.

> "What are you going to do?" she said.
> *"What I have to do."*

Ira was glad to do it. I didn't tell him everything, but I told him that I had made a promise to my wife that I was going to keep if it killed me – and it nearly did. He asked me how much I needed, and I told him twenty-five dollars. He tried to give me more, but I wouldn't accept it. I told him he would have it back in two weeks. It was my first major lesson in *humility,* but the second one was much bigger and not far behind.

The twenty-five dollars took us out to dinner that Friday and even through Saturday. It put enough gas in the tank to get us to church on Sunday morning, but that was it. The rent was paid, and I knew the utility companies would wait because of our good payment record. Our immediate need was for groceries and for gasoline to get me to work. Judi had used every scrap of food in the house to get us through to this time. We had *nothing left* – I mean *nothing* – not a can of anything, not a jar of peanut butter, not a cracker to put it on if we had had it, no milk, no eggs, no cereal, no bread, no dish-washing detergent, no toilet paper – nothing.

> It *was all gone* –
> Mother Hubbard's cupboard was bare.

I still remember our discussion about going to church that Sunday. The church we attended was several miles from our house. We had enough gas to get there and back but not enough for me to get to work the next day.

Grace

♦

135

It wasn't an easy decision, but old habits and a mustard seed's worth of faith won out –

we went.

At the beginning of the service, they announced that we were going to have a potluck and fellowship after services. That sort of took us by surprise because we normally planned those things a couple of weeks in advance. It also put us in a bad spot because we didn't have anything to contribute to the potluck, so my pride made me decide that we wouldn't go.

After services we got the kids and started toward the parking lot. Of course the kids wanted to stay and so did Judi, but my *pride* just wouldn't allow it. It was a real small church and our attempt to leave didn't go unnoticed. When they asked where we were going, we made some excuse about having plans for the afternoon. I guess we should have noticed something unusual about it, but we didn't – we were too caught up in our misery. Everybody insisted that we stay. I mean, it was more than the usual type of encouragement – they *insisted* that we stay and wouldn't take "no" for an answer.

We went back in and went to the basement where our fellowships were held. It was a normal potluck with plenty of food and plenty of laughing and good-natured conversation. When everybody had eaten and things had sort of died down, one of the elders called for everybody's attention. He said that he had a special announcement. While he was talking, the men of the church began to bring out all of these grocery sacks – like forty or fifty of them – all full of groceries. He began talking about this family that was having a real hard time and how much they meant to the church and how loved they were and how the church wanted to show them their appreciation. He said that they had also taken up a collection and he had a check for two hundred and fifty dollars for them and that every family in the church had contributed.

Now I know you're way ahead of me, but *you absolutely must understand* that while he was talking, all I could think about was who it could be and why they hadn't told us about this so we could have helped too. *You must believe me* – because if you don't understand that, you will not understand my complete shock and confusion when he called Judi and me to come up and get the check.

I don't remember much about the rest of that afternoon. I was so *embarrassed* – yes, that is the *exact word;* in fact, *humiliated* is even more accurate, although I am ashamed of it now. I believe that Judi handled most of the *acceptance speech* – I was too dumbfounded to respond. When it came time to load the groceries, I tried hard to decline. Judi rescued me again, whispering to me that *ingratitude was as great a sin as pride,* and I knew that she was right, but I was filled with both, especially the latter, because this was different from Ira's twenty-five – I could and would pay that back – but *this would never be paid back* – it just couldn't be done and I could see that – I would be *indebted* to these people *forever.*

It was one of the hardest things I ever did. I felt like a total failure, like I had betrayed my family. I thought over and over about my dad, and I really began to appreciate him. I said, *"Dad, forgive me, I guess there comes a time when a man just has to do some things."*

I'm sure he understood.

Many of the hard things I have done since that time might seem to shrink this event into insignificance, but they don't. If I made a list of all the hard things I ever did, this would be in the top five.

There are many disclaimers that I would like to make about this story, and I suppose there are a hundred ways to misunderstand what I've said. I hope that it's obvious that I believe in the validity of the principles of "paying your own way" and trying to earn what you receive. I also hope that it's obvious that those things can lead to pride and a *works salvation mentality.* They can give us a false sense of personal value and worth that make it hard for God's Spirit to convict us of our lostness and need.

True humility comes hard to us, and the more filled with pride we are, the harder it is to accept *grace.* And that's what it is, you know – it's *grace* that I was dealing with. A person whose pride can't or won't let him accept the generosity of other people when his need is real is going to find it very hard, *when conviction of sin and lostness is upon him,* to accept God's generosity – especially when he realizes –

> that there is no way
> he's ever going to pay it back.
> Make no mistake about it –
> *grace is charity!*

Home on the Range

The other night I had a dream. I don't suppose there is anything note-worthy about that except that I don't dream much anymore – at least, if I do, I don't remember them. I was impressed by how real this dream was. You can smell, taste, and feel in a dream. I think you can even *learn!* In my dream, I was visiting a prison. This was a women's prison – at least all the people in my dream were women. I don't know if there is anything Freudian about that or not – I simply record it as a fact.

In my dream I was going from one cell to another, teaching and coun-seling. At one point I stood in front of several cells, arranged in a half-moon setting, and preached a brief but inspired message on grace. (I wish I could remember it – I have never preached one that good in real life.)

Off to one side, in an isolated cell – a particularly dark, cramped, and dingy one – sat an elderly woman. Her hair was long, gray, and stringy. She was very old, and her face was so deeply wrinkled that her features were dis-torted. While I was talking, I noticed that she was now standing with her face wedged so tightly between the bars that it pulled the corners of her eyes back, making them mere slits, which heightened her already grotesque appearance. She was pressing herself forward and gripping the bars overhead with both hands. She peered intently – never taking her eyes off me – lis-tening to every word. She was so thin that I thought she might actually slip between the bars.

When I finished my lesson on grace (I guess my fundamentalist back-ground influenced my dream), I started to sing "Oh, Why Not Tonight" as an invitation song. It was real dumb because they couldn't respond even if they wanted to. As I was about to begin the second verse, she spoke. It was so startling, because her voice was not like her appearance at all – it was low, melodic, and vibrant, the kind of voice you would expect from a much younger person.

"Sing '*Home on the Range,*'" she said.

"I don't think that would be appropriate," I responded.

"'Oh Why Not Tonight' isn't very appropriate either," she said, not unkindly. "I know 'Home on the Range' is not exactly a *church song,* but it would mean so much to me to hear it again, and surely God wouldn't grudge me that."

I was ashamed of having refused her – and of talking to her about pro-priety – when she was so obviously moved by my speaking about the grace of God. And so I said I would, and I began to sing – very softly.

> "Oh give me a home,
> where the buffalo roam,
> Where the deer and the antelope play.
> Where seldom is heard,
> a discouraging word,
> and the skies are not cloudy,
> all day.
>
> Home, home on the range,
> Where the deer and the antelope play.
> Where seldom is heard
> a discouraging word,
> and the skies
> are not cloudy all day."

I watched her mouth the words, like a silent prayer, and then softly, she began to cry. She cried all the way through, and I was so moved I sang it twice. I moved over to her cell, and through the bars, I embraced her and I cried, because I understood how a heart, sick with sin and longing, reach-ing for God, yearning to find a spiritual expression, might find it in that song.

> There is more to seeking for God
> and expressing our desire for Him
> than most of us suspect.

That was the end of the dream. I wish I could tell you more. I awoke a better man – with a little different view on appropriateness – the grace of God – and what *home* means. I also awoke wondering if God still speaks to us in dreams. I've been humming "Home on the Range" all day – I might suggest it for an invitation song one Sunday, but it would only be *appropri-ate* to those who understand what it means to be –

> *homesick.*

Free at Last

"There is therefore now no condemnation
for those who are in
Christ Jesus."
—Romans 8:1

They were high school sweethearts. They married the summer after they graduated. That fall, he entered college and she went to work. For two years things went pretty well, and then an *unexpected* and *unwanted* son came. It is only fair to say that although the son was *unexpected* by both – he was only *unwanted* by the father, and he only felt that way because the baby's birth was *terribly inconvenient.* She worked until two weeks before he was born, and two weeks later she was working again. She worked long hours, she cooked, cleaned, washed, and raised a baby. She typed her husband's college papers, and she smiled and encouraged him when he was depressed.

He carried an extra class load every semester and went to summer school. His entire life was controlled by classes, papers, tests, labs, and projects. He spent more time in the library than at home. He was determined to finish five year's work in four –

and he succeeded.

Toward the end she grew very thin. Although she remained cheerful, she was tired most of the time and often not well. The pressure of his class load made him irritable, critical, and insensitive. They argued, sometimes loudly. He graduated on schedule. Two months later she came home from work one day and found a note. He had left her. They tried reconciliation and counseling, but mostly it was *she* who tried – *his mind was made up.* He divorced her, and two months after that he married a nineteen-year-old girl who had been his lab partner in chemistry.

His wife never got over it. After the divorce she went to live with her parents, but she simply was unable to cope. Her physical condition deteriorated, and severe mental depression left her unable to deal either with the past or the future. The baby was raised by the grandparents.

I met her ex-husband five years later – he was twenty-nine. Although I knew him slightly, he came to me for counseling because a mutual friend had recommended me. He had developed a serious drinking problem, which was causing negative reverberations both at work and in his present marriage. He was desperate. He had tried everything else – spending a fortune on psychiatrists, counselors, therapy, and drugs – and he was worse. I gradually pieced together the above story over a period of about five or six sessions. It was very painful for him. Often, he would halt for long periods of time – sitting silently – his mind working feverishly; and when he started talking again, it was obvious that he had skipped over something in the chronology that was too painful or embarrassing for him to verbalize.

He was physically thin, anemic looking. He was nervous – constantly changing his posture, folding and unfolding his hands – even his speech was broken and halting. He would often begin a sentence, lose it, then begin another. His eyes shifted constantly, and he could never, it seemed, look steadily at anything, especially me. Often he just stared vacantly. His favorite phrase was, "I'm not crazy, you know." That phrase was injected constantly into his narrative, no matter what the topic –

"I'm not crazy, you know."

He wasn't a Christian; in fact, he wasn't religious, but he had so violated whatever personal or family sense of morality he had, that it was a festering wound in his vitals. It simply would not heal. The wound was all the worse because –

he could not make it right.
No amount of self-sacrifice
or self-abasement
would cure either her sickness –
his son's questions –
or his guilt.

If he sacrificed his present marriage and became a celibate . . . if he gave every cent he made to maintain his wife and son . . . if he gave his body to be burned . . . nothing would ever erase the pain he had caused – the anguish and suffering he had imposed upon his former wife – or the fact that he had abandoned and neglected his own son. It wasn't just what he had done that crushed him – many have done equally bad or worse – it was the terrible finality of the realization that –

he could not undo it.

At the climax of one session, he stood up – slammed his open hand down on my desk – and screamed, "I can't! Do you understand? I can't! There are two people out there whose lives are ruined because of me, and *I – can't – change it!*" He fell back into his chair exhausted and sobbing. He was the most wretched man I had ever met –

and he was *absolutely right.*

So it was out, and now I had the ball. It was all so marvelously clear, so beautifully simple to me. The reason I write about it is because of its clarity.

It is *every man's* situation,
it is *my* situation and *yours!*

The problem is that you and I rarely ever see our helplessness as clearly as this man did. Consequently, we spend our lives trying to fix things. We try to *make things right* or pay back. We even try apologizing or confessing fault, but somehow, even that doesn't *undo* or give the kind of satisfaction we need. And so, all of our efforts leave us empty, even though we occasionally feel better.

I told him that he was absolutely right about himself — that he was one of the most miserable, detestable, despicable, rotten, wretched examples of humanity I had ever met — that he didn't deserve to live and wasn't worth the dynamite it would take to blow him up. I told him he was also right about his helplessness — nothing he could do would right the wrongs or erase the suffering he had caused.

I told him that he had two options. His first option was to become hardened to his sins and the grief of others and say, "that's life in the big city" or "that's the way the old cookie crumbles." And in his hardened state, he could pursue relief: He could seek *physical relief* through work, athletic efforts — busyness. He could seek *mental relief* through movies, television talk shows, books, and conversation. He could seek *emotional relief* through drugs, sex, alcohol, psychiatry, twelve-step programs, and support groups. But something would still be missing —

and he would know it.
It would be
spiritual relief —
and *none* of the above things can give that.

His other option was to accept the grace of God, to see his life for what it was, and to admit that the answer was neither in himself, me, nor any other human being. What he needed was *forgiveness* — hopefully from his wife — eventually from his son — and then from himself — but first and most important, from God. He needed to be saved —

not from his *guilt*
but from his *sins.*

Salvation only comes from one source. Psychology couldn't save him, counseling couldn't save him, group therapy and motivational tapes couldn't save him. Drink, drugs, partying, work, sports, and all the marvels of the computer age and modern medicine couldn't save him, but when he heard the

♦

message of grace and the call of God through the good news about Jesus, he said –

"Can it be that simple?"

"Simple?" I repeated. "I guess not; it's never simple. You have to understand what it cost God to make you this offer and what he's going to demand of you in return. You see, God loves you so much – He wanted so badly to give you this chance – that He allowed His only son to be murdered by some people just like you. Jesus died because of what *you did to your wife and son!*

"Now you need to know that God doesn't take His Son's death lightly, and the offer he has made you isn't cheap. What He wants from you is your life – yes – He wants you to give Him *your life* – the old life, that is – and He will make a new you. This 'making new' process is going to be *very painful* – especially at first. From then on you will have times of great joy and peace – with some pain mixed in – and the pain and the joy will last for the rest of your life here, but the pain gets less and the joy gets more as you get closer to the end – or the beginning, actually."

"What have I got to lose?" he asked.

"Absolutely nothing of value," I said.

"Well, where do I start?" he said.

"Right here. Do you believe that Jesus Christ is the Son of God?"

"With all my heart."

I immersed him that night in the name of the Father, Son, and Holy Spirit, and he began a new life.

By God's grace,

he was reckoned righteous. I never met or knew a man to whom salvation – cleansing – meant more. He truly experienced the exhilaration of the now famous Negro spiritual –

"Free at last!
Free at last!
Praise God almighty,
I'm free at last!"

SEVEN

P
Pride

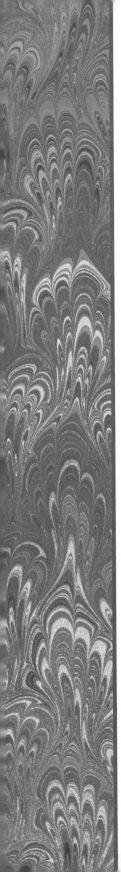

The ancients believed and taught that not only was *pride* the first sin, but that all sin was rooted in that quality which we seem to so much admire. While I can think of few things that I would rather not be true, I know of few things that I personally recognize so much as being true – the ancients were right. It never ceases to amaze me that the very quality we have so little *reason* to have is the very one that dominates most of our decision making. If love for money is the root of all kinds of evil, pride is at the root of that love.

Why should we love money? Because money is power, and power is independence, and independence is control – and control is what we all seek because control is the only thing that will satisfy our pride. Why do we steal, lie, covet, slander, and commit sexual immorality? Are these not vain attempts to satisfy the insatiable thirst we have to control our own destiny, to be our own God? Why does Scripture constantly warn us against idolatry? What is at the heart of man's desire to worship created things rather than the creator of things? The central issue is that we want a God we can manipulate and control. All idolatry is rooted in pride because it is rooted in self-adulation. Deep within all of us is that lurking lust –

to be God.

That is exactly what Adam and Eve wanted. That is the carrot that Satan dangled in front of them – and he constantly dangles it in front of us too. Didn't he say that if they would eat the fruit of the tree that they would "be like God"? Isn't that what he offers us – the ability to be like God? We are no wiser than our parents; we too throw caution to the wind and grab and eat, because we want to be like God. Only pride could so betray our good sense and cause us to be so stupid as to believe that. Adam and Eve's pride fueled desire, and that desire is at the root of what causes us to act like fools and do those things that lead us into sin.

Pride is the antithesis of godliness. It is the anti-God state of mind. It is epitomized in our stated cultural philosophy, "Do your own thing" – a phrase that unwitting Christians mindlessly parrot. Pride will never allow us to be servants. It calls us to seek not the will of God, but our own will. Pride stands squarely between us and the mind of Jesus – it stands squarely between us and agape love – between us and better marriages, better churches, better parents – better people. Pride is the root of all sin.

I am disheartened by the equivocating and disclaiming that is done by well-intentioned people on this topic. Preachers and teachers, who should know better, are so concerned about offending either some worldly parishioner or their own lifestyles that they are willing to offend God by apologizing and groveling – by emphasizing the exceptions – by talking about the fact that pride can be a good thing – by saying that everybody needs some pride. They are so soothing and diplomatic that the basic lesson about the ungodliness of pride is totally lost.

Beware of pride!

Gertrude

My son Lincoln and I had been to the town of Frankenmuth, Michigan, to fish. He was about eleven at the time. The town is nearly world famous for its breweries and for Zenders, a national monument to fried chicken and sauerbraten. It is much less well known for salmon fishing, but that's why we were there. The Clinton River is dammed there, and the Lake Huron salmon collect below the dam.

The town is only about fifty miles from Flint, where we lived. We had left right after school, hoping to fish a couple of hours before dark. It was late fall. When we headed home after a very successful trip, it was very cold and very dark. We were speeding along a narrow, twisting country road when, suddenly, my headlights revealed a white piscovey duck (I couldn't find *piscovey* in the dictionary, so I spelled it by ear) in the road. I can't imagine what it was doing in the road at that time of night. I thought ducks were like chickens and went to sleep as soon as it got dark – and this one should have. I was going much too fast to swerve, and there was no time to stop. I heard the sickening *whack* and *crunch* of the duck hitting the underside of the car repeatedly.

It isn't easy to explain my next action – in fact, it's a little embarrassing – but I have to try, or I can't tell the rest of the story. You need to know me personally, and you need to understand the way I was brought up. In my family –

nothing was ever wasted –
it was a sin to waste.

I turned around and went back to pick up the duck so we could take it home and eat it. It was lying in a heap, sprawled out in obvious death in the middle of ten thousand feathers. I pulled up alongside, reached out my door, picked the duck up, laid it on the floor behind my seat, and we headed home once again. I was driving a compact car. It was a Buick Opel with bucket seats.

Lincoln was very quiet as we drove, but completely alert. Normally, he would have been sound asleep in ten minutes, but the incident with the duck had totally captured his imagination. I noticed that he kept looking behind my seat. A few minutes later, he said,

"Dad, do ducks have souls?"

"No son, ducks don't have souls."

"What happens to a duck when it dies?"

"We eat it."

"I mean, where does it go?"

"It doesn't go anywhere. It just *isn't* anymore."

"Oh." He thought for a few minutes and then he said, "Dad, is it okay to pray for a duck?"

"I guess so, but why would you want to?"

"I feel sorry for it."

He lapsed into a thoughtful silence, and I assumed that he was praying. He kept his eyes on the duck, and a few minutes later he spoke again.

"Dad?"

"What son?"

"God just answered my prayer; that duck's alive."

"God doesn't do things like that anymore. The duck is dead."

A few minutes passed.

"Dad? Why doesn't God do things like that anymore?"

"Because the age of miracles ceased when the apostle John died."

"Dad, are you sure of that? The duck is alive. I just saw it move."

"No, son, the duck may have moved from the motion of the car. I know that you feel sorry for the duck, and I do, too, and I know you prayed for the duck, but we have to learn to accept bad things in life. *The duck is dead.* You heard it hit the car, didn't you?"

"Yes, but, Dad, the duck just moved again, and it's not the motion of the car. *It's looking right at me.*"

"Son, this has gone far enough. You mustn't allow your imagination to run away with you. I've told you that the duck is dead. *It is dead!* No amount of wishful thinking can bring it back. Trust me. I'm your father, and when *I* tell you that the duck is *dead,* you can believe me.

The − duck − is − dead!
Now, I don't want to hear any more
about that duck;
do you understand?"

"Yes Sir."

"Quack."

"What was that noise?"

"I think it was the dead duck, Dad."

I turned around, and sure enough, there was the duck, standing up and looking rather puzzled by its new surroundings.

"Son," I said, "the age of miracles just started again, because that duck was dead!"

We took it home, fed it, found a marvelous place for it to stay − in our swimming pool, which was closed for the winter anyway − and we named her (I guess it was a her) Gertrude. About a month later we went back to Frankenmuth. We took Gertrude and released her as near to the spot where we had found her as possible and went on our way.

I offer this comment on our fetish for being right and how foolish we appear when we state that rightness in unequivocal terms. The problem is that when the *facts* prove us wrong, our *pride* forces us to continue to defend our position. In no area of our lives are we more prone to making unequivocal and uncompromising statements about rightness

than in religion.

And in no area is there more inclination for our pride to cause us to continue to defend our position long after both experience and the facts have proved us wrong

than in religion.

We need to make very sure that we are standing squarely on what God has said, not simply exonerating our egos.

Pride

♦

⚜

God Has Worn Me Out

"If I speak, my pain is not assuaged,
and if I forbear, how much of it leaves me?
Surely now God has worn me out;
he has made desolate all my company.
And he has shriveled me up."
—Job 16:6–7

Bill Odell (he pronounced it *O*-dell because he was from Arkansas; I always said o-*Dell* because I was from Michigan) was a very sick man when I met him. His wife Hazel and their daughter Linda were faithful members of the church where I preached. Bill didn't go to church. He had at one time not only gone, but had been heavily involved. A few years before I came, he had a falling out with a couple of brothers who still attended,

and he had never gone again.

The Odell's lived in a mobile-home park just outside of town, and Judi and I were regular visitors there. When I first met him, he seemed jovial, personable, and reasonable in every area of conversation except one – the church. At the slightest mention of church, he would withdraw – become bitter, cynical, and negative. As his physical condition worsened, this tendency increased with every visit.

The day came when he finally went to the hospital for what appeared to be the last time. The cancer was raging unchecked through his stomach and vital organs. He was a mere shadow of himself, shriveled and emaciated. His business was a shambles, his friends were estranged, and a disease – far worse than cancer – was eating at his soul and destroying the only sustaining strength a man has in those hours.

I visited him often, read to him, and sat long hours in silence with him, hoping he would speak. It was on his mind. It never left him. It was on the edge of every word. It tormented him –

but his pride
was greater than his need.

On Saturday night, July 22, 1965, I stayed very late. The end was near, and he seemed anxious for me to be there. The doctors had given him pain killers, but he fought against sleep – fearing, I know, that he might not awake. His eyes stared intently from two dark holes horribly recessed in his head. About 2:00 or 3:00 A.M., I told him I had to leave. He nodded and made a motion that I should pray. Six-thirty found me there again. He had not slept.

His breathing was labored, and talking required concentrated exertion. Just as I was going to leave for services, he beckoned for me to lean over him. My ear was almost touching his lips.

"Tell Nate and J.V. that I'm sorry. I was wrong and I want to be right – with them and with God." On his face there was a single tear. If every salty drop in the Pacific Ocean is a tear, there is not one more precious than that penitent one that fell from the cheek of Bill Odell.

I went directly to the church, and of course, I was glad to make the announcement, and of course, there were many tears and much rejoicing. The two men went directly to the hospital –

but Bill was gone.
Gone!

Pride

♦

152

Bill was the perfect example of a man, like Job, whom God had worn out. Why did he wait so long? Only his stubborn pride kept him from the joy and affirmation of fellowship for all those years. Bill missed a hundred potlucks, a thousand hymns of praise, five hundred hopeful remembrances of our precious Lord's sufferings and glorious resurrection. He missed ten thousand laughs and the pleasure of genuine goodwill from those who shared his faith, his struggle, and his hope.

And it was so easy.

He was gladly forgiven.

No one wished to carry the burden of those wrongs. How grateful – happy – they were to be released. What a joy it would have been could they have embraced and loved each other like God meant for them to.

If God had not worn him out, his stubborn pride would have taken him to eternal condemnation, where he would have suffered the loss of those things forever.

How much is your pride worth?

Is God wearing you out?

The Price of Pride

His name was Herbert, but we all called him "Herbie," and he was a bully. He was very good looking, with sharply defined features, a clear complexion, and long, dark hair. I did not like him, and I avoided him whenever possible. We had fought on three separate occasions, and he had whipped me every time. I knew he could do it again if I crossed him. I knew it the first time when I tackled him in the sixth grade because he was bullying a fair-haired, anemic-looking boy named Eric, who was slightly crippled from polio. Eric was completely inoffensive, a weakling – and he had a beautiful sister named Grace, whom I much admired. Although I *might* have defended Eric because of the first three qualities, the last one tilted the scales drastically, and I waded in. I don't remember ever being more soundly thrashed. Ah – the things we do for love – but Grace's gratitude made it all worthwhile.

In the seventh grade, Herbie's bullying took on a more serious tone. He demanded our lunch money. Money was a scarce commodity. The second and third time he whipped me was over lunch money. I simply would not give it up without a fight. The first time he got it because I had it in my hand when he grabbed me. The second time he got it because he forced my arm up behind my back until it nearly broke and I agreed to give it to him. I couldn't use my arm for nearly a week.

I think one of the happiest days of my seventh grade year was the day I saw Herbie handing a blue sheet of paper to all our teachers for them to sign. That meant he was moving! My prayers had been answered. I felt as free as a released prisoner. No longer must I walk home in constant fear. No longer must I watch my every step during lunch hour, never knowing when I would be grabbed or tackled by Herbie. He was gone – finally and for always gone! There was much rejoicing in Mary Lyons Junior High that day.

I was looking at a picture of our sixth-grade class today, and I got to thinking about Herbie. Even now I smile as I remember how glad I was when he moved, and I wonder whatever happened to him. I strongly suspect that if we met today –

he would be embarrassed.

The other thing I thought about was how lonely he must have been, and what a poor substitute for acceptance and friendship his victories and the pennies he took were. He might have been a good athlete, he certainly was strong and quick, but he never got the chance to prove it.

Nobody wanted him on their team.

The only way he ever got to play was to threaten us, and even then we often defied him, because he couldn't whip *all* of us. Of course, when he did play, he had to bat first and pitch. If we were on his team, we lost deliberately – striking out and dropping the ball – it made him crazy with anger at us. Often, we would make it up between us to act like we were going home, and when he left, we'd all come back and play –

I'm sure he knew it.

I can only imagine what he must have suffered within himself for his arrogance and pride. To have no friends, to always be outside, to be an island – to never admit need or want, to never confess or say "I'm sorry" – it is a marvel that he did not, like Judas, hang himself. And why did Judas hang himself? Was it because he could not say –

Pride

◆

154

"I'm sorry;
I've done a terrible thing."

Why is that so hard? Is it not true? How about you? Does your *pride* – your self-esteem – keep you from the blessings of family, friends, forgiveness, and acceptance – from being on the team? Do you find it hard to say, "I'm sorry; I've done a terrible thing." How much is your pride worth?

Would it make everybody happy
if you moved?

Something to Make You Feel Better

Occasionally there are those real-life events that make you aware of the need we all have for a sense of humor. Very few of God's great gifts are so critical to maintaining a sense of balance and a more rounded perspective on life than the ability to see both ourselves, others, and situations in a humorous way. I want also to say that *pride* is the greatest deterrent to a sense of humor. It is our false sense of personal importance that prevents us from seeing the humor in situations. We cannot laugh at ourselves for fear that others will laugh also and injure our pride.

The following incident is a perfect example of this. I confess that at first it was not funny to me – and if it had ended sooner, it probably would have left me angry and resentful for days. It was my pride that kept me from seeing the humor in it sooner. This is an embellished attempt to reconstruct the chain of events.

I had taken my daughter's car to the dealer where I had purchased it to have the front end aligned. I left it there at 7:30 A.M. and was taken to my office by a young man named Gilbert. He told me to call the dealership later in the day and tell them what time I wanted him to come and pick me up. Accordingly, I called them about 10:30 to find out if the car was finished and to tell them that I wanted to be picked up at 3:00 P.M.

First call − 10:30 A.M.:

Female voice: "Frank Brown Pontiac-Honda."

"Service Department, please."

"Pontiac or Honda?"

"Pontiac."

"One moment please."

"Thank you."

Two minutes later − female voice: "Pontiac Service Department."

"My name is John Smith − I left my car to be repaired this morning. I was brought to work by a young man named Gilbert. Would you tell him to pick me up at three o'clock this afternoon?"

"Would you hold please?"

"Yes."

Two minutes later − male voice: "Who are you holding for?"

"I honestly don't know."

"Okay."

"Okay what?" − Silence.

Two minutes later − female voice: "Gilbert is not here, you need to talk to John Markham. Would you hold?"

"Yes."

Four minutes later − male voice: "Who are you holding for?"

"John Markham."

"John Markham works in the Honda Service Department. You need to call back and ask for the Honda Service Department."

"Okay."

Second phone call − 11:15 A.M.:

Female voice: "Hello, this is Frank Brown Pontiac-Honda; how may I help you?"

"I need to speak to the Service Department."

"Pontiac or Honda?"

"Honda."

"Thank you. Would you hold please?"

"Yes."

Three minutes later − male voice: "Who are you holding for?"

"The Honda Service Department. I need to speak to John Markham."

"John who?"

"John Markham. I was told he worked in the Honda Service Department."

"Who told you that?"

"The lady who answers your phone."

"Oh, you must mean John Meachamp; we don't have a John Markham in Honda."

"I don't *mean* anybody. I just want to leave a message about being picked up."

"Well, if you want to be picked up, you need to talk to Gilbert."

"I was told that Gilbert wasn't there and that I should speak to John Markham. *I really don't care* who I speak to; I just want to be picked up at three this afternoon, and *I don't care who does it."*

"Would you hold please?"

"No, I *won't* hold please; don't you *dare* put me on hold." – Silence.

Two minutes later – different female voice: "Who are you holding for?"

"Dwight Eisenhower" – not very *creative,* but *effective,* I thought.

"Dwight doesn't work here anymore. He quit last week and went to work for Colonel Sanders."

"Well, how about John Markham then?"

"Would you hold please?"

"No! Absolutely not! Under no circumstances will I hold! Have I made myself clear? Do not put me on hold!" – Silence.

One minute later – different female voice: "John doesn't answer his page. Which department does he work in?"

"I thought *you* might know that. The last time I asked for him, you said he worked in the Honda Department."

"Would you hold please?" – Silence.

Two minutes later I hung up and went to lunch.

Third phone call – 2:30 P.M.:

Female voice: "Hello, this is Frank Brown Pontiac-Honda; may I help you?"

"My name is John Smith. *Please* don't hang up or put me on hold – I left my car there this morning to be worked on, and I just want to know *if you still have it* and how I might get it back. I need someone to pick me up – Gilbert was supposed to, but he's not there – John Markham was supposed to, but you don't have an employee by that name. I just want to be picked up at three o'clock; it's two-thirty now, and by the way this is going, I may not ever see my car again. Would *you* come and pick me up?"

"I would *love* to come and pick you up, but I don't have a driver's license. Would you hold please?"

"Please, *I'm begging you,* don't put me on hold or I'll blow my brains out – no, that wouldn't do – it would take me three days to find them, and by

Pride

♦

157

then I wouldn't be able to remember why I had done it; better yet, I'll blow yours out — no that would be impossible." — Silence.

One minute later — different female voice: "Who are you holding for?"

"Michael Jordan." I felt I needed to use a household name.

"We have a Harold Jackson — that's pretty close, don't you think? Could he help you?"

"Are you a real person or an android?"

"I don't have an Aunt Roy. I have an uncle named Roy, but no aunt. My aunt's name is Clara, but my uncle doesn't work here — neither does my aunt. The reason is that they're both dead, but if they did work here, I would really love it, because then I could live with them and save rent money — but they don't, so I don't — but I really appreciate your interest in my family. Could someone else help you?"

"Is this *really* Frank Brown Pontiac-Honda?"

"Yes, I used to work for Fast Eddie's answering service, but that was two years ago; now I work here, for Fred Jones."

"I'd like to speak to Gilbert or John Markham or, better yet, why don't you just pick someone — I don't care who — just pick a name."

"We have a Leo Fogarty. Don't you think that's an interesting name?"

"Sure, let me talk to him."

"Would you hold please?" — Silence.

Two minutes later — male voice: "Hello, this is John Markham; how can I help you?"

"Is this really John Markham? Are you sure you're not Leo Fogarty or President Bush or Uncle Roy?"

"Who is this? Are you all right?"

"This is John Smith — I think. I left my car there for repairs this morning. I wanted to be picked up at three o'clock today, but it's three o'clock now. Is my car ready?"

"Well, actually, Mr. Smith, we had some problems with our alignment equipment today, and you're going to have to bring your car back tomorrow. Gilbert will be out to get you in twenty minutes."

Pride

♦

158

Are You Someone Else's Idiot?

"When he was abused,
he did not return abuse;
when he suffered,
he did not threaten;
but he entrusted himself
to the one who judges justly."
—1 Peter 2:23

Pride

◆

159

How did Jesus pull that off, I wonder? I think I know, but the answer condemns me. It was because He was totally without pride. That is why his life was sinless and mine is not. What follows is not an extraordinary event – I wish it were – but God knows – it is far too common.

What started the whole thing was that I forgot something I needed. I had fine-tuned my schedule to the point that the slightest hitch would begin a *late cycle*. I drove into Sam's parking lot. (I do not mean *drove* in the sense of calm, vehicular motion – I mean *drove* in the sense of "he *drove* a nail" or "the halfback *drove* between two opposing linemen.") Like I said, I *drove* into Sam's parking lot – scattering people in every direction – ran inside, located the item I needed in seconds, and headed for the checkout. I measured each line carefully – appraising not just the length, but the individuals – which ones would pay by check, who would question prices, who wouldn't be able to find their driver's license.

Suddenly, just to my left, they opened a new checkout line. Like the above-mentioned halfback, I reacted immediately – but I made physical contact with a rather bullish, forty-fivish, linebacker type, who rocked me back on my heels and filled the hole in front of me. He only had three or four small items, so I stepped in behind him with only a minimal protest.

As the girl rang up his purchases, he took out his checkbook. My heart sank a little. Being so close, I could see that his check was one of those temporary types, the kind they give you when you first open an account and your *real* checks haven't been printed yet – you know, the ones with your name, address, phone number, social security number, fingerprints, hair sample, and dental impression – which, by the way, is all totally useless unless you have at least three major credit cards, can prove you are in debt for a minimum of $250,000 and are on a first-name basis with the bank president.

The checkout girl took one look at this guy's check and nearly had a coronary. "We can't accept checks like this," she said rather indignantly.

"I'd like to know why the (bleep) not?" You could tell by his reply that this guy wasn't going to take any stuff from anybody – this was a personal offense. I looked at my watch; I was in deep trouble.

"The check doesn't have proper ID on it," she said firmly.

"I have all kinds of ID." He opened his wallet, and plastic cards tumbled out in profusion. I also noticed that he had a rather large amount of cash. His purchases were less than thirty dollars.

"Your personal ID doesn't matter – it's this check. There is no ID on the check." Now she was efficient, businesslike.

Pride

♦

160

"I'd like to see your boss, right now! I buy lots of things here, and I'm sure they don't want to lose me as a customer."

She was not intimidated.

Personally, I thought they would love to lose him as a customer. The boss came, and he verified what the checkout girl had said. The customer wanted to see his boss – he wanted a personal interview with Sam Walton, his state senator, and Rush Limbaugh – the process was repeated – and I waited. This idiot wouldn't give it up. He was in the limelight, everybody was looking at him, and people who had checked out were standing and waiting to see the outcome.

I was in a hurry.
I wanted to strangle the guy.

My resentment, my indignation, my sense of personal injustice grew to the bursting point. The other lines moved steadily. People who were still shopping when I got in line were now headed for the parking lot while I stood behind this –

self-centered idiot.

You are probably wondering why I didn't just change lines? I hope you are wondering that – it is my reason for writing. There are two reasons: The first, simply stated, is that I was too *proud*. I didn't want to lose face. People who had seen me jump in this line ahead of those who waited in other lines would sneer and see some kind of providential justice administered against me.

I wouldn't give them the satisfaction.
Why should I *make their day?*

The second, *more pride.* I was next in line, here. If I moved to another line, I would be fourth or fifth, and I dreaded the thought that I might move, the conflict here would resolve, and I would be in another line waiting and looking very foolish.

The *idiot* in front of me eventually made his point by returning his purchases and storming indignantly out of the store. When I finally left, I was seething. I was looking for any situation on which I could vent my wounded sense of fair play and vanity. Consequently, for the rest of the day I treated anyone who got in my way unfairly. I was totally insensitive to anyone's needs but my own

— I became *their idiot*.

Instead of stopping the cycle, I increased it.

"When he suffered,
he did not threaten;
but he entrusted himself
to the one who judges justly."
—1 Peter 2:23

Beware of pride.
*Beware of becoming
someone else's idiot.*

The Tree

One of the reasons he bought the house was because of *the tree*. Although it was only a *middle-aged* tree (about eighty or ninety years old) – its symmetry was nearly perfect. It had grown slowly and carefully. The lower limbs were very thick and reached out horizontally nearly fifty feet, but so strong were the branches and so deep and firm the roots that they hardly drooped at all. The tree gave cooling, protective shade to the house, and birds came there – every kind and color and call. The locusts and the katydids sang their love songs there, the squirrels built their nests, and the name *Live Oak* was appropriate.

When he bought the house, he was young, strong, newly married, and happy. During the fifty-one years that he lived there, many things happened to him. He lost his youth, his strength, his marriage, and his happiness. In the third year, he had a son; in the fifth year, a daughter; in the ninth year, another son. The last son was weak and sickly from birth, and in the eleventh year – he died. In the twelfth year, he went through a bitter divorce, and his wife took his daughter to another man's house, far away – and he never saw either of them again –

although he could have.

Pride

◆

162

The older son stayed with him, and the final blow was when this son was killed in the twenty-first year in a motorcycle accident. He never remarried, and gradually he withdrew from all social involvement. He became bitter – cynical – he was a man to be avoided. He asked no forgiveness or comfort – he gave none – he received none – *except from*

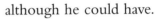

the tree.

The tree became a sort of town monument. It was the largest, the most beautiful tree anywhere within a hundred miles. Folks liked to walk by in the evenings and stop and look at it. When out-of-town company came, they always took them by *the tree.* They would park their cars and take pictures, exclaiming at its magnificence. It is true that they were not always as observant of property rights as they should have been, and it is also true that they dropped occasional gum wrappers, film cartridge boxes, a pop can or two, and left a bit of a mess.

It began to bother him. He began to resent it. It wasn't just the mess – it was deeper than that – it was a *personal violation.* At first, when he was happier, he had been rather proud – often going out to visit with those who stopped to admire – and he shared the history of the tree. But now he felt much put upon, and a different kind of pride began to dominate him. He decided to do something about it.

The first thing he did was to ask the city for a parking restriction in front of his house, which was granted, and *No Parking* signs were posted. Not satisfied, he put up *No Trespassing – Violators Will Be Prosecuted* signs in his yard, and he stood in his doorway and glared defiantly at the lookers. Finally, he built a fence, an extraordinarily high fence. The city council appealed to his civic sense – his community pride – in vain. He said it was *his* tree and *his* property and he was mighty tired of folks taking advantage of him.

He was retired now and had little to do but fret about the tree and brood over the wrongs he had suffered. The tree had become his reason for being – he had nothing else. He made his fence even higher. He lost patience with the squirrels, who were noisy and messy and got into things around the house – and were far too happy – so he patiently, methodically, systematically caught and

killed every one.

Of course, no fence could truly contain the tree, and every day, when the cars passed slowly or the walkers – careful not to step off the public access – stood and looked, he resented it more and more. He wanted the tree for *himself;* it was *his* tree, on *his* property, and everytime someone else enjoyed *his* tree, it struck deeply into *his* heart.

In the fiftieth year – when he was seventy-four – a most horrible thought occurred to him. It came one afternoon, right after he had mowed his yard. He felt a terrible, paralyzing pain in his chest and left shoulder, and he could not get his breath. He staggered to a nearby chair where it gradually subsided. It frightened him. He knew what it must be, and the realization that he might not have too long made him aware that *the one thing of value* that he had would become the property of others. He would die, and others would come and tear down his fence, take down his signs. The thought filled him with bitterness –

he was going to lose *his* tree,
after all.

He thought of making a will – he could make provisions assuring that this would not happen – but he knew that in time those provisions would weaken and fail. He could not rest, and only a few days passed before there was a second chest pain, worse than the first, and he knew he had to act.

There was only one solution.
And the last moment of true pleasure
he had on this earth
was when it occurred to him.

When the tree service company came, they did everything possible to talk him out of it. He was adamant. It was *his* tree, on *his* property, and the final right of ownership had been proven by his right to destroy what was *his.*

They cut it down.

They cut up the limbs into firewood. They took the massive trunk, now more than seven feet in diameter, to a sawmill for oak lumber. It was amazing how quickly – less than twelve hours – what had been growing for well over a hundred years was totally removed, with only a twelve-inch high stump remaining.

And the walkers no longer paused to look –
and far fewer cars passed by –
and no one stopped or made a mess.

When he awoke the next morning and saw it gone, something went out of him. The satisfaction was gone and only a terrible emptiness remained – *an emptiness that nothing would ever fill again.* He lived a few more months – into the fifty-first year – and one spring morning, when the air was clear and the birds were singing and the sky was blue, he walked outside and saw the vast emptiness where the tree had been, and it came again, and this time it did not subside. It gripped and tightened and increased. He made no effort to call for help; he rather stumbled and finally crawled to the place where the tree had been and lay face down on the stump.

As he drew his last agonizing breath, he stared vacantly into the earth – and there – just inches from his face – he saw a miracle – a magic that had been at work for years. The squirrels had buried the acorns everywhere – against the hard winters – and now, with the rain and the sunshine falling where it had not been able to reach for fifty years – right there – right below his nose – was a tiny shoot – a new live oak. Its symmetry was perfect; its tiny trunk, its miniature, transparent leaves and branches were tribute to the genes of its ancestor.

What he learned in those dying moments, what he saw – the incredible light and understanding that filled his mind would fill several books. *He knew that he had never seen anything clearly.* His dying words – spoken to no one, heard by none, were –

"My God,
I have lived only for my pride,
and now
I have nothing."

And he was perfectly right,
you know.

What sort of tree occupies
your life?

Pride

♦

164

EIGHT

Humility

This introduction will be short. I'll let the stories speak for themselves. I've had problems with humility all of my life. That is a fact. It isn't easy for me to understand why I have a problem with humility, because if anything ought to come naturally to me, it should be humility. What I mean is, all I have to do is take even a casual look at my life – all of the blunders, stupidity, forgetfulness, regrets, second guessings, and "if I had it to do over again I'd sure do it different" statements – to figure out that I'm not too bright and deserve to be pitied more than scorned.

The recognition of our humanity – the brevity of our time here, our failure to learn anything from history (which leads to the endless repetition of tragedy), our inability to alter our lives or change our personalities (although God can do both) – should produce humility in all of us; but it doesn't. That is why we go on making the same mistakes.

I know of nothing that would ease our journey more than a good dose of humility.

Laughter – Good Medicine for Pride

I used to live in Lubbock, Texas. The reason that's important is that Lubbock, Texas, is one of the few places left on earth where things like this happen.

One day, I was on my way to meet someone for lunch, and I was running a little late. I got behind an old Ford truck – I mean an *old* Ford truck – about a 1947 or '48 vintage. This truck was not one of those chopped-down, hoodless, magnesium-rimmed, fat-tired, two four-barrelled, super-charged, chrome-plated, flame-painted, T-bucket, 427, hot-rod Chevys that occasionally graces the streets of this fair city and wreaks havoc upon the mental serenity of its sober, stable, and conservative citizenry. No, this was a genuine, fresh-off-the-farm, original-condition, original-owner, original-driver, legitimate work truck, with *real cow manure* in the bed. It was driven (perhaps "pointed" would be more accurate) by a white-haired, bib-over-hauled, toothpick-chewing, cowboy-hat-wearing, red-faced farmer, whose neck had more wrinkles and creases in it

than a topographical map.

He was in my lane, both hands gripping the steering wheel, moving sedately at about fifteen miles per hour. Because there was traffic on both sides, I could do absolutely nothing, except blow my stack and my horn at the stupid clodhopper who had the unmitigated effrontery to impede the progress of such an important personage as myself. About thirty yards from the next intersection, the light turned yellow. *I* hit the accelerator – *he* hit the brakes. He stopped. So did I – but not very gracefully – about two inches from his back bumper. All the papers that were sitting on the passenger seat slid onto the floor in mass confusion. I saw him look at me in his rearview mirror and slowly shake his head in a sort of sad, condescending way.

As we waited for the light to change, I noticed this sticker on his tailgate –

"I may be slow,
but I'm ahead of you."

Well, that absolutely did it. When the light changed, I jammed the accelerator to the floor. Burning rubber with both tires, I jumped into the right lane between two cars, veered into a right-turn lane, and blew past the car on my left. Just as I was running out of turn lane, I cut back to the left, in front of the car I had just passed, and then pulled in front of the Ford truck. I felt like A. J. Foyt just winning the

Indianapolis Five Hundred.

I broke every speed law ever invented in a determined effort to make the next light – and I would have – except there was a police car sitting at the next light facing me. I locked up all four wheels and screeched sideways to a stop about halfway through the intersection. I sat there with blue smoke from my tires drifting and gathering around me. Then I had to suffer the humiliation of having to *back up* in order to clear the intersection. Traffic had stopped in every direction, and I was the object of much horn blowing, head shaking, and unwanted attention from *the man in blue*. It's really hard to act cool and nonchalant in situations like that. About fifteen seconds later, who should pull up next to me but my toothpick-chewing friend. I tried so hard not to look in his direction, to ignore him, to act casual, but I had my T-top removed and my windows down, and I could *feel* him looking at me.

Finally, I looked up, right into two watery blue eyes.

"Where ya goin', *Sonny?*"

It was the emphasis on the "Sonny" that got me. Too embarrassed and frustrated to make a clever reply, I said,

"Absolutely nowhere."

"Well," he said, with a West Texas drawl, *"I'm sure you'll be the first one there."*

There are few things in life so absolutely *humbling* as the full realization that –

you have made a complete fool of yourself.

There are several distinct ways of dealing with this realization, but the most satisfactory way of dealing with it is to laugh. I don't mean to smile or chuckle – I mean a doubled-over, tears-streaming-down, thigh-slapping laugh that leaves you choking and breathless. It is even preferable that you relate your foolishness to someone else and let them laugh with you, or *at you*. What's wrong with being laughed at? Only our ego-centered *pride* denies others the pleasure of laughing at our foolishness.

Humility, on the other hand, has the ability to save us from ourselves and bring relief to our frustrated and stressful lives. *Humility* allows us to receive grace from God and to accept it from others. *Humility* gives us, and those about us, unlimited access to one of life's greatest pleasures –

laughter.

Laughter is one of the cheapest and most healing medicines that God has ever bestowed upon His people. How sad that this healing balm is denied – both to ourselves and to others – by

our ridiculous pride.

Waiting on Tables

I was having lunch with an attorney, an educator, a banker, an insurance salesman, and a politician. I assure you, I left my wallet at home and refused to agree or disagree with anything anybody said.

When I received the invitation from the lawyer, my first reaction was to decline – especially when he offered to buy my lunch. I was reminded of that wise maxim that says "there is no such thing as a *free lunch,*" but then I remembered that Jesus ate with publicans, harlots, and sinners. That made me more comfortable, because I was sure that everyone in this group would fit into at least one of those categories.

We ate at a very nice restaurant, but our waiter was slow – not only of foot, but also of mind – he forgot us periodically. I do not only mean that he forgot to take our orders, bring our food, fill our glasses, and bring our check – he did that, all right – but he also forgot *us* – I mean that he forgot we existed –

we had to go and find him three times.

All of this led to waiters and service being the topic of discussion during lunch. I was glad – it was a *safe* topic *because none of us were ever likely to find ourselves in that role* – and in a crowd like that, there aren't many safe topics.

Both the attorney and the educator stated vehemently that if they were waiters, they would be rich because *they knew what people want in a waiter.* They assumed, of course, that what *they* want in a waiter is what *everybody* wants and that by *putting on servant's clothes* they could *put on a servant's attitude.* They also saw service not as *a way of life* – not as having any intrinsic value in itself – not as an expression of purpose – but

as a means to wealth and, therefore,
as a means to stop *being* servants,
and as a means to *be* served instead.

One of the problems with *being* a servant is that you are surrounded by people who are not servants, who have never been servants, who never will be servants, but *who know exactly what a servant ought to be* and so are constantly demanding that those who are servants live up to a nonservant's expectation of servanthood.

Three of the men at my table actually stated that they could make more money as waiters than at their professions.

> *Of course,*
> *none of them put on an apron.*
> And they were wrong –
> they would have starved to death
> as servants.

Service is an attitude, an approach to life. You cannot take it off and put it on with an apron. Jesus was servant to all, and he never saw it as a means to anything but a closer walk with God and greater service. He knew who He was and why He was here, and He never forgot it. He knew He could pick up other people's trash, carry out the garbage, clean their toilets, serve their meals, and wash their feet – and *never* lose His identity as the Son of God. He never had to *act* humble –

> because he *was.*

Following Jesus

> "If any man would come after me,
> let him . . . take up his cross
> and follow me."
> —Mark 8:34

He was a ninth grade English teacher, and he was a Christian. He was a large man, with an athletic and intimidating physique. The school he taught in was located on the *bad side of town,* and the kids were loud, tough, crude, vulgar, and unappreciative. Although his students liked him well enough, they thought he was an odd duck because he really believed that education was important and therefore took his duties much too seriously. His habit of referring to them as "Mr." or "Miss" was too much. They ridiculed him for it constantly. He told them it was a sign of respect.

It was the hardest year of teaching he had ever had, and although he had put everything he had into it, signs of progress and rewards were few. One afternoon, during the last period of a very long and difficult day, he overheard one of the boys make an extremely crude and suggestive remark to one of the girls. It wasn't that he hadn't heard it before. Maybe it was because the school had no air conditioning and he was hot, maybe it was because he had a splitting headache, maybe he was just tired and fed up – it's hard to say –

but he reacted.

"Mr. Hutchens, I am sick of your filthy mouth, I want you to stand up right now and apologize to Miss Devore."

It was quiet; Mr. Hutchens did not move. He stared at the teacher with unbelief and defiance. He had never apologized to anyone in his life, and to do so under these circumstances would be a tremendous loss of face. He remained in his seat.

"Mr. Hutchens," the teacher rose from his desk and moved to the row the boy was sitting in. His growing anger made his voice dangerously quiet – almost a whisper – and he was trembling. He was conscious of two opposing things simultaneously. First, he wished he had not made a public issue out of this, and second, he was glad he had and he didn't care. "Mr. Hutchens, I told you to stand up – and *I mean it!*"

Mr. Hutchens remained seated, glaring insolently. The teacher grabbed him by his shirt front and jerked him to his feet. The boy's legs hit his desk, and it turned over with a terrible crash, spilling books and papers everywhere. A girl in the next row bent to pick them up. "Leave them where they are Miss Johnson. Mr. Hutchens will pick them up *after he has apologized.* Now Mr. Hutchens, I – am – waiting – for – your – apology – to – Miss – Devore, and I will not wait very long." He was spitting the words out, and his anger was out of control.

"Miss Devore?" the boy chuckled with an emphasis on the "Devore." "Don't you mean Miss De_____?" He used a rhyming, common, vulgar expression for girls with loose morals. The class erupted in laughter, and he looked at the embarrassed and angry girl with an arrogant, triumphant smirk.

The teacher still had the boy's shirt grasped firmly in his left hand, and using that grip for leverage, he jerked the boy toward him and slapped him. He slapped him with every ounce of strength and energy he could muster

Humility

♦

173

– slapped him right across that smirking, sneering, defiant mouth. His thumb must have caught the boy's nose, or it may have simply been the tremendous impact, but the boy's nose began to bleed profusely, and there was a thin trickle of blood in the corner of his mouth.

The blow was so powerful that it stunned the boy. Angry red welts sprang to the surface of his face immediately, and he staggered and would have fallen if the teacher hadn't held him up. The only sounds in the classroom were whispers of awe and admiration from those who were impressed by the force of the blow.

The teacher's anger and resentment were quickly replaced with crushing disappointment. He marched the student, still groggy and struggling with his equilibrium, to the principal's office, seated him, explained briefly to the school secretary, and returned to his classroom. The low, excited buzz that had begun when he left was silenced at his return. He righted the desk, picked up the books and papers, and tried to return to the lesson. Fortunately, the period ended almost immediately. The students rushed into the halls to spread the news, and he went back to the principal's office to call the boy's parents and to explain in greater detail.

The principal was understanding and supportive. The boy's father came immediately, and when he· heard the story, he told the teacher he wouldn't have any problems from him, that his son had gotten exactly what he deserved, and that he hoped it would teach him a lesson.

The teacher had thought it would certainly cost him his job. He knew it had already cost him something of far greater value – his self-respect and much of what he had for all these weeks been trying to teach – that Jesus makes us different. In this school, his action was much admired by the students. They spoke of the force of the blow with awe and respect in their voices – "Did you see Dick's head snap back when he hit him? It looked like he hit him with a brick." They thought more of their teacher because he had reacted *according to their standards of manhood* – "never take anything off of anybody."

He went home utterly defeated.

It came to him that night what he must do. Although there was no cafeteria, most of the kids ate sack lunches every day on the bleachers in the gym. He called the principal that night and asked him to call a school assembly the next day at noontime.

The teacher stood before a quiet, solemn student body and made a very sincere apology – not just to Mr. Hutchens, but to the faculty, the principal, and to every student whom he thought he had disappointed. He asked the forgiveness of all. When he finished, he walked toward the bleachers, his shoulders slumped, his heart heavy with failure. There was a stirring among some of the students, and from the crowd came Mr. Hutchens. He and the teacher met about half way across the floor; the boy was close to tears. They shook hands, and then the boy turned to his fellow students.

"I want to apologize to Mr.____. What I did was wrong, and what he did was right." He paused; he was trying to work up to something, and it was tough. "I want to apologize also to Nan – Miss Devore. I'm sorry I said what I did, and I want her to forgive me." The student body stood and cheered and applauded.

The healing seemed to melt and run through the whole school. It became the "in" thing to call everybody "Mr." or "Miss." Many good-natured jokes and wisecracks came from it, but there was much goodwill too.

I wish I could say that humility always works, but it doesn't. Jesus was the most humble man who ever lived, and it got Him killed. But there is a great victory in the cross – the cross of Calvary and the cross that He has called us to bear. *There is healing and power in humility,* in foot washing, in going the extra mile, in self-sacrifice, and in turning the other cheek. Most of us never experience that healing or power because we don't have the *humility* to do those things, we're too busy –

defending our rights.

"If any man would come after me,
let him . . . take up his cross
and follow me."

His way is never easy,
but it is always best.

Please Take My Umbrella

"Dear children,
let us not love with words
or tongue
but with actions and in truth."
—1 John 3:18

It was right after class, and it was raining. I was standing just outside the doorway but under the protection of the overhang to the entrance of May-bee Hall. I was looking wistfully at the rain and debating whether or not a dash to the student center for a coke was worth it. As I was pondering this deep, theological problem, a young man addressed me from the crosswalk about thirty feet away. I couldn't understand him, so I just smiled and waved. He changed directions and came toward me, his dark face peering out from under a rather tattered, much used, worse-for-the-wear umbrella. I couldn't help but notice his worn sneakers and ill-fitting trousers.

He addressed me again, and although his English was broken, obviously a second language, I understood that he wished to loan me his umbrella. I didn't know him personally, but I knew that he must be one of several Nigerian students who were on our campus. Since I didn't really *need* to go anywhere, I indicated that I could get along all right without it. I could tell immediately that he was actually hurt by my refusal. I mean –

he really wanted me to use his umbrella.

I didn't want him to get wet just so I could go and get a coke, but see-ing the look on his face and knowing how difficult it would be to explain, I asked how I could return it to him. "In this room, let it be," he replied. "After my class, I will come for it." He placed it in my hand with a look of genuine pleasure, and without another word, he bounced out into the rain and ran lightly across the grass. "Thank you very much," I shouted after him. He stopped and turned to wave, and his smile showed the enjoyment and goodwill he obviously felt. He warmed my heart. He acted as though *I* had just made *his* day.

Although this happened many years ago, I still think about it. It left a last-ing impression on me. One thing that occurs to me is that this young man *noticed me.* There were hundreds of students passing by, most with umbrellas, but this young man from Nigeria was the *only one* who offered – he was the *only one* who spoke – he was the *only one* who saw me. The rest had their heads down, looking for puddles. Their minds were filled with thoughts about *themselves, their* classes, *their* tests, *their* ride home this weekend, keeping *their* shoes and *their* clothes dry, *their* grades, *their* problems, *their* love interests, *their* popularity, *their* schedule.

They were so full of themselves
that there was no room
in their consciousness
for anyone else.

This young man saw me because he was not thinking about himself. He was looking for me — not me specifically, you understand — but for someone like me — someone he could help. This young man left his room that morning thinking, "This will be a good day to help somebody." The rest of us left our rooms thinking only

about ourselves.

I think about my own feeble attempts at generosity. I realize that the good things I do are seldom the result of planning, of thinking ahead about the needs of others. With me, it's more of an accident. Occasionally, I am so confronted with someone else's need that I am shaken from my own world long enough to respond. Even then, I am often halfhearted in extending my help. When I offer financial assistance, to coach a little league team, a ride to the store, to pick up someone's child from the dentist, to clean up after a dinner — I wonder if I offer in such a way that my insincerity is apparent? When my help is rejected,

am I relieved?

When we offer to render assistance, is it obvious that we are simply trying to be mannerly — to show the *outward form* that is expected of us? "If I can help in some way, let me know." "Come and see us sometime." "Could I pay for this?" These statements are not necessarily hypocritical, but they are often trite, meaningless, polite ways of saying,

"Don't bother me
unless it's an emergency."

One other thing: Sometimes I do the right thing *naturally*. It's not often, I'm afraid, but in the case of the umbrella, I praise God that I had the humility to allow this young man to help me. Don't let your ego stand in the way of someone else's pleasure.

"Dear children,
let us not love with words
or tongue
but with actions and in truth."
—1 John 3:18

Humility and Fear

Harold was *tough*. He was tough in the classic sense of the word. He was also mean. There wasn't an ounce of compassion or sympathy in him, and he was only in the ninth grade. He was nearly seventeen, stocky, very strong, and he might have been good looking except his eyes were a shade too close together and his complexion was bad. He was in my English class. It was a *tough* school, full of *tough* kids, where the degree of survival was equated with the degree of *toughness* –

and Harold survived very well.

I had taken this job about one-third of the way through the school year. The previous teacher had simply walked out of her classroom and into the principal's office and had announced her immediate, final, and irrevocable retirement.

She didn't even finish the day.

I needed a job badly, and when this position was offered to me, I took it quickly – too quickly. After the first day, I understood why she had quit and almost decided that I didn't need a job *this badly*. They were monsters. Every imaginable negative adjective applied strictly and specifically – loud, profane, immoral, uncaring, vulgar, crude, undisciplined, and unfeeling. They screamed the grossest profanities right across the classroom. The boys mouthed lewd suggestions openly and the girls made even more lewd comments in return. It was an eye-opener for this small-town boy.

Harold was the ringleader. He set the tone. He defied anyone to match his disgusting behavior. On one occasion, he took the crutches of a permanently crippled boy, smashed them to pieces, stuffed the pieces in a trash can, and went off laughing, leaving the crippled boy helpless in the bathroom. On another occasion, he threatened and cowed a much smaller boy, forcing him to break all of the windows out of the principal's car, then he reported him. These are the things I can write about; there were other things – much worse.

I really tried with Harold. I tried to love him; I prayed about him often. I showed him every conceivable kindness. He thought I was weak, afraid of him, and he scorned me publicly. He threatened to "chew me up," because he said I was *"soft and gutless."*

My principal, who was one of the finest men I ever met, called me one Saturday morning quite early. He told me that Harold was in the hospital, that he had been severely beaten, and had mentioned my name to his parents.

I went to see him, but –

I never would have recognized him. "Beaten" does not adequately describe Harold's condition. He had several broken ribs from being kicked and stomped. He had a broken arm, a broken nose, and a fractured skull from having his head pounded repeatedly into the pavement. One of his ears had been somehow cut to ribbons and was barely attached to his head. His face was so swollen and discolored from bruises, abrasions, and lacerations that he had no discernible features, and he could barely see from only one eye.

He was a changed young man. He had encountered *fear* – something he had produced in others, but knew little of himself. He was afraid, and that fear had made him *humble.* He talked little and only in a whisper, but there was a haunted tone in his words – and none of his old arrogance. I didn't know what to say, and I was uncomfortable – so was he – but he didn't want me to go, and so I stayed. I asked him if he wanted me to pray. It took him a moment as he fought with his old pride and his disdain for anything that expressed need or dependence, but finally he nodded yes. I stood by his bedside, and I prayed. I prayed as fervent, as heartfelt a prayer as I have ever uttered. I prayed that God could show Harold that He loved him, and that Harold could be changed and healed.

At some point during that prayer, I felt something touch my arm. I can feel the prickly sensation yet. It was Harold, trying to find my hand. He was just a frightened little boy after all, all his *pride* reduced to *humility* by a real, practical fear that led him to seek comfort outside himself.

Not all people come to God in this way – the way of *humility* learned through *fear* – but many do, and for some –

it is the only way.

Humility

♦

180

To One of These Little Ones

"Whoever gives even a cup of cold water
to one of these little ones
in the name of a disciple—
truly I tell you,
none of these will lose their reward."
—Matthew 10:42

It was one of those nights when I simply could not go to sleep. Every time I got close, some new idea would rattle through my brain and I would pursue it until another one crossed that track and took me in a different direction. It was raining very hard, which normally helps – but tonight nothing helped. I finally got up and went to the living room to read. It was 1:30 A.M. I always have several different books I am in the process of reading, but tonight I decided to read the Bible. I was deeply engrossed in Second Kings five, the story of Naaman, when the phone rang. Who in the world would be calling me at one o'clock in the morning? When I picked up the receiver, I knew immediately what it was, and a hard core of cynicism crept over me.

"Is this the pastor for the Church of Christ?"

"Yes," I said.

"I'm not a member of your church. I'm a member of the Faith Gospel Church, and – well – I've been to my brother's funeral in Arizona, and we're on our way home. We had some unexpected transmission trouble in Gallup, New Mexico, and our funds are very low."

Why is it always a funeral, and why is car trouble always *unexpected?* I mean, it is the nature of cars to break down. Isn't all car trouble to be expected. I waited for the punch line.

"But that's not the reason I called."

"Oh?"

"Well, sir, we've had a bit of bad luck."

"Yes," I thought, "and so have I."

"We've had a flat tire, and my jack won't work. There are no service stations near us, and we desperately need help. I have to be at work in the morning, or I'll lose my job. I know it's late and it's raining, but I will pay you fifteen dollars if you will come and help us. I called two service stations, but they said it would cost forty dollars, and I don't have that much. I've called a Baptist minister and a Methodist. They told me that people shouldn't get out on the road without enough money to cover emergencies. I'm wondering if you would help us?"

I know it sounds dumb – but after being conned at least six thousand times, I decided to help this guy. Maybe it was because I found it odd that I was sitting here reading my Bible at one o'clock in the morning when I would normally be asleep when this guy called. Maybe I felt a little guilty about my hard-heartedness and cynicism, but I found out where he was and hung up.

As I rummaged in my closet for some old clothes, I heard the sleepy voice of my wife – "Who was that on the phone, Honey?"

"Oh, some guy with a flat tire wanting help."

"What are you doing?"

"Oh, I thought I'd go and sort of assess the situation." Do you understand how ridiculous that sounds? The next time she spoke, she was much more alert.

"It's nearly two o'clock, and it's raining," she said – as if I didn't know.

"I know," I said.

"Who is this person?" she said.

"Just a guy."

"Do you think it's safe? Remember that story last month about the people who stopped to help someone and what happened?"

"I'll be okay. *I've got a feeling* I ought to do this."

"John, I wish you wouldn't. *I've got a feeling, too,* and it would mean a lot to me if you wouldn't go."

"*I have to go.* I promised the guy I'd be there in fifteen minutes. He's got a family."

"*So do you,*" she said.

Humility

♦

"It'll be all right. I promise I'll be careful."

I found the guy, all right, and he did have a family. He was skinny, very poorly dressed, dirty, soaking wet, exhausted, and defeated. He was driving a black and green '64 Buick Electra, loaded to the max with luggage, a wife, and three of the chunkiest kids I've ever seen. He was desperate. He was a decent, simple man – a good man – who was struggling against the insurmountable obstacles thrown against him by a society that sets no value upon either goodness, decency, or simplicity. He *had* been to his brother's funeral, and he *had* had transmission trouble in Gallup.

His jack was broken. The only jack I had was a small hydraulic one that had to go under the rear axle. It took me over an hour to change his tire, and when I finished, I was filthy dirty and soaking wet from crawling under his car.

When I finished, I said, "Well that does it. You can get back on the road; I sure hope you don't have another flat." He motioned for me to walk over to the light of a nearby convenience store. He fumbled awkwardly in his front pants pocket and pulled out some wet, wadded, and crumpled bills. In a halting voice and with shaking fingers, he began separating, straightening, and counting them – out loud – a five and ten ones. It was the last vestige of pride he had – proving that he had the money – and then with a trembling hand – he offered those soggy bills to me –

and he really meant it.

As he extended his hand, I backed away from him so suddenly that it startled him. I protested that I couldn't possibly take his money. That money was like a holy thing – like David's jar of water from the well near Bethlehem – I knew my hand would turn white with leprosy if I touched it.

"God will strike me dead
if I touch that money,"
I thought.

I thought of the beautiful house I lived in, of my beautiful wife and children – healthy, dry, and safe at home in their beds. I thought of how good life was for us and of all the advantages I had. They had never been so precious to me as at that moment. It was an honor to be chosen by God for this task tonight – a blessing, a priceless treasure had become mine because of this experience. To take money would cheapen it.

I ran to my truck. I need to tell you this – first because it's true and second because I do not wish for you to think me a better person than I am. When I left home I had placed my wallet under the seat – fearing a robbery. I had eighty-seven dollars in my wallet. I took out the seven dollars and

Humility

♦

offered it to him. He refused. I begged him to take it in Jesus' name, *for my sake*. He reluctantly took the money, and I tried to tell him what a blessing he was to me.

His name was Dewitt, and he was from Gardendale, Alabama. He told me that if I were ever close to Gardendale, to please stop and eat with them. I have never witnessed such heartfelt gratitude. He told me how great it was to meet a preacher

who acted like a Christian.

He meant it, and I believed him. I believed him because I chose to, and I believe I gave "a cup of cold water in the name of a disciple."

In a world filled with cynicism, skepticism, isolation, and distrust, our Lord Jesus Christ gave me a special blessing that night. But it occurs to me that I only received the blessing because I had the humility to accept the task. In fact, just before I went to sleep – or maybe it was just after – I thought I heard Him say,

"You didn't do too badly tonight John.
In fact,
I was rather proud.
*I might make something
out of you yet.*"

Humility

♦

183

One Cherry Tree

"Unless you eat the flesh of the Son of man
and drink his blood,
you have no life in you."
—John 6:53

When I was in high school, I dated a girl whose name was Gwendolyn Brandtsen. Of course, that is not her real name, but it's close. No one ever called her Gwendolyn – we called her Gwen. This story is not about her, however; it's about her parents. During the time we dated, which lasted into my first year of college, I became very attached to her parents, especially her mother, so much so, in fact, that even after Gwen and I stopped dating, I visited and corresponded with them.

Years later, after Gwen and I had both married – not each other, obviously – I learned that Mr. Brandtsen was very ill, and I determined to visit them. Gwen's folks had moved to Traverse City, Michigan. When I arrived, I learned that Mr. Brandtsen was more ill than I had thought and that he was extremely depressed. Although his illness did not incapacitate him, he spent nearly all of his time in the house, and there he confined himself to an upstairs bedroom. He was morose, unconversational, and negative, and he spent most of his time brooding.

It was spring. My trip to Traverse City *providentially* coincided with the blossoming of the cherry trees, which grow in profusion on the shores of Grand Traverse Bay. Miles and miles of cherry trees, row after row, stretched upward from the roadside to the tops of the hills. The blending of pinks, whites, oranges, greens, and lavenders – the smells, not only of the blossoms, but of the rich, black, loamy soil – the sounds of buzzing bees, robins, red-winged blackbirds, orioles, and canaries – the deep blue bay itself reflecting the cotton candy clouds – the small, green-shuttered, white cottages across the bay – the harbor with its thousands of graceful sailboats – it was, well, it was quite beautiful, breathtaking really.

No camera could do it justice. Cameras do not record the singing of birds or the smells that rode the breeze that swept up off the bay, a breeze that was so rich with the nectar of life that it carried nourishment and impregnated those who inhaled it with youth, vigor, and invincibility – making you feel that you could live forever –

and you can, you know.

Mrs. Brandtsen and I drove out to the bay very early the two days I spent there. We returned laughing, uplifted, and animated. Mr. Brandtsen would not go. We begged him; he was resolute. They had a single cherry tree in their front yard, and it also was in bloom. He could see it easily from his upstairs bedroom. At one point, as I pleaded with him to go with us, he pointed to the tree, and with that singular, dismissing wave of the hand that he used to brush away all disagreeable things, he said, "Oh, John, you're just a romantic. *If you've seen one cherry tree, you've seen them all.*" But it needs to be said that even if that were true, and –

it is not true –
he hadn't *seen* that one either.

My main purpose in this visit was to talk to Mr. Brandtsen about eternal considerations – about his soul. *It was no easy task.* He listened – he wasn't rude, but he was totally apathetic. My attempt to find some responsive chord met with that same disinterested, dismissing wave of the hand and, "Oh, John, you're a good boy, and I appreciate your coming all this way, but you know I never did have any use for stuff like that, and –

I haven't any use for it now."
And he didn't.

Mr. Brandtsen's trouble with the gospel was directly associated with his trouble with the cherry trees. A mind-set that says, "If you've seen one cherry tree, you've seen them all," is also going to say,

"How can a man be born when he is old?"
"How can this man give us His flesh to eat?"
"What is truth?"

Those are pretty good questions – penetrating questions – and Jesus does not give the kind of explanations that would satisfy us. He only affirms their truth by saying,

"No one can enter the Kingdom of God
without being born of the water and Spirit."

"Unless you eat the flesh of the Son of man
and drink His blood,
you have no life in you."

"I am the way and the truth."

Although Mr. Brandtsen's statement about cherry trees has some truth in it, I hope you also recognize that *there is something terribly wrong with it.* But what is wrong, and why is it wrong? How can a thing be both right and wrong? Is it not because there are *two kinds of truth?* Perhaps "two levels" of truth would more accurately convey my meaning. There is that truth which is confined to the physical senses – truth that is logical, literal, legalistic, rational, finite, earthy, and terribly inferior to the second, which is spiritual truth. Spiritual truth is transcendent, unbounded, and abstract (though no less real). It is truth that incorporates all senses, emotions, and reason but is infinite and heavenly, transcending the first just as the light of the sun transcends that of a flashlight. That is why Mr. Brandtsen's statement is true in the first sense of truth and totally false in the second. Talking about it is difficult. Writing about it is even more so. That is why the teachings of Jesus are called

hard sayings.

When Paul says that the "natural man" cannot receive the truths of God because they are "spiritually discerned," he knows exactly what he is talking about, because when he was Saul of Tarsus, he was a "natural man." When he was Saul of Tarsus, he always knew the answer and he could have proven it with fourteen syllogistic arguments and eleven undeniable affirmations, because he knew "the truth of the Law." But by his own admission, *he did not know God* because he says, "Who are you Lord?"

As Saul of Tarsus, he would have asked with Nicodemus, "How can a man be born when he is old?" and with those unbelieving Jews, "How can this man give us His flesh to eat?" and with Pilate, "What is truth?" When Saul, by the grace of God, is forced to his knees — both physically and spiritually — by that great, blinding, supernatural light, when he hears that cosmic voice calling, "Saul, Saul," and when he says, "Who are you, Lord?" he is well on his way to becoming the Apostle Paul, who no longer asks such ridiculous questions or says things like —

> "If you've seen one cherry tree,
> *you've seen them all."*

Mr. Brandtsen's problem was that he was a "natural man," and consequently, he could see only with his eyes and not his heart. He lacked the *humility* that is necessary to believe that there could be a truth greater than himself. But God did not intend that he stay that way. It was God's will that he become *a spiritual man* by being born again and beginning the process of putting off the natural, fleshly man. Then the Holy Spirit would have opened his eyes and his heart would have been enlightened to a new and higher sense of truth and beauty.

Mr. Brandtsen said, "Oh, John, I've never had any use for that stuff." In his pride, he *could not believe* that he was going to hell because he *would not believe* that he could to go to heaven. What I saw in Mr. Brandtsen was a man who had so nearly lost every semblance of the divine nature, who had so little appreciation for life, for beauty, and for truth that he was closer to being an orangutan than a saint.

Mr. Brandtsen could not conceive himself better or worse than he was — not bad enough to be lost or good enough to be saved. There is enough sadness in that to cause a mountain to weep. Since he lacked the humility to see himself as he was, he had no dream of becoming something infinitely better. After all,

> "If you've seen one cherry tree,
> you've seen them all."

Being born again would have opened Mr. Brandtsen's eyes. I believe he would have understood that the glory of one blossoming cherry tree is multiplied and enhanced by the glory of other blossoming cherry trees. Although he might not ever have had the faith to look about him and see the mountains full of horses and chariots of fire – or better yet, the heavens opened and the Son of Man standing at the right hand of God – he would certainly have learned that before a person is qualified to make any unequivocal statements about cherry trees in general, he must first –

see one cherry tree.
And I don't think he ever did.

Humility

♦

187

NINE

Love

"There is a time for everything,
and a season
for every activity under heaven."
—Ecclesiastes 3:1

This chapter is about love. If you have read my first book, you may remember a chapter I wrote called "Why Is Love So Hard?" If you didn't buy the book, you obviously won't remember the chapter, so run out and buy it right now and read it. Although love is the greatest thing in the world, it is also one of the hardest things in the world. The amount of pleasure and the amount of pain we experience in this world is in direct proportion to our willingness to invest in others, and that is why this chapter is here.

I have known much of love. When I was a child, I was taught to love God. I did so without much thought. I was also taught to love people – at least some people – but it was a child's love, so it wasn't personal or based on the kind of deep-seated convictions that are required for intensity or longevity. As I grew older, I began to think that loving God was a lot easier than loving people, and it has only recently occurred to me that the two things are tied together. Loving has been a slow and painful process for me – a type of *impossible dream*.

I was much loved by my parents, and I have known the love of friends, family, children, admirers, students, colleagues, and women. I came to know that there is no joy – especially with women – like love reciprocated and no pain like love unrequited.

For sheer, abject despair
and brutal, unrelenting hopelessness,
love for a member
of the opposite sex
not returned
has no equal.

But the great thing about love is that in the very worst moments of the wretchedness that it sometimes brings, love will pray for bright days, warm nights, and lasting peace for the beloved. Love makes everything it touches larger. Love increases. Love wants to – seeks to – forgive, excuse, believe in the goodness, and if not in the goodness, at least in the *need* of the beloved.

And love will hope –
against all reason –
against impossible odds –
love will hope
that one day . . . ?

And that is why it is
the greatest thing
in the world.

The God of This World

Very Young Love

"The god of this age has blinded
the minds of unbelievers,
so that they cannot see
the light of the gospel
of the glory
of Christ"
—2 Corinthians 4:4

Her name was Barbara, and she was quite short – especially for a sixth grade girl – but she was more *physically mature* than most of the other girls, who, though they were taller, were less "developed." Her short, dark hair was very, very curly. She was the first of the girls to wear lipstick and makeup, and the boys – *myself included* – thought she was daring and exciting. She was sort of the class sweetheart, and nearly every sixth-grade boy was in love with her – in a sixth-grade, awkward, confused, embarrassed sort of way. *I was no exception.* When we square danced in P. E. class, I just couldn't wait to "Do-Si-Do" with Barbara.

She lived just down Maxwell Street from me, so we sort of walked home – if not together – at least in the same direction. I showed off for her every day – doing the crazy, ridiculous things a sixth-grade boy would do to attract attention. I frog-hopped fire hydrants, turned cartwheels, threw insects on her, knocked her books loose, insulted her, accused her of being in love with the most unlikely prospects, argued with her, and even sang songs for her. She enjoyed it – encouraged it – and made me act twice the fool I was already making of myself. She didn't give a flip for me, but I never ceased trying to be her favorite.

Grace, on the other hand, liked me.
I always knew that –
she didn't try to hide it.

She was taller than I, with long, straight, blond hair, and a very fair complexion. She wore no makeup, and her seamless, nondescript, gingham dresses totally concealed any figure she may have had. She spoke with a light accent and pronounced her last name "Yonson." Her speech patterns were constantly corrected by our teachers, and she complied in every area but her name – there she persisted. Grace was a quiet, shy girl, a very pretty girl – I know that now – and when I look at our class picture, I wonder much about where my head was in the sixth grade.

I liked her well enough, but she was almost like a boy to me. She did not *act* like a girl – like Barbara – she didn't giggle or flirt or do other preposterous things; in fact, she didn't *act* at all. She liked me – she didn't try to act as if she didn't – she didn't send her girl friends with notes or messages – she talked to me directly, in a friendly, interesting way.

We ate lunch together almost every day. She would find me on the playground, and we would open our sacks together and exchange goodies and talk. She spoke of her home in Norway, about school, about things she liked or did – and she did it so naturally. She laughed quickly, easily, genuinely, and I was always at ease with her and never acted ridiculous. When she was accused of liking me, she readily assented.

Love

♦

194

> But I paid no attention to Grace,
>   and I let her go –
> while I vainly pursued Barbara.

What I want you to see is that in many ways, I haven't changed much since the sixth grade – and I wonder if you have. I still catch myself going for the big names, for the lipstick, the makeup, the sequins, the bright lights and noise. I fall for the slick promotions, the full-page, full-color ads – "the ultimate driving experience" – yet they don't care a flip for me. But they encourage me and lure me on; they *act,* and I *react* by doing ridiculous things – making a fool of myself, trying to win them and be a part of their gaudy world. I wonder if I want so badly for that world to be real that I am willing to be deceived.

When John tells us not to "love the world," he speaks to me about Barbara and Grace. In my juvenile way, I thought I loved Barbara, and I wanted her to love me. I didn't know much about love, in fact, I guess the story proves conclusively that I didn't know anything about love at all.

Our culture keeps trying to sell us a concept of love that is self-defeating and has the seeds of destruction built into its very fabric. I have learned some things since then – I hope I've learned to look deeper and in different places than I used to. Love isn't always pretty, and it's seldom found where I would have looked. Love is sort of shy; it doesn't peddle its wares on the street or on billboards or in magazines. It doesn't seek to attract my attention by appealing to what is base in me – my animal instincts. It doesn't entice me to burn all my energies or exhaust and waste the best I have in a fruitless pursuit. It doesn't so absorb me that I totally overlook the simple beauty of much that is worthy, honest, and true – things that are all around me.

When Paul writes of the unbelievers of his day, he says that "the god of this age has blinded their minds" (2 Cor. 4:4). What had Satan blinded their minds to? I think it was to love. We are all too willing to accept a cheap imitation, because the real thing requires more effort.

❦

Pay Attention

Young Love

I was preaching for a church in Northern California. They had no youth minister, no singles minister, no education, college, or involvement minister – so I was all of them. In my *youth* minister capacity, I decided to take the young people on a canoe trip down the *Rushin'* River – actually, it's the *Russian* River. *This was a very bad decision.* The water runs very fast, and it is not to be trusted. My only excuse is that I was very young and consequently can plead both ignorance and temporary insanity. The brochure that was sent to the church made it sound like a nice adventure – fresh air, exercise, natural wonder, excitement, scenic beauty – get close to God and to each other – all the necessary ingredients for a spiritually exhilarating church outing.

We left before daylight, three carloads of us, about twenty-five people in all. In my *involvement* minister capacity, I had planned on there being several adult chaperons to give spiritual guidance and to keep some of the more active boys and girls out of the bushes. Every one of my adults had last minute *emergencies* which *providentially* hindered them from being involved.

In my *singles* minister capacity, I had planned for there to be an equal number of boys and girls. My thinking was that there should be at least one boy and one girl in every canoe – the theory being that not only is that romantic, but deep in every male's genes there is a primordial instinct for how to handle a canoe – and a girl – in rough water. Both theories proved to be totally wrong – especially the one about the handling of a rough girl, I mean a girl in rough water – but you must remember that I was young. I ended up with two more girls than boys. Neither of them had ever been in a canoe before.

It was a beautiful day – as bright and warm and promising a spring day as you can imagine – which just goes to prove once again that Mother Nature is not to be trusted. She is deceitful, lulling you to sleep, so she can take full advantage of you when you least suspect it.

The first warning of potential trouble was when we arrived at the canoe rental headquarters. There was a long and heated discussion among the people behind the counter. They talked in strong whispers, and it was impossible to tell just what the debate was about, but I overheard things like –

"I don't think we should."
"Remember what happened the last time we did this?"
"Well, I'm not going to be responsible!"
"I don't think we'd lose *that* many."
"We could get *sued!*"

I thought the problem was with our reservations and the deposit, or maybe they didn't have enough canoes, or maybe they didn't have enough staff to pick us up at the end of our trip, but it wasn't too long before I discovered that it was the –

condition of the river.

Some torrential rains at higher elevations, coupled with an exceptionally heavy run-off of melting snow from the Sierras, had seriously raised the level and the velocity of the river. Apparently, those staffers who thought that making money was more important than safety won out, because our trip continued.

When we reached the departure point, my alarm grew. The river was obviously out of its banks, the noise of the muddy, foamy, turbulent water was deafening. When I saw large trees, boat docks, and dead animals floating down the river, I expressed my apprehension. The person in charge assured me that this was no cause for concern; he said that it was – *perfectly normal*. We launched twelve canoes into that rushing flood.

I had decided to take the two *odd* girls with me. I do not mean *odd* as in *strange* or *peculiar* – any more so than any man would view any female – I only mean *odd* in the sense that I had no boys to pair them with. They were college age and attractive enough to turn heads. My parting admonition was, "Now, let's stay together."

I'm sure they tried.

We hadn't gone two hundred yards before disaster struck. Every canoe had tipped over at least once. Lunches, sunglasses, seat cushions, paddles, shoes, an assortment of life jackets and articles of clothing, along with a few kids were floating down the river, much of it never to be seen again. I was trying to be everywhere at once – trying to get canoes upright, trying to find lost articles, trying to find lost kids, trying to find the bank of the river – and failing miserably at it all. There were several other groups on the river, and it was impossible to tell who and what belonged to whom and which.

Gradually, things began to settle down. The kids began to get the hang of canoeing, and the water became less turbulent as the river widened, and the descent became more gradual. The trip became rather enjoyable, except for those kids I couldn't account for. I didn't know if they were

ahead of me, *behind* me, or
under me.

At some point, I began to notice another canoe – not of our party – that contained two young men. Now these young men had not only been astute enough to *notice* the two young ladies with me, they had also observed that they were not *with* me, in that special sense of boy-girl *with*. It sort of frosted me a little, and I made it as difficult as possible for them to advance their cause. However, their persistence and dogged determination was admirable.

Only one thing can make men act like such fools –

love!

As we neared the end of our trip, there was a particularly wide stretch of very calm and placid water with beautiful oak trees lining and overhanging both banks – it was lovely – enchanting – and it drove those love-crazed boys to the brink. Their time to *score* was very limited, so they made a desperately bold and determined advance against the rather flimsy fortifications the girls had thrown up. They drew their canoe up so close to ours that I could see the little beads of erotic perspiration that *desire* had placed on their foreheads – these boys had such a bad case of the *spring itch* that they were broken out with little red blotches – like hives or bee stings – all over their faces –

they were pathetic.

They began the oldest song and dance in history; it was disgusting –

but it worked!

That is why it's so old. However, they were so absorbed by their objective and so excited by their success that they forgot two things of great importance – they forgot where they were, and

they forgot me.

The stretch of calm water was narrowing to one last rapid. Pretending to pay no attention, I slowly, carefully maneuvered my canoe, and consequently theirs, toward a large rock, just above the rapids. *Love is a marvelous thing.* It not only blinds us to the faults and blemishes of the beloved, it blinds us to impending disaster —

they never saw it coming.

About ten feet before the collision, I spoke for the first time. In a very conversational tone I said, "Boys, you are about to pay the price that all men pay when they allow women to divert their attention — you are about to look very foolish," and I pointed to the rock, which was now looming over their heads.

They looked up, paddled frantically, screamed wonderfully, then one of them bailed out of the canoe in a marvelous acrobatic display of sheer panic. The other, determined to see it through to the end, clung to the sides of the canoe, thinking it would save him -

it didn't.

The prow of their canoe struck the rock and reared high into the air; the rear end filled with water, and then it disappeared beneath the surface with its lone occupant still clinging fiercely to the sides. Both boys went down into the water — both they and their gear were baptized, and the river carried me away, and I — I saw them no more, but

I went on my way rejoicing.

I hope the dunking cooled their ardor somewhat and made them more rational. I'm sure it cured their *rash,* and I'm sure the experience did them much good. I have often wondered how *they* told this story, and in what endearing terms and memorable language they described me.

I had a marvelous moral in mind when I began this piece. It was about love, I think. Whatever it was, I forgot it. You probably would too — so just laugh and appreciate God's gifts, and don't take yourself

too seriously.

Staying in Love

Not Quite So Young – But Still Young – Love

I was teaching English at Auburn University in Montgomery. It was right after class, and I had gone to my car in the parking lot. I saw him standing casually by his car, and it made me wonder a little because it was very cold – no time for loitering. I couldn't tell too much about him, except that he had a lot of dark, curly hair sticking out from under his baseball cap. His jeans were old, and his jacket looked a little *worse for the wear*. When I saw his face light up, I followed the direction of his gaze and – *I saw her*. She was blond and cute. She was wearing a heavy tweed coat with a white scarf hanging down the front. He was waiting for her. It struck me, even then, that he could have waited in the car where it was warmer, but then I remembered what it was like to be young and in love, and looking at her –

I would have waited outside too.

He walked toward her as she came across the parking lot, and when he got close he smiled, like he was really glad to see her, and she smiled too – right up into his face. They didn't say anything; they just stood there in the cold, looking into each others eyes and smiling. Then suddenly, he reached out his hand toward her face – he did it so quickly that I anticipated her reaction – flinching, ducking, or slapping it away – but she didn't. She never moved; she just stood there, eyes wide open –

smiling and trusting.

His hand stopped about an inch from her face, and then he extended his index finger and touched her – right on the tip of her nose – to tell her it was red from the cold, I guess – but he might have done it even if it hadn't been. They both laughed and linked their arms around each other and walked to the car, skipping a little. When they got there, he opened her door, and when she got in, she slid way over so that they'd be close when he got in. It was so clean, so natural, so beautiful. I went to my car a little warmer. As I drove away, I saw them again, still in his car –

sitting close and laughing.

I hope they never forget how important it is to do the little things – the natural things – to smile, to touch noses, to trust, to link arms, to sit close, and to laugh –

because if they remember,
they'll always be in love.

Love

♦

199

It's not the big occasions – anniversaries and birthdays, things easily remembered – that count. It's the little, everyday kind of things that are so easily overlooked that sustain relationships.

Love

200

Boy Blue

Parent Love

It was 1968. We lived on Chevrolet Street in Flint, Michigan. I was in my last semester at the University of Michigan. Our two sons, Lincoln and Brendan, were about three-and-a-half and nine months. I was sitting in my favorite recliner one evening, studying, Judi was cleaning up the kitchen, Brendan was in bed, and Lincoln was playing in his favorite place – underneath the studio grand piano, which occupied about one-half of our living room.

Lincoln's bedtime came, and Judi told him to go upstairs. He came to my chair and kissed me goodnight, and I watched him slowly climb the stairs, one at a time on his hands and knees. He was wearing one of those light blue pajama-type jumpsuits – with the *emergency flap* on the back side. I remember how out of proportion the size of his bottom looked because of the diaper.

After he had gone, I noticed that he had left his toys under the piano – a small steel dump truck, three matchbox cars, some plastic, army-type figures, and a small, stuffed animal.

I don't know why that inconsequential incident should have left so deep an impression on my memory that I still recall it after all these years – except perhaps for these two things. First, as I watched him go up the stairs, it occurred to me that this was a time to be treasured, because I remembered that he had been Brendan's age only days ago, it seemed. It also occurred to me that *you can't hold on to things,* no matter how hard you try, and I saw a glimpse of the future – I mean, I became aware, for a few moments, of the importance of what I was doing and the awesome responsibility before me. My eyes filled with tears as I thought about how much I loved my son and what I wanted him to be.

Second, I remembered some snatches of a poem – a simple, but lyrical rhyme – that etched that moment forever in my memory. When you read it, you will see immediately why I associated it with this event and why I remember it. I have since learned it all. It seems that the author of the poem went to look at a cottage that was for sale. The previous owners had closed it up after their small son died, and it remained as they had left it. As the author wandered through the long, empty house, he discovered some child's toys left in the seat of an old rocking chair, and he penned these words.

Love

♦

201

"The little toy dog is covered with dust,
But sturdy and staunch he stands.
And the little toy soldier is red with rust,
And his musket molds in his hands.
Time was when the little toy dog was new
And the soldier was passing fair,
And that was the time when our Little Boy Blue
Kissed them and put them there.

'Now, don't you go 'till I come,' he said,
'And don't you make any noise.'
So toddling off to his trundle-bed,
He dreamed of the pretty toys.
And as he was dreaming, an angel song
Awakened our Little Boy Blue,
Oh, the years are many, the years are long,
But the little toy friends are true.

Ay, faithful to Little Boy Blue, they stand,
Each in the same old place,
Awaiting the touch of a little hand,
The smile of a little face.
And they wonder, as waiting the long years through
In the dust of that little chair,
What has become of our Little Boy Blue
Since he kissed them and put them there."
—Eugene Field, *Little Boy Blue*

As my son went up the stairs, it occurred to me *how fragile life is* – that neither he nor I might live through this night. I thought about my plans and realized once again how totally dependent I was on the grace, the providence, and the steadfast love of God. I knew that not even death could destroy my love for my son, and I went to bed with a renewed faith in Paul's statement that *love abides,* because it is the greatest thing of all.

We know that God loves the world, and we have been told that God loves us – personally and individually. How does He love us? There is much about God's love that is infinitely deep and mysterious – it is food for the philosophic meditations of sages and thinkers. But there is also that about God's love that is marvelously, beautifully simple – though no less profound and mysterious – so simple that it is often missed. Although we have *experienced it,* we have not recognized it, because we have not yet learned the meaning of that great truth –

that we are made in His image.

Love

◆

202

Kicking against the Goads

Parent Love

It was late February or early March. James and I were playing at the gravel pit. It was a cold, windy, overcast day, with a few flakes of snow flying, but we were having a great time. I had on my first pair of genuine boots – rubber footwear that you could actually stick your foot right down into with no shoes on, and you didn't have to buckle them. They were black with red soles and a little too large for me (my mother had bought them at a sale, and neither size nor comfort was a major consideration). Even with two pairs of socks, I "clumped" in them considerably. They came almost to my knees and looked like firemen's boots.

I was exceedingly proud of them.

There was a little thin ice at the edge of the gravel pit, and we were breaking that ice by stomping on it and then splashing through into the shallow water beneath it. I had been doing this for some time when I found a small pool, covered with what we called "rubber ice." It was not actually part of the gravel pit, but it was connected by a narrow neck of water. The ice would actually give with your weight and then spring back – a sort of trampoline effect. You can imagine what fun I had with it. Suddenly, it gave way, and I fell into some sandy water unlike any I had ever been in before. I sank immediately over my boots up to my thighs. Terrified, I began to struggle, but simply could not extricate myself. This produced a fear that resulted in an absolute frenzy of effort to get out. The only noticeable result was that I was nearly up to my armpits within a minute or so.

I did not know that I should remain calm – I simply wore myself out struggling. Finally, I had no energy left, and the absolute futility of further efforts overwhelmed me. James heard my cries and came to help me, but he quickly realized that he could be of no assistance. He stood completely helpless, within ten feet of me. As I grew more calm, I noticed that I wasn't sinking as fast. I told James to run and get Elmer Russell. He was a well driller, and I knew he was home because I had spoken to him on my way to the gravel pit.

When they returned a few minutes later, I had sunk past my armpits. I was numb from the effect of the freezing sand and water and was quite concerned about my condition. Elmer had brought a rope, and he got a circle of it over my head, and I grabbed it with my hands. Being an extremely powerful man, he pulled me out with relative ease. Unfortunately, he pulled me right out of my boots. It was about a mile or so to my house, but I ran all the way –

in my socks.

I thought I would receive the whipping of my life – if you have read my other book, *My Mother Played the Piano,* you will understand completely why I felt that way – but you know, the funniest thing happened. When my mother first saw me – soaking wet, mud and sand right up to my ears, my boots gone – she was real upset. I tried to tell her what had happened, but it was a less than convincing story. Just about the time I finished my explanation, the phone rang, and it was Elmer Russell calling to see if I had gotten home all right. He talked to my mom –

for a long time.

When she hung up, there were great tears in her eyes, and she came and hugged me and kissed me. She helped me undress, got the washtub, heated some water, and made me take a hot bath – it wasn't even Saturday – gave me some hot tea, and put me to bed. I couldn't make any sense out of it at

Love

◆

all. When my father came home that evening, I thought sure I was going to catch it good.

For some reason, they went to their bedroom to talk, which was really unusual, because normally when I messed up they talked right in front of me – so I would know what was coming, I guess. I heard her say, "Oh, Fred, Elmer told me that another five minutes and he would have been gone. *We almost lost him.*" When my dad came out, he never said much, but I noticed that when we prayed at supper that night, he mentioned me several times and told God how grateful he was that He looked after me when he couldn't.

On Sunday afternoon, he and I walked over to the gravel pit, and I showed him the place – I guess he wanted to look for my boots, but they were nowhere in sight. He stood there by the little pond of water a long time and looked, and again he didn't say much, but I thought I noticed him wiping his eyes a time or two with the back of his hand, and I wondered about it, because the wind was hardly blowing –

and it wasn't that cold.

The lesson is – I know you see it – how the threat of loss makes all that we hold dear more precious – how it moves the love in our hearts. *God loves us.* The Father grieves when He sees us struggling frantically to find meaning and purpose in our lives, yet always ending in greater lostness. How pleased He is to circle His great arms around us and rescue us from certain death. When He carries us home, He says, with great concern, to Jesus and the angelic host –

"You know,
we almost lost him."

P.S. Late that fall, I was playing at the gravel pit one sunny afternoon with James (I told you I wasn't real bright as a youngster – some might argue that age hasn't helped substantially), and we found one of my boots sticking right up out of the ground. I pulled it out and took it home, but it wasn't much good. I always wondered what happened to the other one.

I Knew You'd Come

Brother Love

I heard this story from George Romney, then Governor of Michigan, in 1955 when I was a junior in high school. It made a deep impression on me, and I have never forgotten it. It is a story about love. I have made up the names, but the rest of the story is told as I remember him telling it.

In the great Ohio Valley, where the fertile, black, loamy soil produces the wheat, corn, potatoes, and other staples for the tables of Detroit and Chicago, there is a small town called Steubenville. It is an old town. Two hundred years ago – and before that – the area was settled by German immigrants who were dissatisfied with life in their native land. What they found, they liked. They cleared their land, they built their homes, they established towns, schools, churches, they had their families – and they stayed.

There is a very old family there named Hansen. It is said that there have always been Hansens in Steubenville. The Hansens are good citizens, close-knit, solid, dependable, courteous, loyal, and helpful. It is a great tribute to the Hansens that whenever a Hansen son or daughter is sent to school, every teacher and administrator is pleased by the prospect.

Some years ago – in the early forties, actually – Lutz Hansen and his wife, Gwendolyn, had two sons in successive years. In fact, they were born eleven months apart. One, the older, they named Travis; the other, James. They had other children – older and eventually younger – but between these two, there developed a closeness, a relationship – a tie – that even in a close-knit family was remarkable – they were inseparable.

Blond, sturdy, intelligent, both were good athletes and good students – and they were always together. They worked, played, even studied together. They were a year apart in school, but with his parent's permission and understanding, Travis stayed out his freshman year of high school so that he and James could play sports together and graduate together. Stories are still told of the way they blocked for each other in football and passed to each other in basketball, how Travis pitched and James caught in baseball, how they always double-dated, and how the girls said it didn't matter which one you went with, because you had a feeling that you were out with both of them.

When they graduated, it was the time of the Korean conflict. They both registered for the draft, and when inducted under the "buddy system," they went to basic training together and later were assigned to the same unit, the

Love

♦

205

same company. They arrived at the Yalu River, north of Panmunjom in January, 1961, in time for a major offensive.

Normally they took their duties together, but one night, James was assigned to a routine perimeter patrol designed to prevent enemy encroachment upon their position. The patrol was ambushed, and only two members struggled back to the camp to report the disaster.

James did not come back.

When word reached Travis, he went immediately to his commanding officer and requested permission to go and search for his brother. It was denied. The place of the ambush was assumed to be in enemy control, and it would be suicide to send a rescue squad. Travis quietly explained his need to go, and even here, in this cold, barren, forbidding setting, a commanding officer realized that there was something unusual here, something not to be treated with normal rules. He also realized that the boy was going to go – with or without permission.

He finally said that although he could not grant permission, he would not prevent his leaving. Travis spoke to the two men who had made it back, learned the location of the ambush, and set out. It was completely dark, it was unbearably cold, it was a hopeless task, and even if found, his brother had little chance of being alive.

All through that dark night he searched, and just at gray light, he located the place. He moved quickly from one frozen, shattered body to another – not him – not him – and then he found him, nearly frozen, mortally wounded, but alive. He cradled the head of his dying brother in his lap and wept. James opened unseeing eyes, and with the last of his strength whispered –

"Is that you, Travis?"

"Yes."

"I knew you'd come –
I've been waiting."

It was the last thing he said. A short time later, he died.

Do things like that really happen? Does love that strong really exist? When Governor Romney told the story, I believed it with all my heart. I want badly to believe it now. Sometimes I need something like this to restore my faith in man's power to do good. Governor Romney didn't say whether or not these boys were religious – I have always believed they were.

James trusted his brother because of the love between them, because love always produces a covenant of trust. He waited because he knew that if the situation were reversed, he would come or die trying. Because of his

absolute faith, not just in his brother, but in the power of love itself, he found the strength, had the hope to stay alive – to wait for him to come.

We trust God because He has shown us and taught us love. His love has created a covenant between us and Him. We trust God because we know Him and believe that He loves us. We trust each other for the same reason. Because of our absolute faith in God's unfailing, steadfast love, we find the patience and the courage – in the hour of our greatest need – to overcome this world and to wait for Him to come.

> When every other reason fails,
> love will find a way.

> "The steadfast love of the Lord never ceases,
> His mercies never come to an end;
> they are new every morning;
> great is your faithfulness.
> 'The Lord is my portion,'
> says my soul,
> 'therefore I will hope in Him.'"
> —Lamentations 3:22–23

> "Is that you, Lord?"
> "Yes, John."
> *"I knew you'd come –*
> I've been waiting."

Remember Me for This

Friend Love

When I lived in Indianapolis in 1962, I met and baptized a lady with the singular name of Hazel Whitecotton. She had terminal cancer. Hazel lived for four or five weeks after her baptism. I went to see her often. After the initial greetings, there was always a strained silence because she was so weak that it was an effort for her to talk. She asked me one day if I might read to her. I was glad to do so and asked if there was anything in particular that she would enjoy. In addition to several portions of the Bible, she loved Shakespeare and Robert Frost. We became friends.

She lay on a daybed in the living room, where she could look out over her tree-lined, flower-filled yard, as the afternoon sun slanted brilliantly through the front windows and door. Three or four afternoons a week, I went faithfully to visit and to read. We talked very little. There wasn't much to say. She was dying. We both knew it – had admitted it – we had cried and prayed –

and it was all right.

How precious those memories are now. We shared a Savior, a family, a hope, even a love for Robert Frost's New England. We shared a vision of birch trees, stone walls, peck-fretted apple trees, woods on a snowy evening, and "The Road Not Taken." Hamlet, Caesar, Richard II, and Romeo and Juliet all lived again, and we became good friends. Often there were other things that I would have *preferred* to do – sometimes things that I felt I *needed* to do –

but I went to see Hazel.

I went with mixed emotions. I was honestly glad to help, and Hazel was a pleasant, though often silent, companion. I looked forward to the reading – to the characters, places, and events, as they lived and walked again in my mind – but I found it very hard to look at Hazel. She was – emaciated. Her hip bones stood out sharply under her dress, and the wrinkled, discolored skin on her arms and legs was almost transparent. I wondered how a body with so little left could live.

Toward the end, the cancer was so advanced that her flesh actually began to decay and the odor was overpowering. More than once I excused myself from the reading to go to the bathroom and retch violently until my nausea subsided. Doggedly, I returned to Hazel and the books.

I gave something to Hazel, the most precious gift I have, something beyond reckoning, not confined by time or space. We call it *giving of ourselves.* But the words are not enough – they will not satisfy. We must *experience* that gift – both in the receiving and the giving – to know it, to recognize it as a small reminder of that great gift He gave us.

I gave her my love.

There is a great redeeming and strengthening power in this kind of loving. We are at our very best when we do so, and it is almost impossible to engage in it and simultaneously be proud, selfish, or immoral. How sad that we find so little time to do it – that we are often so uncomfortable with it. Perhaps we seek to avoid it because it seems weak and is a *death thing*—it has so much to do with dying to self and to the world – and so we think of it as less important than doing *living things.*

God could have chosen to do some cataclysmic feat to demonstrate the power of His love – but He is best seen washing feet, talking to women at wells, in still, small voices, weeping at cemeteries, and nailed to a cross on Calvary between two common thieves.

I am very conscious of the sins of my youth – and my present ones as well. I am often burdened with my materialism, insensitivity, and lack of evangelistic fervor. Occasionally, I think of good things I have done. In the midst of my anguish over sin and my penitence for the heartache I bring to the Father, I remember that I loved Hazel Whitecotton completely and unselfishly, and I cry with Nehemiah,

> *"Remember me for this,*
> *O my God."*
> —Nehemiah 13:14

"I Buried Her There"

A Love Story

In the land of Egypt, Jacob – 147 years old, feeble, blind, sick, and near death – called for his son Joseph and his grandsons, Ephraim and Manasseh. When they appeared at his bedside, he told the story of his life – his history. He told the story one last time in the hope that it would be repeated to succeeding generations and that the memory would stir their hearts and souls.

> "When I came from Padan,
> Rachel died, to my sorrow,
> and I buried her there,
> on the way to Bethlehem."

His sightless eyes clouded over, and his voice trembled at the mention of his beloved Rachel. He paused as though he were finished. Ephraim was relieved and turned to leave, but gentle pressure on his arm from his father made him stand patiently and wait.

Jacob was gone – he was living it again, living it in his mind as he had lived it in his flesh. He was seeing Rachel in his mind as he had seen her in the flesh. He was feeling the pulsing chemistry in his memory as he had felt it in his flesh, that first time, there by the well in Haran. The memory was so real that he reached out his hand to touch her – and though she beckoned to him with her eyes –

her image slowly receded.

He tried to follow her and almost succeeded – but she finally disappeared into a dimension he could not yet penetrate. He was a long time finding his way back.

"Joseph, you should have seen her – she was the most beautiful, the most daring, exciting, teasing – yes she was," he laughed. "You didn't know her then. She was a tease, your mother – I loved her from the first moment until the day she died.

"I worked for your great Uncle Laban for seven years to make her mine, and then he tricked me. Your great uncle was a very clever man, Joseph – a good business man and a hard bargainer. He got me to drinking on my wedding night and brought Leah, Rachel's older sister to my tent. It's a little embarrassing, you know; but I was so drunk I didn't know the difference. When I got up the next morning, I was furious and desperate. I felt sorry for Leah, it must be an awful thing to not be loved. Laban knew I was mad enough to kill him, but he also knew how desperately I loved your mother, so he got me to work for him another seven years. When Rachel became mine, I was the happiest man on earth.

"She was terribly jealous of Leah you know. She didn't have any children for many years, and Leah had several. It didn't matter to me – there was never anybody for me but Rachel. Leah was a good woman – pleasant, kind, a good wife and mother – and I loved her for her goodness – but your mother, Joseph –

ah, *your mother was special.*

Love

◆

210

"When you were born, Joseph – how can I tell you our joy? Your mother was so happy. She thought that now I would love her more, and I did, but not because of you as much as because being a mother awakened a whole new element in her that I had never seen. Those next years were the best of our lives.

"I saw the trouble coming between you and your brothers, and I tried to tell you not to do things to provoke them. You never understood the depth of their jealousy. When we lost you – that day Simeon came with your robe all torn and bloody and told of your death – I knew that Rachel would not live. Everything died in her, and when that happened, the light went out in my life too.

> The light has been gone
> for a long time,
> but that time is nearly over.
> The light will return.

"Your brothers could never understand. We thought no less of them – each was important – we loved each of them in their own way – but you, Joseph, you were us – the fulfillment of our love.

"When she was pregnant with Benjamin, it just wasn't the same. We had never stopped grieving for you, so there was no joy in it. Things were hard for us with all of the moving, and your mother was not a young woman anymore. She was not well, and her grief sapped her strength, and her resolve weakened. It made everything harder. I worried – I worried myself sick – for your memory and for Rachel. What if I should lose my love –

> my Rachel?

"On the way from Bethel, long before we got to Ephrath, she went into labor. It wasn't time. The trip had been very hard, she was tired, discouraged, and she had no hope. Your brother was born after an awful labor, but Rachel took no joy in the baby. When she saw that it was a son, she named him, 'Ben Oni' – the son of my sorrow – and then she died. We did everything to save her, but she didn't want to live anymore. I couldn't bear to call him 'Ben Oni', so I renamed him 'Ben Amin' – the son of my right hand. I still cannot look at him without tears, Joseph; he is the very image of your mother.

"Life was never the same. When Rachel died, something went out of my life – it has never returned – and it never will. The years have dragged on – so much has happened. Here we are in Egypt. I never liked it here, Joseph, and *you must not bury me here."* He raised himself up, and reaching out his hand, he gripped Joseph's arm with surprising strength. He shouted, "Hear me Joseph, and promise me that *you will not bury me in Egypt.* This is not our home Joseph – not yours either. You must bury me in the land God gave us; promise me that. Bury me beside your mother. I'll rest well there."

"I promise father," Joseph said solemnly.

"Never, never forget your mother, Joseph. Never forget this story. Teach it to these boys; make them repeat it until they know it by heart.

It's all I have to leave you.
It is my legacy to you
and to my grandchildren."

The old man sighed, released Joseph's arm, gradually laid himself back on the pallet, stopped talking, and lay still. And then, like one who suddenly awakens, he shook himself, wiped his eyes, and said, "Now where was I? Oh yes – when I came from Padan – Rachel died, and I buried her there. I buried your mother beside the road – the road to Bethlehem – Rachel died and things were never the same – I buried her beside the road to Bethlehem – because, you see, there was no other place; we had to go on. It wasn't easy you know, I didn't want to leave, but I had to, you see –

God made me."

❧

Hosea Loves Gomer

Married Love

I have often been troubled by the story of Hosea. I mean, it's a good story with a great moral – *if you're a long-range observer, or if you want to use him as an example for a lesson you're teaching.* But Hosea was a real person who had to live his life one day at a time with no sneak previews of how it was all going to turn out. He was a man with feelings and frustrations, a guy who loved his kids, baseball, fried chicken, and rooted for the home team. I wonder how he felt about being used as a *symbol* – an analogy, a proof text, an illustration – a walking sign board –

> "Hi, my name's Hosea,
> and I married
> the town prostitute."

I wonder how he felt when God told him that He wanted him to select a wife from the *red-light district?* What a slap in the face when she left him for her old way of life. I'm sure he thought he had done her a big favor by taking her in the first place (which is what a lot of husbands think). I mean, he thought she had a pretty good situation with him. I wonder how he felt when all of his friends *felt sorry* for him or, worse yet, when he overheard the jokes they told about his *shady lady.* I'm sure they all felt he was crazy and that nobody could possibly *love* a woman like that.

I'm sure that he had some reservations about the whole deal, and I wouldn't be at all surprised if he argued quite a bit with God before he actually did what He told him. I bet he said, "Lord, let me make sure I heard You right. Now, did I, or did I not, hear You say that You want me to marry a prostitute? I mean, let me get this straight. You always told us to *stone* people like that, and now You want me to *marry* one?"

I think one of the real lessons from this story has to do with Hosea's willingness to obey God against all human wisdom and judgement, against all of his own desires, against his religious convictions and moral standards – and with his willingness to trust God for the outcome and to be ridiculed by everyone for God's sake. I want to say that that is what we all must do in our marriages – we must place that relationship in God's hands and trust him.

A second lesson has to do with the fact that apparently Hosea actually came to *love* Gomer – I mean, he really got attached to her. If he didn't, then this story loses much of its purpose because it's supposed to demonstrate God's never-failing love for His people in spite of their sins. Hosea learned what it's like to love someone in spite of their faults, and again, that's what every marriage is about – loving someone in spite of their faults.

Gomer became an inspiration to Hosea's life – every time he looked at her, he was reminded of God's love; and the more he loved her, the more he loved God and understood Him. He understood why it was so important to God that Israel do right and that they love Him, because

> more than anything,
> Hosea wanted Gomer to do right
> and to love him.

Love

◆

Isn't that what we all want? And you know what? I think maybe she did come to love him. It may have taken her a long time to *understand that kind of love*, but when she did — I mean, when she understood how much she was loved and what love really is — I believe she knew that it was the greatest thing that had ever happened to her. I want to believe that she became a beautiful person — that she blossomed into all that she was meant to be —

because that's what love
and marriage
are supposed to do,
you know.

Love

♦

TEN

Life

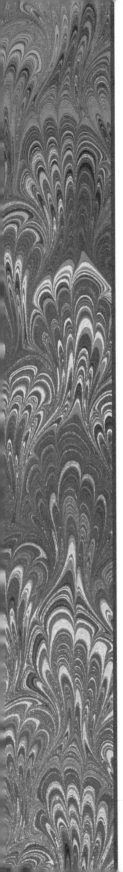

"What is your life?
You are a mist
that appears for a little while
and then vanishes."
—James 4:14

Not long ago I found a list of "Things to Do Today" in the pocket of a seldom-used jacket. In fact, it is more than four years old – the list, that is – the jacket is much older. It read as follows:

Call Ricardi for dirt
Call phone company
Call Bob Skupien
Go to hospital – see Donna
Take door to Copeland
Watch Brendan's game – 5:30
Office – pay bills
See Paul Harper – price on truck
Go to Hill Bros.
Talk to Johnny at Tire World
Take boots to Kogers
Take $20 to Mrs. Rucker
Picture for yearbook
Cash checks
Call Jaime at Dolan Springs
See Jim Knell
Lunch – Bob Nichol

Many of the items have lines drawn through them, which I assume indicates that either I did them or they became unimportant. Others, apparently, never got done.

I wonder if
they were important?

The dirt was to level the front yard. Why I needed to call the phone company, I can't remember. Bob Skupien wanted me to referee a basketball

216

tournament. Donna died; I preached her funeral. The door was a brand new one, but the glass was cracked. I don't remember if I got to Brendan's game or who won. I guess I paid the bills; nobody sued me or turned off my utilities. Paul Harper's price was too high, so I didn't buy the truck – so was Hill Brother's. I bought new tires from Johnny at Tire World and kept the old truck. Kogers resoled my boots. I sure hope Mrs. Rucker got her $20. I don't remember her or it. My picture is in the yearbook. I'm sure I cashed the checks; I *know* that I spent the money. Jaime wanted some firewood, but he didn't want to pay what I thought it was worth, so – I kept it. Jim Knell probably wanted to be paid for working. Bob Nichol divorced his wife and left the church.

The list reveals much. It tells of the things that were important to me at that time. It is significant that none of those things are very important to me now. I wonder if I read my Bible or prayed that day? My present days are all too similar –returning calls, sending faxes, putting gas in the car, counseling troubled marriages, writing bulletin articles, making plane reservations – the nuts and bolts of my existence.

What is my life? I want to live thoughtfully, purposefully, incisively. I want to grasp every moment, to wring meaning from it – to rise above the ever encroaching whirlpool of minutia that sucks and pulls me down. I fight the forces that seem constantly to break my days into ever smaller fragments – the sum of which *never adds up to twenty-four hours*. I want time to read, to think, to pray – time to consider my life, my purpose, my direction. I do not wish for my life to be measured out in cups of coffee.

What is my life?

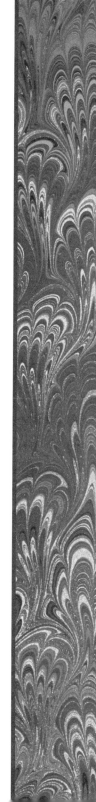

217

Susan Edgin

December 19, 1967 – May 19, 1995

The Life of Susan Edgin

She was the older sister of my son's wife, and her name was Susan. She was a nice girl – a good girl. She was *good* in the traditional sense that she loved her family, her friends, her dog, obeyed her parents, studied hard, slept late, was kind and thoughtful of others, sang in the church choir, cleaned up her messes, made good moral decisions, loved God, was silly, laughed a lot, cried some, and all in all, was the kind of daughter that every parent dreams of having. She loved life and lived it to the fullest every waking moment. She took good care of her body, watched what she ate, exercised regularly, was neat in her appearance, and went to great pains with her hair and clothes.

I think that at first glance she would be judged as no more than average-pretty, but if you looked too deeply into those large, luminous, all-telling eyes or listened too long to that intriguing, animated voice, it would soon occur to you that she was quite beautiful. She was a tall girl, lithe, athletic, and graceful in all her movements. She carried herself well – with dignity, style, and verve. She never took herself too seriously, but she was interesting to talk to and thoughtful enough to be introspective when the occasion called for it. She was a loyal friend, a great lover of children and the simple things of life, and she sang beautifully.

I know you think that I am just romanticizing, but I'm not. My son put it this way: "If you went anywhere I have ever lived, you would find someone who didn't like me, but that wasn't true of Susan. I never met or heard of anyone who didn't like Susan Edgin."

For the short time I knew her, we spent a fair amount of time together. Susan was so refreshingly open that you didn't need to be around her long to feel that you were her best friend. Once, when I was staying at her house, we went running together. She thoughtfully adjusted her pace to accommodate my aging legs. Susan talked the whole way. (I am tempted to make a pun and say she kept up a *running conversation* the whole time, but I won't.) I don't talk when I run. It isn't that I am concentrating or unfriendly; it's that talking requires breath and energy, and I don't have any to spare when I'm running. After about four miles, I was nearing exhaustion. We came at last to the bottom of the long, steep hill that led to her house.

As we approached the incline I said, "Susan, I just can't make it, you go ahead."

"Sure you can," she said, "just follow me, and do what I do. I always save a little for the end – for this last hill – you can borrow from me."

Life

♦

219

I followed her.
I did what she did,
and I borrowed a little
of what she had saved
for the end.

When we got to the top, she turned and laughed and said, "See there, you can always do a little more than you think —

especially if you have someone with you."

Life

♦

220

She's gone now. She died on May 19, 1995, in an automobile accident near Augusta, Georgia. The car she was traveling in spun out of control on a wet road and slammed sideways into a guard rail. Susan was crushed. In the short time she lived after the accident, calls went out for prayers. We poured out our hearts to God in agony, begging him to save her. The doctors tried everything that medical science could do, but she died.

It doesn't seem fair, you know. Here I am still plodding up hills, and I'm thirty-five years older than Susan — it doesn't seem right. I thought about all the slimeballs, the thugs, the drug dealers, the rotten, miserable, low-life wretches who don't even know they're alive and really don't care and wouldn't be missed. I wondered why it wasn't one of those who had died instead of Susan. You can't help the nagging doubts; they are an integral part of a growing faith. I started asking those questions a long time ago. The only answer I've found is to trust God. It hasn't been easy, and I still ask the questions, but I know that I don't have a clue — so I trust him.

What is life?

I think I know. Life is a gift — a precious, beautiful, gift. Yes, that is exactly what life is. It is something to hold — but not too closely — because it isn't ours. That is why Jesus instructed Mary not to hang on to him. God gave Susan to us for twenty-seven years, and he let us know her and love her and bask in the glow of her vitality — but *she was never ours.* That is the great mistake we make. We become so used to things that we begin thinking that they're ours. That's what leads us into asking stupid questions about justice and fairness and —

"What if . . . ?"

Life originates with God. Even our personal lives are not our own. Life has nothing to do with fairness, and its value or justification cannot be measured by longevity. It is not sad to die young. What is sad is to die and never to have lived, to have been alive and never to have seen anything or known God. We don't feel that kind of sadness for Susan. Susan lived a full life because she saw the created world through eyes of faith and because she knew the God who made it.

Susan was a gift – and the only proper response to a gift – is gratitude.

"Thank you,

O Lord of the Universe,

for Susan."

As I stared into her grave, I thought, "Anybody who can come face to face with the awesome, impending power and meaning of what it means to die and still hate another person or maintain petty, selfish, intolerance and meanness has totally lost touch with the divine voice within them."

Life

I honestly don't remember the last time I saw her or what we said. We didn't try to make it important because we thought we'd see each other again – soon and often. I guess it really wasn't too important, because we will see each other again – soon and often – and we'll pick up right where we left off.

Susan has climbed her last hill – it was a long, steep grade – even for young legs, and she didn't know if she could make it, but when she started the assent, she found Jesus beside her, and he said –

"Just follow me, and do what I do.

I always save something for the end –

for this last hill –

you can borrow from me."

And so she followed Jesus, and she did what he did and borrowed some of what he had saved, and they climbed the hill together and passed over to the other side. And it's true, you know –

it is easier,

if you have someone with you.

Ah, Susan, Susan. What was there about you that should cause our God to call you to Him so soon? Was it that you were so little of this world that it could hold you no longer? Was it something that you were – or were not – was it something that you are or are to become?

"The Lord gave,

and the Lord has taken away;

blessed be the name of the Lord."

—Job 1:21

Life is a gift.

Will I Be Missed?

It's softball season again. I don't enjoy it the way I used to. I don't get excited when the guys talk about getting up a team. I don't run so fast or hit so far as I used to, and no matter how hard I try, the thrill of winning doesn't exhilarate me and the blow of defeat doesn't depress me so – not like it used to. I've become philosophical, which I guess is what happens when you can't "cut the mustard" anymore. Did you know that "cut the mustard" came from the restaurant business? It has to do with people ordering a hamburger or a sandwich and not wanting any mustard. The waitress would tell the cook to prepare the sandwich, but to "cut the mustard." It came to refer to someone who doesn't have what it takes to handle the challenge – they can't "cut the mustard." Put that in your trivia department.

I really didn't set out to write about softball – or *cutting the mustard,* for that matter. What I wanted to write about was J. D. Fairly. It was softball season that made me think of him. I was missing him today. I miss him when I'm preaching sometimes, because I look where he should be sitting and he's not there. It's funny about things like that. He never even went to church where I preach now, but sometimes when I look at the audience from a certain angle, I still know right where he ought to be and –

I miss him.

I miss him when I think about softball. He used to come to every game. He never clapped or cheered – he never even said much – I'd just look up and there he'd be, sort of like at church. He'd smile and wave, and it made me feel good – and important too. We weren't a very good team, so it wasn't the game he came for. I think maybe he came to the games for some of the same reasons he came to church –

he liked it,
and he enjoyed the folks.

Anyway, I miss seeing him, although I suspect he still never misses a game – or a church service. Sometimes when I'm preaching, I want to say, right out loud – *Did you hear that J. D.?* J. D. was dependable. I pray that I may be more like him in that regard. I wonder if he ever played softball? You know,

I never asked him. But the next time I see him, I sure plan to do just that. Like I said –

I miss him.

It's a nice thing to be missed. I hope they'll miss me. I hope when basketball season starts or when they sing "Almost Home" or "When the Roll is Called Up Yonder," they'll say –

"Boy, I sure do miss John."

I think that being missed is as great a tribute to a person's life as there is. I believe with all my heart that when the apostles met each other on occasions during their travels – after dinner was over and their companions had gone to bed, when they were at last alone – they would look earnestly at each other and say –

"Do you remember that time –
I sure do miss Him."

Will you be missed?

Life

♦

223

Why Do You Jump?

One of the things that made a visit to my Uncle Clarence's farm in Maynard, Arkansas, so much fun was a dog he had. His name was "Shep" – like a zillion other dogs during that time. He looked more like a collie than anything else, but beyond that, his looks were rather nondescript, as were his duties around the farm. He was friendly – and I think I would like to say that he struck me as being *happy.* He was a great jumper. Uncle Clarence had a fence around his house that I suppose was meant to define his yard and keep the farm animals out. I never ceased to be amazed at Shep's ability to jump it.

I would stand on one side of the fence and call him, and he would come sailing over, clearing it by a foot and a half. As he came bounding over, I would run back through the gate, close it, and then call him to the other side. After about ten minutes of this game, he would be standing on the opposite side, tongue lolling, sides heaving, and I would call. He would hesitate a moment, and I would think, "He's not going to do it," but suddenly he would crouch, gather himself, and come flying over. He never seemed to tire – in fact, most of the time –

I quit before he did.

I thought that I was very clever and that Shep was dumb – after all, he was doing all the work. *I also thought he was jumping for me.* I was quite surprised one day when I looked out the kitchen window and saw him jump the fence with no one around. I learned that Shep didn't jump for me, *he jumped because he liked it* – for the sheer, unadulterated pleasure of jumping.

Why do you jump?

We all do, you know. Why do you go to work, get an education, eat too much, attend church services, give money to the girl scouts, stay faithful to your mate, tell lies, vote in elections, pay taxes? Why do you wrestle with fears and failures and jump through the hoops of societal expectations? There is an amazing statement in Hebrews 12. Paul writes that Jesus endured the cross and despised the shame –

"For the *joy* that was set before Him."

People who live their lives or practice their religion only out of a sense of duty or obligation – who never do anything hard simply for the pure pleasure there is in sweat and effort –

will never jump one extra time
or run another mile,
just for the fun of it.

And when a little extra is needed – when the situation requires something beyond the normal – when neither need, duty, nor self-discipline will carry us, we fail because we have not discovered the secret of doing the unpleasant –

for the fun of it.

I have never enjoyed running. It is an act of discipline that arises out of a sense of duty to my health.

I do, however, enjoy playing basketball.

When I run, I set a goal. I decide beforehand that I am going to run three miles. The last mile is always agony. If someone asked me to go another mile *just for the fun of it,* I would tell them in no uncertain terms that they are mentally deficient. When I play basketball and my breath comes in ragged gasps, my knees are rubbery, my shirt is soaked with sweat and someone says, "Let's play one more just for the fun of it," I stagger back out there, grinning from ear to ear.

It is unrealistic to believe that I can perform out of joy every time in either religion or sports, but I want to affirm that joy must be an integral part of our overall motivation. If it is not, we will ultimately stop participating, and we will never be able to take those extra steps – *just for the fun of it* – which often make the difference between success and failure.

Why do you jump?

⚜

Peace and Safety

"While people are saying,
'peace and safety,'
destruction will come on them suddenly,
as labor pains on a pregnant woman,
and they will not escape."
—1 Thessalonians 5:3

I believe it was Leo Tolstoy who told the story of a man, living in a remote section of Russia, who is being pursued by a pack of wolves. In his flight he comes across an old abandoned well. He cannot see the bottom, but there are vines growing on the sides, and in his desperation, he seizes them and climbs down inside. As his eyes become more accustomed to the half-light of the well's interior, he sees that the bottom is dry, but there are several poisonous snakes there. He is hopelessly trapped between the waiting wolves above and the poisonous snakes below.

He realizes that he must find a way to relieve the stress upon his arms, or he will soon fall to the bottom. Because the well shaft is quite narrow, he is able to brace his back against one side and his feet against the other, temporarily freeing his hands and arms. This relief allows him to examine the walls of the well more carefully.

He discovers, by moving up and down and by pulling the vines apart, that the walls have decayed badly and that large chunks of the smooth, ceramic like surface can be pulled loose. By doing that and then using one of the hardened pieces as a digging tool, he soon gouges out a sizeable hole, a hole large enough to allow him to sit quite comfortably – at least in comparison to his former plight. Occasionally, he still hears the muffled growls of the waiting wolves, and now and then one of them peers cautiously over the lip of the well. Below him, the snakes, quite agitated by the dirt and debris showered upon them by his digging, have begun crawling about, even venturing up the sides on the vines.

His temporary safety allows him to consider his plight. He observes that there is something shiny on the dark leaves of the vines, and upon investigation, it proves to be honey. With some excitement, he begins to pull the leaves and lick the honey. It is delicious – he is famished. As he pulls away more and more leaves, he uncovers the now abandoned hole that the bees once used for their hive. He plunges his entire arm into the hole and finds a veritable trove of golden brown honeycomb, dripping with the precious fluid.

And so we leave our hero sitting in relative comfort, licking his sticky fingers, now almost totally oblivious to the peril of the wolves above and the snakes below.

Now, I am sure you are saying to yourself that this is the most ridiculous story you have ever heard and that no one would ever be so stupid, but I beg to differ. There are millions of people who live daily in such circumstances – blissfully, willfully, and purposefully unaware of the imminent disaster that awaits them, a disaster that is obvious to any discerning observer but to which they are totally oblivious.

You may be one of them.

Let me tell you of another man, a man whose daughter dresses like a punk-rocker, who has had an abortion, but is now on the pill. She has been picked up by the police and charged with DWI, and occasionally she exhibits the telltale signs of drug and alcohol abuse.

His wife shops at the mall, plays bridge two nights a week, goes on sightseeing excursions, and does volunteer work for the American Cancer Society, the Red Cross, and the Women's League of Voters. They appear together periodically at social functions, hold hands, and are extremely polite. He is entangled in a rather sordid affair (and suspects that his wife is too) from which he wishes to extricate himself, but he lacks the decisiveness to do so because of potential embarrassment and complications.

He is well employed by a paper mill. Their production processes are somewhat outdated and consequently they dump large amounts of chemical waste and other by-products into the nearby river. Their boilers spew even worse pollutants into the air. The government, through the EPA, is threatening to close the plant down, but through legal maneuvering, cover-up, deliberate misrepresentation, and the very real threat of destroying the financial base of the entire area surrounding the plant, they have postponed the inevitable crisis that must ultimately put them out of business. He has high blood pressure and consults the corporate psychiatrist twice a month.

In the midst of all this, he has a plan. For years he has kept a secret bank account. He has invested well, and every month he comes closer to the financial independence that will allow him to walk away to the mountain retreat that he purchased years ago, where he will be safe from present problems.

And every evening on his way *home* – if such a sacred word can be utilized to describe a dwelling place that is anything but that – he stops for *happy hour* at a gentleman's club where he drinks and socializes until ten o'clock. When he gets home, he changes into something comfortable, takes a sleeping pill, unplugs the telephone, locks and secures the doors, and turns on the television. For the next hour or so he smiles, he frowns, he experiences the lust of sensual pleasures, he sees the cops win and the mafia lose. He dozes off during the news, awakens, flicks off the set, and slips into an uninterrupted sleep, thinking, "The world's not such a bad place, and when you get right down to it, I'm no worse than average and better than many."

Yes, there he lies in peaceful slumber. Even his dreams are dominated by visions of safety and security. He licks the sticky sweetness from his fingers while the wolves prowl restlessly outside his windows, and there is a whisper of movement from the snakes under the floors. Oblivious to the vast eternity that stretches endlessly before and behind him, oblivious to his wife, his children, his sins, his community, his earth, his soul – his accountability – he has retreated into the world he had in his mother's womb – the world of himself – and there he is secure. But outside, the wolves and the snakes wait, because they too are secure in their knowledge that their prey is now assured.

Now, you may think that no such person exists, but I assure you that not only does he exist –

you probably know him.

Life

♦

227

Staying Busy

Some time ago, I took a trip to Pepperdine University in Malibu, California, for a lectureship. My flight was in three parts: Montgomery to Atlanta, forty-five minutes; Atlanta to Dallas, ninety minutes; Dallas to Los Angeles, one hundred ninety-five minutes. Flying is very boring for me. Going to Atlanta, I read the *USA Today* that I bought in Montgomery. When I got to Atlanta, I started to buy an *Atlanta Constitution,* but the real news is always about the same, so I bought a book by Bill Cosby titled, *Fatherhood.* He knows much more about fatherhood than any psychologist. I read his book between Atlanta and Dallas – it barely lasted. I slowed down my reading, fearing I would run out before we landed. What was I going to do between Dallas and Los Angeles? I decided to write some letters.

Just as I was about to begin, they served a snack. Snacks take time, and that is a far greater blessing than the snack, which is normally airtight, sanitary, packaged in New Jersey, and wrapped in plastic – you generally can't tell the difference between the food and the wrapper. Anyway, I was going to write to my niece who lives in Chattanooga and who is one of my favorite people on the whole earth – because she's a *real person* – when the snack arrived. It was some pieces of honeydew melon *(honeydew,* by the way, is a superlative name and should be recorded in the "name" hall of fame), a bagel, a container of Philadelphia Cream Cheese, and some Smucker's strawberry jam – which at first appeared to be a most unlikely combination, but actually proved to be quite tasty –

it was delicious,
in fact.

I tried to take my time with this snack, *spreading it out,* so to speak – which is a pun, in case you're slow on the uptake. I know you're wondering where this story is going – I'm wondering myself, but since I know the ending, let me assure you that it turns out fairly well and should be worth your time – remember, most of the joy of marriage is in the anticipation, and so I heartily recommend long engagements – but that is another topic.

I carefully cut my bagel in half – following the dotted line – so I could take twice as long eating it. I spread the Philadelphia Cream Cheese on first. The cheese was quite cold and difficult to spread at first, and I was trying hard to make certain that I didn't use more than half of the cheese on half of the bagel, because I didn't want to leave half a bagel with an inadequate amount of cheese. Anyway, I was spreading the cheese, and it sort of got to be a challenge – working it around – smoothing it – covering every square millimeter of bagel. As the cheese warmed, it became quite pliable. The plastic serrated knife they had given me made really neat little swirly designs as I smoothed it – and then I began to spread strawberry jam on the white cheese on the brown bagel. My fellow passengers were beginning to notice – poking each other and pointing – they were envious, too, because they had finished theirs and I still had mine. With a few light strokes of the knife, I finished my creation and received a round of applause. It was a shame to eat it –

but I did.

When I finished my snack, I returned to my writing. But it occurred to me that I am always saying that I never have any time, and then when I did have it, I couldn't wait for it to pass – I guess because I had no earthly idea how to relax. This warns me that I am not at peace with myself, but must constantly be about some business to absorb my attention lest I begin to think – and my thoughts lead me where I do not wish to go. I wonder, do I stay busy because

I fear
the alternative?

Salt and Light

Life

♦

230

"Blessed are you when men revile you,
and persecute you, and say all kinds of evil
against you falsely, on account of me.
Rejoice, and be glad,
for your reward in heaven is great,
for so they persecuted the prophets
who were before you.
You are the salt of the earth. . . .
You are the light of the world. . . .
Let your light shine before men in such a way
that they may *see your good works,*
and glorify your Father
who is in heaven."
—Matthew 5:11–16

Jesus tells His disciples that they are salt and light. I think that although all Christians believe that, they find it difficult to translate that concept into their lives in any practical way. What does it mean to be salt and light? Is that what my life is?

I thought at one time that I was "salt" because I was doctrinally correct. My *saltiness* was predicated upon my belief that I had a right understanding of the word of God, and that idea certainly has value. It is important to understand God's will correctly – a person's salvation can depend on it. Yet, I have come to realize that the world will not be saved by doctrine alone. *Doctrinal correctness is not enough to be salt, and it is not enough to define my life.*

I have thought that I was "light" because I am a meditative and introspective person. There is great merit in contemplative thought. I believe that modern Christians do altogether too little of it. Being alone with my ideas is very constructive, but my real spiritual battles are seldom fought in isolation. Although meditation and prayer bring much light into *my* world, they do not diminish the darkness of the people around me. The meaning of life is not to be found in isolation.

Am I salt and light because of my good works? At first, I was tempted to say yes, that good works must be the answer. But then it occurred to me that the Jews were zealous for good works – as are many philanthropic organizations like the Red Cross, the Lion's Club, and the Royal Order of Moose. Although doing good works is an essential part of a faith response to the gospel, good works do not in themselves guarantee that I will be salt and light for God's kingdom.

It seems that what is necessary, then, is a balanced combination of a correct *understanding of the word of God, prayerful meditation,* and *good works.* That means that my quest to be salt and light will require some plan of action. Yet, when I say *plan of action,* I am aware that most of the critical things that happen in my life are impossible to plan for. What I mean is that life is never simple. It seems that I can never really relax – that no matter what I do, even the most innocent and nonthreatening situations bring some crisis to me.

When I was teaching at Lubbock Christian University some years ago, I left my 7:30 A.M. English class at 9:00 to go to the hospital to pray with a ninety-year-old lady who was about to have eye surgery. I anticipated that this would be an extremely traumatic event. She was very apprehensive and distraught, and you can understand why. As it turned out, her whole family was there. We gathered around her bedside, we held hands, we prayed with her, and what might have been a very disconcerting situation was actually a very heartwarming and encouraging one.

When I left the hospital, I went to the farmer's market. In Lubbock, they have this big open building, where local farmers sell fruits and vegetables from their gardens off the tailgates of their pickups. I went there because they have

real tomatoes.

I mean tomatoes with juice in them and cracks around the bottom. They have dirt on them where they have actually lain on the ground. They are not raised in total sterility and isolation in a "hothouse" in New Jersey, then picked green, stored in a gas-filled warehouse where they turn bright red on the outside and to tasteless mush on the inside. These tomatoes have taste, like the ones you picked right out of your own garden when you were a kid. You may remember – they grow on big, green, leafy bushes. Well, anyway, a trip to the farmer's market is not usually a spiritually threatening excursion.

At the farmer's market, there is this little Mexican-American guy that I like to buy my stuff from. He's very friendly, and he has a neat network of wrinkles around his eyes from squinting in the sun and laughing a lot. His vegetables are always good. His English isn't too hot, and his math is very bad – he always gives me too much change. But we always laugh about it, and it's part of what makes me like him. I mean, this guy grows all this stuff on his own land, and he's sort of close to the earth. He wears old, faded coveralls and denim shirts and a baseball cap. When I'm around him, I watch his fingers hold the tomatoes and the melons. It's kind of like they are his children or something, they give him status and worth and a measure of pride, and I think humility too. Anyway —

I really like this guy.

Today there is a guy in front of me, and that's okay, except that this guy is a loudmouthed white guy, and I don't like the way he talks to my farmer friend. He talks in a very condescending, very big-shot way. He says things like, "I don't know why I come here — Mexicans don't know how to raise vegetables," and he says that the tomatoes are too small and that they are not ripe and that the melons are overripe and that they have dirt on them. This guy is really provoking me, and it's all I can do to keep my mouth shut. I also begin to notice that Loudmouth is deliberately trying to confuse my friend. He says things like, "How much are these?" and "How many more could I get for another fifty cents?" And he says, "If I buy four melons, two baskets of tomatoes, three cabbages, and a sack of beans, how much is that?" And I am watching, and I'm listening to everything.

When Bigmouth makes his purchase, he gives my friend a ten dollar bill, but the little farmer is extremely confused by this time. He puts the ten in his little box that he keeps there on the tailgate of his pickup. He takes out far too much change, and he hands it to this guy who not only pockets the change but tells my friend that he gave him a twenty, and he points to a twenty, which is also in the money box. My friend apologizes all over himself, and he hands Bigmouth back the ten that he had just given him —

and it's *decision time.*

Now you can say, "Oh, that's easy," but I beg your pardon — it is not easy. Sitting in the church building on Sunday morning or reading this in your recliner at home — yes, it's very easy — but standing there in the farmer's market with a hundred people around and I don't have ten minutes to analyze and to think or to call the police —

it is not easy.

I want you to see that — right here — at this very tick of the clock — an important decision is going to be made about who I am and what my life is and what it means to be *salt and light.* You see, I can either take a great risk, or I can say it's none of my business and nobody will ever know.

My heart is pounding as I step forward and say, "Just a minute. You didn't give him a twenty; you gave him a ten — I saw you."

Bigmouth turns around with this very malignant and evil look on his face — and Bigmouth is *a very big man* — and he obviously does not like me.

"Are you trying to start trouble?" he says to me.

And I say, "No! No I don't want any trouble," – and I don't – "but I don't want my friend cheated either."

Bigmouth's voice is very loud; he has attracted a lot of attention, and I'm very uncomfortable – and now I wish I had kept my mouth shut.

He says to me, very loudly, "Are you saying that I cheated this bean eater?"

And I say, "I'm saying that you didn't give him a twenty – you gave him a ten. I'm saying that he had already given you far more change than you deserved and it hurts me to see people taken advantage of, and I'm saying that you should be ashamed of yourself."

There really isn't much to the rest of the story. As it turned out, I was supported by the people who were standing around me. Ultimately, Bigmouth took his ten, and he left without his purchases.

I was greatly relieved.

Life

♦

233

Life is never simple. And it's good for us that it's not, because if life were simple and predictable, we would never know *who we were* or what our life is.

The Christian life is the process by which we come to know God. But it is also the process by which we come to know ourselves. We make decisions every day about who we are and about what it means to be us. *It is in those decisions that our potential to be salt and light is realized, and it is in those decisions that we define what our life is.* When Jesus says, "Let your light so shine before men," he means that I have some definite responsibility as to how and when my light shines. Jesus talks about the salt becoming tasteless, and He means that it becomes my responsibility to see that my life never loses its flavor.

It's when our guard is down, when we least suspect it, that whether we are going to be salt and light really becomes practical. It is, in fact, when we're angry, tired, sick, excited, offended – *when we can most easily excuse ourselves* – that we ought to be the most ashamed of our failures.

Standing there in the farmer's market, I could have excused myself easily; I could have said, "Well, I just don't have time to think. It's happening so fast, I don't know what is the best thing to do." It's when the pressure is on that I really begin to find out who I am. And it's not until those kinds of things happen that I understand what James means when he says –

"What is your life?"

We Almost Made It

When I think of her now, the first thing I remember is how attractive she was – what a matchless harmony of flesh and bone structure. Large eyes, sensitive, provocative mouth and lips, white, even teeth, and a great, heart-warming smile. She knew how to dress, too, and the way she did her golden red hair . . . it was breathtaking! She was soft-spoken, almost plaintive, and she wanted – she wanted to be wanted – to be loved. She wanted – she wanted what she imagined to be happiness. She wanted to live. She wanted to know what her life was. She had attempted suicide three times because the happiness she sought eluded her grasp every time she seemed to have it cornered.

We talked much – this pretty one, this young one and I – I the unpretty and unyoung. We shared much – or at least we tried. We came from two different worlds. Me – born and bred to religion, to faith, to harmony in family, to security, to love, to joy and friends, reveling in God's providential goodness. She – born out of wedlock, to infidelity, to alcohol, to drugs, to insecurity, to hatred, to selfishness, to being used and abused. And then we were together, and we spoke across the gulf of experience between us – reaching out hands – wanting to touch – to understand. She – wanting help, understanding, salvation. Me – wanting to help, to bridge, to heal, to share Jesus and what I knew He could do for this shattered life – so near to being new life –

or no life.

Dear child, did I fail you? I watched your silent tears and I matched them with my own. I shared your grief for your sins – I grieve for my own – and when you embraced me, sobbing as you left, your tears left dark smudges of eye makeup stains on my shirt. I hate to wash it because they remind me that –

we almost made it.

You were so close – eternal truth was within reach – I could see the recognition in your eyes, and I thought, "Surely now, she will say 'yes' to You, Lord Jesus." And then the light dimmed and the doubt came, and you shuddered as though some terrible, haunting nightmare afflicted you, and you said, "It cannot be." I felt you slipping away and frantically fought to bring you back.

I was crushed when you left, as you have left before, with your quest unanswered – crushed and defeated. I wondered how many more times the Spirit would bring you to the very threshold of life – only to see you – in the very act of reaching out – back away. *But you did come,* and there is the hope. Out of your need – you came – and perhaps we got closer this time. Perhaps – this time – thoughts of the love of Jesus and His forgiving grace may rest a little nearer to your heart as you go back to that other life. Perhaps – when you come the next time, when your need for life with meaning and purpose drives you to seek Him once again – perhaps you'll make it. This time we must settle for –

almost.

> "'Almost persuaded' now to believe;
> 'Almost persuaded' Christ to receive;
> Seems now some soul to say,
> 'Go, Spirit, go Thy Way'
> Some more convenient day,
> On Thee I'll call."

May God grant you another day,
another call,
another quest to find
your life
before it is eternally –
too late.

It Remains by Itself, Alone

"Unless a grain of wheat
falls into the earth and dies,
it remains alone."
—John 12:24

If you leave Tiger Stadium, on Michigan Avenue in downtown Detroit, Michigan, then take the John C. Lodge Expressway north, then exit west onto the Edsel Ford Expressway, which is actually I-94, you will soon leave behind the smog, filth, drugs, and depressing corruption of the murder capital of the Northeast. Interstate-94 eventually takes you through Ann Arbor – home of University of Michigan (my alma mater) and the fighting "Wolverines." The next thirty miles is the beautiful, gently rolling, heavily wooded farm country of Western Michigan.

If you pay very close attention, you will see a sign advertising the town of Chelsea (population 7,045) and Clear Lake (which is their main attraction) seven miles north. If you take the Chelsea exit, but turn south, you will soon come to the experimental agricultural farm belonging to the University of Michigan. It is renowned for innovative approaches to crop production and experimentation with hybrid seeds and pest control. Its fame is much enhanced by the fact that it also contains the source of the Clinton River, which is an extensive marsh, in the center of which is a fairly large, circular body of open water formed by two joining creeks and several natural springs. Although I had no agricultural or historical interest in this farm, I was fascinated by the incredible number of pheasants that have found a home there.

My good friend Ray and I wrangled a hard-won permission to hunt there one year. Ray went to church where I preached, but his real claim to fame was first, his wife Irene, whose name is emblazoned in gold letters in the *top five* of my list of candidates for all-time great cooks and second, for his English setter named Jack. He also owned two beagles, whose names I have forgotten.

The first few days we hunted there were glorious. The birds were so plentiful and so innocent of the vicious ways of man that I was *almost* ashamed to kill them.

There is a remarkably strong instinct for self-preservation among wild things that can be very frustrating. The pheasants learned, with amazing quickness, that by running to the edge of the marsh and flying across, they could escape us. But being what hunters are, we determined to cut off that retreat and, accordingly, just at grey dawn on an extremely cold November morning, I found myself shivering, in spite of my layers of clothing, at the edge of the marsh, waiting for Ray and the dogs to drive the birds in my direction.

It didn't take too long. I could see Ray, his breath plainly visible in the cold air, and I could hear the warning cry of the beagles. I could actually see the tall grass moving as the birds rushed to the water side. When I flushed them, they flew back in Ray's direction and we killed several. One beautiful rooster rose cackling into the first brilliant rays of the sunrise. He was determined to get across the marsh to safety. I let him swing out, away to my right, and then realized, almost too late, that he was over the water. I hurried my first shot and missed, took a little more time and killed him with the second shot. He collapsed in midair and fell with a great splash, about forty yards out.

When Ray arrived, we began to hunt for the birds we had knocked down. With the dogs' help, we soon found them.

"I guess that's it," Ray said.

"No," I said, "actually, there's one more."

"Where?" he said.

"Oh, over there," I said, with a general motion of my hand.

"Over where?" he said calling the dogs.

"Well, actually, you can see it, it's that dark thing floating out there in the bay, just past that patch of duck weed."

"Did you shoot that bird over the water?"

"No, I shot him over the land. The stupid bird flew out there and died over the water just for spite."

"Well," he said, "you can forget that one."

It is not in me to forget anything I have killed or wounded – it seems un-Christian. I believe God has placed the animals here for us, but he has made us responsible for them. His bounty should never be wasted – or taken lightly. If God is concerned about sparrows, then we should also be concerned.

There was no wind blowing, so we had no hope of the bird drifting in. Jack was an excellent retriever, and we threw sticks and rocks in the floating bird's direction and yelled, "fetch" and "dead bird," till we were hoarse, but Jack acted as if he had never heard those words. I figured his problem was that he didn't want to get wet. I told Ray that if he was already wet, he wouldn't mind too much, so we threw him in – at least we tried. We called him, and when he came to us, we grabbed him and heaved him head first,

Life

♦

237

way out over the water. *I had never seen a dog walk on water before.* That dog changed directions in midair and was out so quickly that I don't think he got anything wet but the bottoms of his feet – after that, he wouldn't come close when we called him, and he didn't trust us again for several days.

There was only one thing to do, and when problems are reduced to a single, simple solution, you either do it or walk away. *I began to undress.* Ray told me plainly that I was crazy – I'm sure he was right – it was one of the nicest things he'd ever said to me. I continued to undress. "That water can't be more than forty degrees and this air is probably twenty-five to thirty," he said. "You don't have a chance." Boots, socks, hunting coat and pants, wool shirt, T-shirt, thermal underwear – all in a pile.

I stood naked on the bank for just a moment, shocked by the cold, before I plunged in. Every rational faculty said, "This is really stupid; you could die." But there were other voices too – voices that said, "If you don't do this, you will always regret it and some immeasurable and indefinable internal quality of your personality will be lost and you will never be the same – you must try."

Adjectives are useless. It was mortally, frighteningly, numbingly cold. The first sensation seemed odd, but it was like millions of tiny, red-hot needles. I immediately knew that I had miscalculated how bad it would be, but I had already made ten yards of progress, so I continued. When I reached the bird, I discovered a terrible flaw in my plan. You probably have already seen it – swimming requires two hands. Holding a dead pheasant in one hand leaves only one for swimming – which severely impedes progress. Although I am a very determined swimmer, I am a very poor one. I believe it has to do with the density of my flesh – whenever I am placed in water, I descend slightly faster than a fifty-pound lead weight. There was no time for social amenities or niceties. Having come this far, I wasn't about to go back without that bird. I put its head and neck in my mouth, clamped down fiercely with my teeth, and began thrashing my way back.

Obviously, I made it. The numbing exhaustion is beyond telling. When I reached the shore, I had no feeling in my limbs and could not stand up. Ray dragged me out on the bank. The wires were down between my brain and my hands and feet. It is the most peculiar feeling in the world to look at your hands and tell them to do your bidding – and have them refuse – it was like they weren't part of me. Ray took my T-shirt and toweled me off. He slapped and massaged me and made me keep moving and stomp my feet, and he helped me dress. The hot blood, which had retreated from the extremities of my body due to the onslaught of the icy water, began to make its way back to the surface and I itched everywhere.

Life

♦

The creeping warmth was delicious –

I was going to live!
Life had never been so precious.

I was more aware of myself and my surroundings than I had ever been. I stood there on the bank of the source of the Clinton River, and I looked at things as though I had never seen them before, and I *guess I hadn't.*

Sometimes you can be out of focus
and not know it.

I had never seen such a glorious sunrise. I could see every aspect of the landscape in sharp detail – the stark, leafless branches of every oak and maple stood out in bold relief. The golden, bent grasses and weeds, living out their last days before returning to the earth to decay and bring forth new life – the steam rising from the marsh – the dead pheasants – the dogs – my brother Ray – heat and cold – want and plenty – hope and despair – all of God's eternal gifts were mine at that moment, mine in the sense of actualization. I thought –

"this is life,
and life is very,
very good."

*"Dear God,
I am so glad to be alive,
and I am so grateful
for this moment."*

Would I do it again? Every day if I could. Was it stupid? I suppose that depends on your perspective. Could I have died? Yes.

But is that so important?
There are things far worse
than dying.

Far too many people are so intent on *preserving* their miserable lives that they take no thought for *living* them.

When the disciples of Jesus encounter a storm on the Sea of Galilee that threatens their lives, they awaken Jesus with this question –

"Master, do you not care that we are perishing?"
*"No, not particularly.
The perishing that you speak of
is not serious.
It is easily prevented,*

Life

♦

and is mainly an illusion.
I care much more
that you are indeed perishing
in a far more serious and real way,
and you seem to neither
know nor care."

"Unless a grain of wheat
falls into the earth and dies,
it remains alone."
—John 12:24

What is your life?
Your life is a grain of wheat.

ELEVEN

Death

"But though I have wept and fasted, wept and prayed,
Though I have seen my head (grown slightly bald)
brought in upon a platter,
I am no prophet – and here's no great matter;
I have seen the moment of my greatness flicker,
And I have seen the eternal Footman hold my coat,
and snicker,
And in short, I was afraid."
—Thomas Stearns Eliot
The Love Song of J. Alfred Prufrock

In those dim and somber halls that mark death's presence, our hearts are slowed to a barely perceptible beat by the droning of a distant organ. Its torpid, somber chants hush our laughter, and we begin to speak in furtive whispers – as though we feared being overheard by the Dark Lord who dwells in such places, as though we might offend so as to bring down some unknown disaster upon ourselves. The very air of the chamber creates and sustains an oppressive and darkly mystic mood. The vapid heaviness of the atmosphere, tainted with the demoralizing odors of antiseptic and preservatives, contains barely enough oxygen to sustain respiration. In the place of oxygen are the captured and recirculated dying vapors that lingered in the chests of those lifeless bodies that found their tragic and weary way to this place. Those vapors are named –

Death Breath.

And every person who has entered the halls of the dead has felt its oppressive power. Our ties are suddenly too tight, and though we are not exactly warm, small thin beads of cold perspiration drip from our armpits. There is a nauseating emptiness in our stomachs that is not hunger.

We are greeted at every turn by little cloned, fawning, plastic men in dark suits. They offer cool, smoothly polished, ivory white, patronizing hands to us. They speak their trite, memorized words of consolation so quietly and indistinctly that we are only barely aware that they have spoken. They say

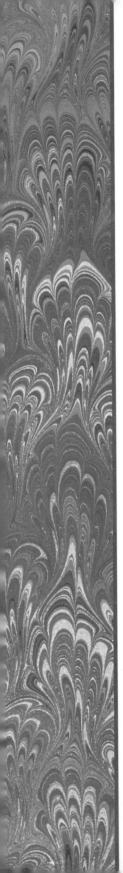

"yes" to every inquiry and go about their business in their own prescribed and efficient way.

We have developed a whole death theology that attempts to shield us from its reality. From the moment, and even before, the lifeless body is whisked away to be prepared for "viewing," an aura of unreality surrounds our death mythology. This theology is characterized by discriminate terminology. Words like death, grave, body, and bury have been replaced with more acceptable ones like "final resting place," "deceased," "entombment," "interment," and "remains."

When my grandmother and uncle died, the women of the family washed and dressed the bodies. Their simple, wooden caskets were kept in the living room of the house. We ate, slept, laughed, and talked in the same room. We dealt with death head on; we saw it face to face.

Death is *natural*. It's like eating, sleeping, laughing, and crying. It's like the seasons – it is natural. *It is not our enemy* – no more than winter is the enemy of nature; it is simply necessary to the continuation of life. What makes winter bearable is the fact that we believe in spring. We know that winter does not last forever because we have experienced the wonder of its passing. And that is exactly what Jesus has done for us – He has experienced the winter of death in our place so that we might rejoice in the everlasting hope of our eternal spring of resurrection.

We need to change our thinking. We were never meant to stay here, anymore than the seasons were meant to remain. Each season serves its purpose in God's majestic plan of life. And so death – our winter – serves its purpose. That is why Jesus says of the "death" of Lazarus, "Our friend Lazarus has fallen asleep, but I am going there to waken him." Is Jesus just trying to soften the blow of death by choosing less dire terminology? Absolutely not! Jesus was speaking the truth about death – *it is not serious, and it is not permanent*. Jesus had less trouble calling Lazarus out of the sleep of death than we have rousing our sleepy-headed children from their beds to get ready for school.

The Hebrew writer says that Jesus shared in death so that –

> "through death He might destroy the one
> who has the power of death,
> that is, the devil,
> and free those who all their lives
> were held in slavery
> by the fear of death."
> —Hebrews 2:14–15

In no way do we more annul the power, purpose, and meaning of the resurrection of Jesus than by our ungodly attitudes toward death. Why do we still treat death as though it were the great enemy? Why do we speak in hushed tones in its presence? Why do we live our lives in perpetual fear of its inevitability. Why does the word *terminal* mean *no hope?* Our attitudes belie our faith.

To the unbelieving, death is not an event – it is *a state of being* – a way of life. To the believing, death is the opening of the door – it is the spring of hope after the winter of despair – it is the final release from all that has separated us from becoming perfectly free from the bondage, the groaning of the flesh.

The following words were written long ago by a man who was in prison because of his faith in Jesus – I urge you to read them slowly and let their truth and beauty sink into your soul.

> After this it was noised abroad that Mr. Valiant-for-truth was taken with a summons by the same post as the other, and had this for a token that the summons was true, That his Pitcher was broken at the Fountain. When he understood it he called for his friends, and told them of it. Then said he, I am going to my Father's, and though with great difficulty I am got hither, yet now I do not repent me of all the trouble I have been at to arrive where I am. My Sword I give to him that shall succeed me in my pilgrimage, and my courage and skill to him that can get it. My marks and scars I carry with me, to be a witness for me that I have fought His battles who now will be my rewarder. When the day that he must go hence was come, many accompanied him to the riverside, into which as he went he said, Death, where is thy sting? And as he went down deeper, he said, Grave, where is thy victory? So he passed over, and all the trumpets sounded for him on the other side.
>
> —John Bunyan, *Pilgrim's Progress*

Death is Satan's final attempt to defeat God's plan for us. Jesus has broken the power of death by the power of his resurrection; it has no dominion – it holds no fear for those who are his.

William Hall

Dear God – Oh Why? Oh Why?

"On a strange and distant hill
A young man's lying very still.
His arms will never hold his child
Because a bullet, running wild,
Has struck him down.
And when we cry
'Dear God, Oh Why? Oh Why?'
Who will answer?"
—Author Unknown

When I was twenty, I had a special friend – his name was Bill Hall. When I think of Bill, one of the first things I remember is him calling me one rainy spring night about 11:30.

"Did you know that the Clinton River is flooding?" he asked.

"No," I said, " and did you wake me up just to tell me that?"

"No, I called you to give you the chance of a lifetime. Let's take a canoe down the river to Yates Cider Mill."

"Sure," I said. "When do you want to try it?"

"Right Now!"

"Tonight? It's pitch dark and the river's flooding!"

"I know," he said. *"Anybody* can do it when it's daylight and not flooding – *nobody's ever done it at night."*

"Well, there's a reason for that," I responded. "The only people who ever tried it never lived to tell about it, and besides, who would be stupid enough to let us use their canoe?"

"We'll borrow the Bordines."

"The Bordines wouldn't let us use their canoe, and besides, they're in bed."

"So, we'll do them a favor and not wake them up – then they won't have to worry because we'll have it back long before they know it's gone."

I told him he was crazy – he thanked me for the compliment. He said that all *geniuses* were called that and he'd be over in thirty minutes. As I was getting dressed, I wondered why I was doing this – why didn't I just say "no"? I still wonder. But as I dressed, Bill's excitement began to captivate me.

It was terrifying. You can't imagine how dark it was or how strong and merciless the current. We took a flashlight, but we lost it the first time the canoe tipped over. We hit submerged logs and other debris and tipped over. When we got too close to the shore, which we couldn't see, we were swept out of the canoe by low-hanging limbs, which we also couldn't see. In two narrow places the river was piled high with dead trees and brush, so we had to climb over the jam and carry the canoe. We spent more time in the water than in the canoe. When we tipped over, we would cling desperately to the canoe and our paddles, trying to maneuver toward the bank so we could get back in and try again.

The water was freezing cold, and the current of the swollen river was so powerful that it bounced and threw us like floating insects. I was soaking wet, shivering with cold, scared out of my wits – and Bill kept yelling, "Isn't this great? – Don't you just love this? –

We're the only ones out here."

When we reached Yates Cider Mill, I was the *happiest camper in town.*

Bill was special. He was full of life and vitality – his energy and enthusiasm swept away all opposition and doubts. He was also a very spiritual and committed young man. He kept a scrapbook filled with all kinds of novelties, newspaper clippings, photos, and mementos. One night I was leafing through it and came across a photo of an old African man. He had advanced leprosy. He had no nose, no fingers, and his facial features were grotesque. I said, "Here's a relative you never introduced me to." Bill took the scrapbook from me, and his face was very sober.

"Do you know why that's there?"

"No."

"That's my inspiration. Whenever I get to thinking too much about girls or cars or success, I look at this picture and I remember that I have pledged myself to do something meaningful with my life."

Bill was my true friend – he was constant, loyal, honest, unselfish – he was a brother to me, the brother I never had – and I loved him. He was compassionate and good but a fierce defender of the people and things he believed in. For two years we were inseparable.

When he graduated from the University of Michigan, he joined the Air Force. His older brother Jim was a jet pilot, and Bill was determined to follow in his footsteps. It was the time of Vietnam – and Bill was sent there to fly helicopters. One night, on a rescue mission to evacuate some wounded soldiers who were pinned down by enemy gunfire – Bill's helicopter was shot down, and his charred, bullet-ridden body was found in the wreckage.

I have watched many people die – people close to me and not close – young ones, old ones, and middle-aged. They died of cancer, heart attacks, leukemia, alcoholism, emphysema, brain tumors, liver disorders, car acci-

Death

♦

dents, and even suicide. I felt that I *understood* those deaths – they were *natural,* and I felt no bitterness or frustration – only pain and sadness.

Bill's death troubled and frustrated me, because I couldn't fit it into the framework of what to me are the boundaries of *natural.* It was to me a senseless, pointless death. I couldn't understand or justify it. How did he get to Vietnam anyway – this boy from Rochester, Michigan? Why should he die in such a bizarre way? The bullets that took his life were not meant for him personally. They were simply fired at random in the general direction of his helicopter.

I also must admit that I believed that, somehow, *Bill's goodness would save him* – that because he was a Christian, because he came from a Christian home, because he prayed and had people praying for him constantly – *and because he was my friend* –

he would be spared –
that God would protect him.

I remember that when news of Bill's death reached me, my first words were, "Oh God – no, not Bill." My confusion and bitterness were heightened because of my faith – or lack of it. When a believer is angry with the vicissitudes of life – *where else can he direct that anger?* I can only speak my feelings to the One who created and sustains the universe – to Him who bids the sun to rise and set, because –

who else *is* there?
No – I mean it –
who else is there to be angry with?

I would like to be angry with Satan, to place all the blame on him – that would be much easier because I could give full vent to it – I could shout and curse and raise my clenched fist and hate him. But Satan is an empty shell, a hired hand – he has no answers – not for me, anyway. Being angry with Satan is like being angry with the postal clerk who tells you that your important letter has not come. Your immediate passion is satisfied, but you still don't have your letter or the reason why. And the reason why is important.

I seek an answer when things don't make sense, and I know that there is only One who knows that answer. And so I say –

"Dear God, Oh Why? Oh Why?"

And what does He answer? What does God say to me? I hear His great voice, though it is quiet and sad. It comes – not as spoken words come in bits and pieces of sound that are pronounced singly – but it comes whole, as a complete idea that emanates and emerges from everything around me – echoing, sometimes loudly, sometimes softly, but never absent.

"He died a *natural* death."

This idea is not newly or personally revealed. It is not as though God speaks it to me for the first time. He spoke it long ago – there at the beginning of time – and I just now hear it, although I am aware that He has been revealing it all along.

It's true, you know. Bill died a *natural death*. Just as Abel died a natural death. Abel died as the natural result of the sin created by Cain's jealousy. Did Adam and Eve view the death of Abel as *natural*? Did they not lift their tear-stained, angry faces to the heavens and cry,

"Dear God, Oh Why? Oh why?"

Death

♦

250

Or did they know that somehow
there was a direct link
between what had happened
in the garden between them and God
and what had happened in the field
between Cain and Abel?

When the messenger comes to tell King David that his beloved son Absolom is dead – killed in the rebellion that he had led to dethrone his own father – David's grief is almost unbearable. "O my son Absolom, my son, my son Absolom! Would I had died instead of you, O Absolom, my son, my son!" Does David not speak for all of us? And is he not saying in chorus with burdened humanity,

"Dear God, Oh Why? Oh Why?"

And yet, it is easy for us to see that this event was predictable, that it was the *natural outcome* of David's failures as a father and Absolom's own pride.

Man, with his awesome living and dying, is predisposed to ruin when sin eliminates the spiritual aspect of his being and so unbalances the delicate framework of his essential nature that the decision-making process is skewed. The terrible reality of our lives is that murder, theft, selfishness, jealousy, adultery, lies, cruelty, war, hatred, addiction, and greed are all *natural products* of man's nature when his *spiritual being* is negated by sin. It is for this very reason that being "born of the water and the Spirit" and the subsequent spiritual regeneration that takes place is so absolutely critical to a right understanding of the meaning of life and death.

Until we realize what it means to "lay aside every weight and the sin which so easily besets us" – until we learn what it means to fight against principalities, powers, and world forces of darkness – until then, we will continue to cry –

> *"Dear God, Oh Why? Oh Why?"*
> And He will say –
> *"I have already told you."*

I Believe

My roommate during my junior year of college was an agnostic, an eccentric, and a bit of a genius, although perhaps not in that order. He was a pretty good roommate, all in all – he kept his side of the room reasonably clean, he didn't let his dirty underwear and socks lie around more than three days, and he didn't ask to borrow money or my car – very often. One thing I remember was that he brushed his teeth with Arm & Hammer baking soda mixed with Roman Cleanser. He always wanted me to try it, and I admit that I was tempted.

> He not only had the whitest teeth in school,
> he never had a stomach ache.

The fact that his tongue was green and had little sores on it did worry me some. I thought that members of the opposite sex might be discouraged by that, and somehow I just didn't think it was worth risking their disapproval.

He was real smart in all his classes, and he thought a lot. On top of that, he was a fairly decent Hearts player (which is a card game – for those of you who never developed the vice), and that was extremely important when there were *room challenges*. The only problem with his Hearts playing was that he cheated. Actually, that wasn't the only problem – it wasn't even the greatest problem. The real problem was that he was very clumsy at it and couldn't carry it off gracefully. I guess, like most folks, he thought himself very clever and never suspected that we all knew he cheated.

We never confronted him – we just anticipated his moves, collaborated, and used our insight to make him lose. Because he thought himself so clever and because he concentrated so hard on his deception, it never occurred to him that we would cheat. We would offer to buy the sodas if he would go and get them – it was quite a trip to the machine – and while he was gone, we would deal the cards and set up his hand.

I don't think he ever caught on.

We had these real deep, philosophical discussions late at night. At least they were deeper than our discussions about girls. I had been preaching for four or five years and thought I knew a lot. He enjoyed the notoriety of his agnosticism, and we played word games with each other – but sometimes we were very serious. Religion was obviously the main issue. He usually took the offensive with these kinds of questions –

"How can there be a God of order when everything is all messed up?"

"If God is love, then why do such awful things happen?"

"If God is so wise, then why didn't He foresee what man would do?"

"If God is all powerful, then how could Satan mess up His plans?"

Some of his questions were the old normal ones, but he would often confront me with everyday stuff like – "If God is no respecter of persons and preaching the gospel is the most important thing in the world, how come this school doesn't allow blacks to come here, and why do they give full scholarships to football players and nothing to preacher students?"

Sometimes his questions
were very difficult to answer.

We had a mutual friend who lived on the second floor. He wasn't especially close to us, but we had played him and his roommate in Hearts several times. We were sitting in our room one Saturday afternoon when the boy across the hall rushed in and said, "Did you hear what happened to _____?" He had gone with some other boys to a local lake and, although he was a very good swimmer, had mysteriously drowned.

We were stunned.

We asked how it happened – as we always do – as though it were important. And then there wasn't much to say, and he shrugged his shoulders and left us alone. The silence was painful. There were big questions on the horizon, but we couldn't get the words right – and didn't know the answers –

so we didn't ask them.

Late that night – long after we had gone to bed – we were still awake – *and we both knew it*. It was so quiet. We had been thinking all evening, and we knew we wouldn't go to sleep without making an effort to talk. Finally, very slowly, he said, "Are you awake?" It was coming.

"Yes, I am."

A long pause.

"He *knows* now, doesn't he?"

An even longer pause.

"Yes – he knows now."

"Oh God," he said,

> "what I'd give to *know.*"

And when the *word games* are all played . . . when the stupid questions are all left unanswered . . . when the hard reality of shattering death comes fresh upon us . . . when all our childish cleverness, our juvenile pursuits after empty philosophy and humanistic justification for life are dashed in the vision of eternity . . . when all our ten thousand questions become one question – faith responds,

> "I do not *know,*
> and cannot *know,* but Oh, Lord,
> *I believe.*
> Help thou mine unbelief."

Immortality

> "I had the world, and it wasn't nothin!"
> —Muhammad Ali, 1988

If you were alive during his reign – when he was king – whether you loved him, hated him, admired or ridiculed him – whether you cursed or blessed him – he dominated our lives for awhile and –

> nobody ignored him.

He was the very best, and he knew it – the best that's ever been – and we gave him all the things – the stuff that the best get. The money, the applause, the power, adulation – the glory. We hung on his words – quoted him – made him greater than he was.

But we couldn't give him enough.
We couldn't give him enough
because we don't have it.

Death

♦

254

When he began to fade, we couldn't give him the incredible foot speed, the lightening jab, the thunderous hook. And even though we tried not to notice for awhile – when we couldn't ignore it anymore – we agonized when he got hit, when he was hurt – stumbling – we did not wish to believe it –

and neither did he.

He wanted to believe he could do it forever, and we wanted to believe it, too, because his youth and immortality were somehow tied up with our own. And when he couldn't "float like a butterfly" or "sting like a bee," when his eyes were swollen shut and his jaw broken, when he stood wounded and beaten, we cried – not just for him, but for ourselves – and for the dream – for what he really wanted from us –

immortality.

Every generation falls into the same trap. They reach for immortality, and they create heroes to give flesh to the dreams of the fountain of youth – Alexander, Cleopatra, Pharaoh, Moses, Napoleon, Hitler, Elvis, Churchill, and Eisenhower. And when the heroes fail – which they inevitably must – when our money, adulation, and applause fails to give them youth and immortality – and that's what Ali wanted and what we want – we are left with only the illusion, and we grieve for our vanished demigods.

There has only been one exception to this broken dream in the whole, sad, bleeding history of the world. After the crucifixion, when two of the followers of Jesus walk to Emmaus, a tiny village seven miles from Jerusalem, they represent the classical, historical image of disillusionment. They, too, have created a hero to give flesh and substance to their dreams of immortality. But their hero fails. He proves inferior to the power of Rome and the hatred of the Jews, and their dreams collapse on a wooden cross with the words –

"It is finished."

So complete is their depression as they shuffle despondently, heads down, along the long road home, that when their hero approaches them, they fail to recognize Him. But when they finally discover his identity at the dinner table, their joy is unbounded, and their exclamation, "It's Him!" is a declaration of the realization of the glory of immortality –

for them –
for us –
for the first time –
the last time –
the only time.

Muhammad Ali said, "I had the world, and it wasn't nothin'" – and it's true, you know – because it wasn't meant to be anything.

"And the world passes away,
and the lust of it;
but he who does the will of God
abides forever."
—1 John 2:17

The Nameless Dread

"As the sun was setting,
Abram fell into a deep sleep,
and a thick and dreadful darkness
came over him."
—Genesis 15:12

When I was small, sleep came quite easily and naturally to me. I never *thought* about going to sleep – I never had to *work* at it or take pills or *psych* myself – I welcomed it like an old friend, and it opened its arms and took me to its bosom like a lost child. I believe it was because both *death* and *tomorrow* held absolutely no waking fears for me. My bedtime prayers were of the "Now I lay me down to sleep" variety. I knew with every bone in my body that I was going to live forever – and that "if I died before I woke," the very same angels who bore Lazarus to Abraham's bosom in paradise would also bear me gently in their arms to God – who would personally receive my soul – and I would slip ever so naturally from one state of being to another – from one life to the next.

As an adult, sleep eludes me – I fight to go to sleep. As soon as my body hits the bed, my mind begins a fantastic, whirling odyssey, and a kaleidoscope of ideas run rampant through my imagination. I have to trick myself into sleep – by forcing myself not to think about it. Even then, I occasionally lack the moral fiber to refrain from resorting to taking pills. When, eventually, I do fall into a troubled, restless, somnambulistic state of uneasy oblivion, I find little rest there, either for my body or my soul. I do not awaken refreshed but weary and wary, as though I am afraid that something was stolen from me in the night.

It may be due, at least in part, to my sins. I have lost my innocence, my faith in both people and tomorrow. I know that I will be betrayed, and I know that I am not going to live forever –

nor do I wish to.

My faith in my salvation is no longer simple and absolute. As a child I did not fall on my knees beside my bed pleading with God to forgive me for all of the rotten things I had both thought and done during the day – only to finally lay down and be reminded of additional transgressions. My going-to-sleep prayers – for myself, my children, the church, and specific others – are often a gut-wrenching agony that leave me sweat-soaked and seeking because I know that we all have much growing to do and that growth only comes through suffering.

Like many children, I had a recurring bad dream. That puzzles me now, especially in view of what I just said about my childhood sleeping habits and attitudes. I would have thought that because of the dream I would have feared sleep, but I didn't. I went to sleep so gently that it never occurred to me that the dream might come. I never learned anything from it either – each time was a new experience. I mean, I never said in the middle of my dream, "Wait a minute. I've had this dream before, and there's no point in being frightened because I'll wake up any minute and it will be gone."

In my dream I was standing on a vast, flat, expansive, endless, unbroken, grassy plain. There were no large rocks, valleys, hills, trees, water, people, or towns – not a single place to hide or seek shelter. I had no idea how I got to this place – it was as though I had been suddenly born there. As I looked about me, I was filled with a sense of dread – as though I were in danger from some as yet unknown source. I slowly became aware of something like

Death

◆

256

a vast cloud bank that stretched from earth to sky and from one edge of the horizon to the other. It moved slowly but purposefully in my direction, becoming darker and more ominous with each moment. It was –

The Nameless Dread!

I do not know how it got that title – it was not of my doing. I only know that from the first time I saw it, I knew that –

that was its name.

My reaction was always the same. I began to run – to seek any kind of shelter. I ran slowly at first, casting my eyes frantically about me, sure that there *must* be – *had* to be – some nook that I had overlooked. Finding nothing, I increased my pace as the dark horror drew nearer. Ultimately, I would find myself running in abject terror as fast as I could until I was totally exhausted – until my breath came in ragged gasps – until my legs simply would no longer move at my bidding. I would scream for help, but my screams could only be heard in my head – never in my ears – and I was aware that in this land, there was no sound, because there was no one to hear. The sound went out, but it never came back.

I was alone.
Alone in a way that I had never known –
alone with
The Nameless Dread.

The creeping darkness was cruelly relentless. It never hurried, changed its pace, or varied its direction. It was absolutely sure of its quarry. Actually, The Nameless Dread wasn't after me – I mean, personally and individually. I was nothing to it – no more than a stone or blade of grass – it simply moved across this plain every day, consuming everything in its path.

At the end of my dream, when I had reached the last extremity of my strength, I would fall to my knees, interlock my fingers, and raise my hands in a supplicating posture and beg for mercy. I would cry and plead for clemency in the most touching, sympathetic, and endearing terms. The Nameless Dread never responded. It did not and could not hear. It never altered its countenance –

it simply came on.

Just as it reached me – just as I was about to be enveloped and overwhelmed by its misty blackness, which I always interpreted as death, I awoke. My first waking sensation was always the vague awareness of light. I would gradually, fearfully open my eyes – assuming that I was dead and wondering what kind of world I was waking to – and the light would grow.

Familiar things – the quilt, the picture on the wall, my chest of drawers came into view. I would look out the window and there would be the chicken coop – right where it ought to be – the well and the pump, the outhouse, the pear tree, and then, down below the house, the misty fog rising from the swamp. I was alive! It had only been a dream.

"Oh God," I would say, "Oh God,
it was just a dream –
it was just a dream –
it was just a dream!"

Over and over I would repeat that phrase as the wonderful, dawning reality swept over me that I was not dead – that I was not awakening to a new and frightening world. I would be drenched with sweat, trembling from head to foot; real tears would streak my face, and my fingers would ache from being clenched for so long. Gradually, I would begin to relax, pulling the familiar quilt up around my chin – its realness assuring me – as the glory of being alive – of living – washed over me.

You cannot imagine the pleasure I took in the simplest things. I would slowly finger my old, worn blanket – made for me by my grandma Smith – tracing the quilted pattern as though I were seeing it for the first time. The chicken coop and the outhouse were not the drab, decaying, ordinary things they had been, they were wonderful, glorious structures – and I took individual pleasure in them. The smells from our kitchen would float into my room, and they were not of ham and eggs but of exotic dishes – ambrosia and the nectar of the gods. All of these things were created anew for me every time I had the dream. Life was born again by the morning – I tingled with it – I wanted to open the window and shake my fist at

The Nameless Dread
and say,
"I beat you."

I wonder if our life here is not simply a process of trying to escape The Nameless Dread – the creeping, overwhelming, relentless, impersonal blackness that Satan constantly uses to discourage us. It has many names and many faces. It comes in many forms, *but it always comes.* We call it aging or loneliness or cancer. We call it fear, heartache, hopelessness, ingratitude, guilt, death, or depression. It is the past – the irretrievable past. It is want – pride – cold – deception – darkness – selfishness – emptiness – betrayal –

it is –
sin.

All of these are The Nameless Dread, and we all run before the ever encroaching darkness; but we know we cannot escape – that sooner or later we must succumb. Ultimately, we reach the last extremity of our strength, and we fall to our knees, begging for clemency, but The Nameless Dread does not know mercy, and the dream of life ends with The Nameless Dread hovering over us.

There are two possible endings for this dream of life. For some, the next sensation will be of light, and they shall open their eyes to familiar objects and familiar faces. "Yes," they will say, "there is the pear tree and there is the chicken coop and there are my loved ones – Jary, Priscilla, Mom and Dad, Judi, Lincoln, Amy, Brendan, Kamber, Kristen, and Debbie. And there is the Holy City – just as John described it and more glorious than I ever imagined it." The alabaster walls reach ever higher, and at the twelve gates, each made of a single pearl, stands a herald to welcome home the children of God. The city stands sparkling in brilliant light – but it's not the sun – this light is a truer, cleaner, whiter, and clearer light than ever the sun knew. There are no shadows here, for the light is everywhere – it is the light of presence – of being – of God's own face beaming in the glorious victory of His Son.

"Oh God," we will say, "Oh God" – and it won't be a word of hope but of reality.

Death

◆

259

> "Oh God, it was just a dream,
> *it was just a dream,*
> and now I am alive –
> more alive than I have ever been –
> and I shall never sleep again,
> and never dream again,
> and never, never again fear –
> *The Nameless Dread.*"

And from the throne there will come a voice –

> "Blessed and holy are those
> who have part in
> the first resurrection.
> The second death
> has no power over them."
> —Revelation 20:6

I wish I could stop there, but it's not quite the end. There are many who shall awaken to a dim and misty light that will constantly grow more sinister but never go out. They will find themselves on a vast and endless plain. There will be no hills, valleys, rocks, or trees, no towns or people — not even a hole. And here they will begin to run — through time and eternity they will run before the ever-approaching, all-consuming blackness of an endless destruction from which they always awake to find the new day more horrible than the last as they come face to face with —

The Nameless Dread.

"And the smoke of their torment
goes up forever and ever;
and they have no rest
day and night."
—Revelation 14:11

Those who awake to the light now understand that grace, forgiveness, and salvation mean *complete renewal,* the recreating of all things, and now they know what Jesus meant when He said, "Behold I make all things *new,*" and they understand why salvation begins with the *"new* birth" and why the dwelling place of God is described as

"new heavens and a *new* earth."

But you must see that the glory of that awakening is in direct proportion to the horror of the reality of our dream of The Nameless Dread. Without the *Dread,* my room, blanket, chicken coop, and pear tree were the most shabby, mean, pitiful, disgraceful, and disreputable collection of low-class poverty symbols imaginable.

Only as eternal condemnation and the reality of the culmination of sin in the hell of fire where worm does not die and the fire is not quenched; where there is weeping, wailing and gnashing of teeth; where all is lost and all is absolute hopelessness; where one dreary day blends into the next; where greed, pride, selfishness, and the worst aspects of the sinful flesh are totally unchecked and every vile, fleshly passion is unrestrained; where brute strength, fear, and survival of the fittest are the only criteria and justification for right — only in proportion to the reality of that nightmare do the promises of God become meaningful.

Christianity's joy is the pleasure of waking up every morning to the glory of grace after experiencing the nightmare of —

The Nameless Dread.

Time and Chance

"I have seen something else under the sun:
The race is not to the swift
or the battle to the strong,
nor does food come to the wise
or wealth to the brilliant
or favor to the learned;
but time and chance
happen to them all.
Moreover, no man knows when his hour will come:
As fish are caught in a cruel net,
or birds are taken in a snare,
so men are trapped by evil times
that fall unexpectedly upon them."
—Ecclesiastes 9:11–12

On May 24, 1984, I was in the Las Vegas, Nevada, airport. As I sat in the gate area waiting for my plane, a flight arrived at the next gate, and as the passengers deplaned, a man who was arriving greeted one who was waiting to leave. They stood within five feet of me, and I heard every word. They obviously had been long-time friends, either as neighbors or fellow workers, but they had not seen each other in some time.

After the initial greeting, they began asking the normal questions about where they now lived and worked. They made various family and recreational inquiries and passed to other general topics. The conversation was winding down – they had covered the trivia and were finding less and less to talk about. They began making the kinds of physical motions – taking a small step, picking up luggage – and saying the kinds of things – like "Been good seeing you," "Give my love to the wife and kids," "Guess I'd better get moving" – that signal the end of the conversation. One of them – almost as an afterthought – said, "By the way, I almost forgot, how's your brother – the one who moved to Portland – I think his name was Ray?"

"Ray died last month," was the quick reply — almost too quick.

"Oh, I'm sorry to hear that; it must have been sudden."

"It was to me. He had a stroke two months ago, but they didn't tell me until they called to tell me he had died."

"You never heard about it at all?"

"Well, we actually hadn't seen each other in five years. We kept meaning to get in touch — *you know how it is* — I guess they figured — you know."

"Yeah, my family's the same way. How old was he?"

"Fifty-five."

"Fifty-five! I thought Ray was in his mid-sixties."

A shadow of unbelief passed quickly across the face of the inquirer, and it occurred to me that he must be close to that age. The looked passed, and the face hardened back into its previous professional, plastic mold. He laughed — a rather hollow, cynical laugh — "Well, Smitty, *I guess it's coming to all of us,*" he quipped.

The word *guess,* left a little room for doubt, and I noticed that *death* had become *it* — when it was personal.

"Yeah, I guess so, but not before I close this next deal, I hope. You know, it's really funny, us meeting here like this, Frank. I was thinking about you last week, and if my plane hadn't been delayed in Dallas, I wouldn't have seen you. *Life sure is funny.*" He was struggling with a thought, but it was obvious that he wasn't given to thinking, so he soon gave it up. "Just a *coincidence,* I guess."

"Yeah, you're right. Life is funny; who knows, maybe we'll meet here again" —

and maybe they would,
but the *odds* were against it because —
time and chance
happen to them all.

Till We All Fly Away

Christmas of 1991 we made our annual pilgrimage to my sister Jary's house. Her house has sort of been the traditional family gathering place for several years. I didn't know at the time how historically significant this Christmas was to be. The trip was a hassle – it was a long way – we only had a day and a half to spend – it really didn't seem worth the effort. To make it worse, we hadn't bought any gifts this year. *That was my idea.* I have become very pragmatic in my old age. I never know what to buy – I hate shopping – everything I buy is the wrong size, the wrong color, out of style, doesn't match anything, not what they really wanted – and so it gets returned and I get mad. It was a mistake – not buying gifts, I mean. It can be overdone, but not doing it

is equally bad –
or worse.

Death

♦

One of the real blessings of having Christmas at Jary's house is seeing Priscilla – she's my niece. Priscilla has a neuromuscular disease that has kept her confined to a wheelchair for thirteen of her twenty-five years. Priscilla and I have a *special relationship* – although I suspect that everyone who has a relationship with her thinks that their relationship is *special* – that's because Priscilla makes you feel that way.

It's important that you know two or three other things about Priscilla if you are to understand what I want to say. I have never known her to use her condition as a tool to manipulate people and get what she wants or make them feel sorry for her. In my work I get manipulated by someone nearly every day – people who want me to *feel sorry for them* – who want to make me feel guilty because I don't have their particular problem. And because they make me feel guilty, they think I will give them whatever they want. Most of them don't have anywhere near the problems Priscilla has.

Another thing about Priscilla is her thoughtfulness, her patience, her sensitivity to others, and her spirituality. Whenever Priscilla and I get together, we always take a walk. I push her in her wheelchair and we talk. *Talking is very hard for us.* Priscilla has to work very hard to talk, and what she says isn't always as intelligible as she would like because her condition has affected her speech. To make matters worse, my ears aren't what they used to be, so between the two problems, we really struggle to understand each other. Sometimes I have to ask her two or three times to repeat what she has said. Even people who can speak easily would get aggravated with me. Priscilla struggles with every word – but she is patient with me – slowly, painfully, she forces out each syllable to make me understand, and then we laugh about it – that's another thing – she has a great sense of humor and takes teasing unbelievably well –

because she is not vain.

When we took our walk last Christmas Day, it was obvious to me that her condition had deteriorated. As we strolled through the neighborhood, we were greeted often by friendly people. *Priscilla asked if I thought that people were more friendly to her because she was crippled,* and I said yes, I thought so, and I was glad for it. Then she asked if I remembered a passage from Charles Dickens' *A Christmas Carol,* where Bob Cratchit was telling his wife what Tiny Tim had said to him on the way home from church on Christmas day:

> "He told me, coming home,
> that he hoped the people
> saw him in the church,
> because he was cripple,

> and it might be pleasant
> to them to remember,
> upon Christmas Day,
> who made lame beggars walk
> and blind men see."

Priscilla told me that she hoped that people would feel the same way about her so that her malady might help folks be more grateful to God for their health.

As we neared the end of our walk that Christmas Day – as we came in sight of the house – with all of the cars parked around it and all of our family inside, she said –

> "I'm so thankful for my family –
> I just don't know what people do
> who don't have a family
> to care for them."

> *That was our last walk and*
> *those were our last words*
> *on this earth.*

Late Saturday afternoon on February 2, 1992 Jary called me and said that Priscilla was in the hospital and her condition was serious. We got in the car and drove the three hundred fifty miles in record time. As I drove, I found myself praying – "O God, please let her be alive when I get there." I really don't know why that was so important to me – but it was. We arrived at the hospital about 2:30 A.M. and went directly to ICU.

> She was alive –
> not much,
> *but alive.*

For the next hour we cried and prayed and remembered, as we stood helplessly and watched her life slip gradually away. It was as it's supposed to be – your family standing around your bed in your last moments. The little blips on the monitor raced . . . and slowed – raced . . . and slowed – then stopped.

> There were no more blips,
> and that meant
> *that she was gone.*

I wouldn't call her back for anything – I am very selfish, but not that selfish – but I miss her. She was good for us. She reminded us constantly of our

Death

blessings – of what we assume so easily. She reminded me of how small I am, and she made me ashamed of my complaining and depression. She never rode a bike, never had a date, never climbed a tree or drove a car. She couldn't brush her teeth or feed herself. She could never go anywhere unless someone took her or carried her. But she loved. She took the greatest pleasure in the simplest things – and we loved her.

And love is, after all –
the greatest thing.
It has lasted.

I had written Priscilla a letter for her 26th birthday, which was February 7th. It was a letter she didn't get to read. I want to share it with you:

January 28, 1992
My Dearest Priscilla,

I've been wondering what to get you for your birthday – outside of a visit from your favorite uncle of course – and I've decided that I'm the world's worst gift buyer. I haven't got a clue. I don't know anything about CDs, or music for that matter. My knowledge of what is stylish in clothes is about thirty years behind – and let's face it – (as your mother will tell you) I never was too much on the clothes scene – even thirty years ago. I am a total flop as an uncle – in the gift-buying department, that is.

So I thought I'd write you this neat letter and we would both feel better – me for writing to you and you for getting a genuine, first-class piece of mail. Now I'm sure that you're going to accuse me of being a cheapskate – trying to get by your birthday with a twenty-nine cent stamp – but just to prove how wrong you can be, I'm going to hand-deliver this essay – which will cost me, I figure, about sixty bucks, plus I'm going to take you out to your favorite restaurant – MacDonalds – right?

Seriously, I wanted you to know that I hadn't forgotten your birthday, and I wanted you to know that I think of you nearly every day – you are precious to me, and I pray that someday in God's providence, we can live close together again – like we used to – and I can see you real often.

Yes – you have one other birthday present coming – I promise to take you on a very long walk and we'll talk – well, I'll talk – and you'll repeat yourself about sixteen times until I understand you. Thanks, my love – for being patient with my bad ears – you know my heart really understands.

Have a specially great day.

Till we all fly away to be with Jesus,
I love you,
Uncle John

Priscilla has flown away to be with Jesus. Now there is yet one more reason to go to heaven –

> where we can live close together –
> like we used to –
> and I can see her real often.

Death

♦

TWELVE

Heaven

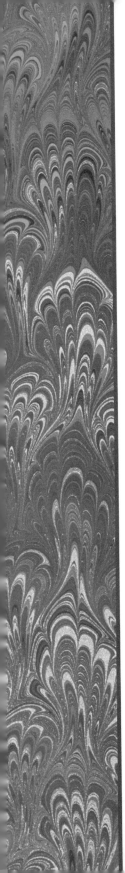

"And the toils of the road
will seem nothing,
When I get to the
end of the way."

I know why that song was my mother's favorite – why it gave her strength to go on. She knew where she was going and who she was going to see. She believed that He had gone to prepare a place for her and that He was coming again to take her there. It is heaven that makes the toils seem as nothing. It is heaven that makes everything we have borne worthwhile.

It seems rather strange to me that I have no vivid memories of sermons preached or classes taught about heaven during my formative years. That fact is rendered even more peculiar by the fact that I have many memories of sermons on hell. It was described to me in three-dimensional, living color – complete with names, faces, climate, activities, and duration – all told in vivid and unmistakable language. When I first started preaching, I preached the same way. I am glad to say that over the years I have sincerely tried to bring these two topics into balance.

You know, hell is much easier to describe – to paint a picture of. Maybe that's why the old-time preachers were more comfortable with it. It also needs to be said that humans are more easily motivated into action by what they abhor and fear than by what they like or enjoy. I am very sorry to say it, but it is simply true. I could use any number of examples, but my teaching experience of twenty years was one long lesson in that fact.

It's really hard to get a handle on heaven – that is because we tend to conceive of hell as being real and heaven as ethereal. Hell has real fire and real torment; worms don't die and the fire is not quenched. There are real tears and real monsters and real gnashing of teeth. But conceptually, heaven has been presented as vague, mystical, surrealistic, and totally beyond both our imagination and experience. We have tended to spiritualize those passages about new heavens and a new earth, streets of gold, gates of pearl, trees, and rivers, while we have taken the hell passages quite practically and literally.

I don't know why. It seems to me that the same rules ought to apply to both. They are both spiritual realms. They are both the creation of God to house those beings who have chosen to live in them. They coexist in the same time frame and atmosphere, and they both house the resurrected and imperishable bodies of those who are no longer in the flesh.

The problem may have arisen from statements like the one Jesus made about there not being any marriage in heaven. I guess it's not conceivable to us that real men and women could coexist without it. We have also assumed that no marriage means no sexual differentiation or desire, but Scripture does not say so.

I would not have you believe that my understanding of heaven is absolutely correct, but you do need to understand that I take the descriptions of it in Scripture quite literally. I mean, what John said about seeing "new heavens and a new earth wherein dwell righteousness" – if those new heavens and that new earth bear no resemblance to the old ones, I see no purpose in calling them that, and John might as well have said that he saw toglat and scrumptard.

The stories in this chapter are based on my faith that heaven is a real place, where real people, with real spiritual bodies live. If God were going to destroy every aspect of our personality and humanity, remake us into something that bears no resemblance to what we are now, it seems to me that this life of preparation serves absolutely no purpose at all and there was no reason to make us so in the first place.

It is my prayer that as you read you will develop a longing for heaven that will brighten your days on this earth and cause you to redefine your purpose for living.

"My Lord, What a Morning"

"My Lord, what a morning.
My Lord, what a morning,
When the stars begin to fall.
No more grief and pain for me,
I heard from heaven today.
Yes my Lord's going to set me free,
I heard from heaven today.
My Lord, what a morning.
My Lord, what a morning,
When the stars begin to fall."
—Negro Spiritual

Babs Durning died the day after Christmas. She was thirty-six years old and the mother of three small boys. She was a fascinating person. Death was a long, hard, painful time coming for Babs, but it was sudden when it came —

because you're never really ready.

Those who were touched by her — who loved her — were caught between the welcome relief we felt, because her pain was over at last, and the frustration of believing that she died too soon. She was a marvelous athlete — a marathon runner and triathlete. She also had a great heart, an instinctive love for people and for life. Babs was her own person — she marched to her own drummer. She was tenderhearted and kind, a good and loyal friend, and a faithful Christian. Babs didn't wear her faith like a hair shirt —

she wore it with a smile.

During the time I knew her, we both lived in Kingman, Arizona. I had a firewood business. One very cold, winter Saturday morning, just at daylight, I was going to cut firewood. *I was feeling very sorry for myself.* I imagined that I was the only person in town out of bed with a long day of hard work ahead. As I turned the corner near my house, I saw a small figure, heavily clothed, trotting along the roadside. It was Babs. Sweatpants and long johns, woolen cap and hood, gloves and muffler — it was Babs, training for her next event. I could see her breath plainly.

I drove up alongside and rolled down my window. "Hi!" I said.

She turned and recognized me. That impish, lopsided grin spread across her freckled face, and she said, "Hi John, isn't this a glorious morning?"

To be perfectly truthful, I thought it was something rather less than that. But Babs called my attention to the sun, just peeping over the Hualapai Mountains, and to the striking gold, purple, and green that reflected from the Black Mountains across the valley. In between, the entire valley lay in that magnificent, sleepy, half-light of anticipation, and it *was* beautiful – *glorious,* indeed. We visited for a few moments, and then she went on with her running and I went on with my woodcutting. But I went on thoughtfully –

because of Babs.

Heaven

♦

274

The Sunday after Babs died, I was on my way to preach at the early service. When I saw the sun, perfectly round and clear, standing motionless on the horizon as if etched on a blue canvas – I first thought of the face of Jesus, which John the revelator said "shone like the sun"; but as I continued looking into that cloudless sunrise, I thought of Babs. I couldn't help but think of the thrill I would feel if I could see that hooded, muffled, bundled figure, trotting beside the road.

I miss her!

It is my faith that when the Father calls me home and I begin my first tour of the heavenly city, the New Jerusalem, the eternal dwelling place of the redeemed, where it is always a *glorious morning,* I will need no introduction to that figure I see trotting along the side of those streets of gold. And when I come up alongside, she'll turn and recognize me, and that impish, lopsided grin will cross her freckled face, and she'll say,

"Hi, John, isn't this a glorious morning?"

Babs didn't run for glory; she didn't run to win or to maintain her figure – Babs ran for the love of it – because God gave her the gift and because she found meaning in everything she did. She ran because it made sense to her. As you run the race before you, it is my prayer that you will run for the love of it, because it makes sense to you and because God has given you the strength to do so. I also pray that as you run, you will think of Babs Durning – a great lady with a great heart. And if you will be very quiet and listen very carefully, you just may hear her say,

"Hi, isn't this a glorious morning?"

"Still round the corner there may wait
A new road or a secret gate;
And though I oft have passed them by,

A day will come at last when I
Shall take the hidden paths that run
West of the Moon, East of the Sun."
—J. R. R. Tolkien, *The Return of the King*

I Wouldn't Miss It for Anything

I recently returned from a Bible lectureship at the beautiful Pepperdine University in Malibu. I was sorry to leave because I hated for it to be over. It was an event I had long anticipated, and the expectation had motivated me for many days before I actually went.

There are few places that combine the ethereal, scenic beauty and the balmy, tropical temperatures of Malibu, California. But the lectures are more than that. There is the gathering of old friends, the making of new ones, the excitement of thoughtful and intelligent discussion of Scripture. There is the challenge of new ideas, the affirmation of old ones, and the emotional exhilaration of the gospel message proclaimed from the heart. There is the new awareness of efforts to increase our mission effectiveness and community service. The encouragement to study, to give, to be more thoughtful, more tolerant, more committed is ever present.

One of the main reasons people go is *reunion*. They get to see people they haven't seen since last year, or maybe longer. And at the end of every lectureship, we embrace each other and sing an old familiar refrain – "see you next year." Just to meet fellow strugglers and be aware of their existence, just to know that in their communities Jesus lives, the Word is being proclaimed, and the church is alive – is both comforting and encouraging. And of course,

there is the singing.

I get excited about going to the Pepperdine lectures. I am excited by every single aspect I just mentioned. Those things are real to me, and so,

> I make sacrifices in order to go.
> *I wouldn't miss it for anything.*

How "real" is heaven to you? Are you *excited* about going there? Wouldn't you like to see the oyster that produced a pearl so big they made a gatepost out of it? Would you make sacrifices in order not to miss it? Is hell more "real" than heaven? Is your motivation toward a *vague* heaven more a desire to avoid a *real* hell?

Heaven

♦

276

If living in heaven will be a "Casper the Ghost" nebulous type of existence, where you float around on a white cloud, listen to harp music, sing the same Stamps-Baxter songs over and over, and hear Paul preach till midnight – I can't get too excited about it. If heaven is a place where you bowl, eat tuna-noodle casserole, listen to rock music, play Dominoes and Trivial Pursuit – I think I'll check my alternatives before I make a final decision.

Most of us have some notions about heaven. Personally, I like Revelation 19:11–21 – I can get excited about *that* heaven. And then I like Revelation chapters 21 and 22 because they talk about a whole different dimension. Every time I read those chapters, I get new ideas about the trees, the rivers, the streets, and those white stucco buildings (alabaster), and I want to see some of that transparent gold and meet Abraham.

It'll be great to know that the murderers, liars, and other bad folks are "outside" and that you don't have to lock the doors or worry about whether the police chief is on the take or the fire department is on strike. And I wonder about how they'll handle the trash – maybe there isn't any trash because in heaven you eat the "cores" and the "peels" – or maybe they don't have any of those either. And there can't be any fouled-up city government because they don't need streetlights because there's no night and the water comes from the river and nobody fouls it up because there are no refrigerators or cars because everybody eats room-temperature food and walks, which means no factories – and I can't imagine what that means.

And about every thirty minutes someone will say, "Hey, let's go down to the church and have a singing." And while you're there, *He* comes in – I mean He just walks right in and says, "Hey, what are you guys doing? Singing? I'll tell you what, John, you sing tenor, and I'll sing bass." But for a while, I don't even want to sing; I just want to look at Him – *because it's really Him,* you know. And after I look for a while and listen to Him sing bass, I get excited about singing tenor. Boy, does He like to sing! And then about a hundred years pass while He teaches us some new songs, but nobody cares how long it takes, because *He's* there, and wherever He is, we all want to be. And of course,

there is the tree of life.

I guess I got carried away, but it's pretty exciting when you think about it, and I hope you do.

> I have to make sacrifices to go,
> but *I wouldn't miss it for anything.*
> And I think that's
> what it takes to get there.

Doc Brachitt – Office Upstairs

Author's note: I heard Charles Coulston, who was the preacher at Redwood City, California, tell the following story at Sierra Bible Camp in 1972. I have written it down as I remember him telling it. The names and the incident are completely ficticious, but the parable is true.

It was a typical western Oklahoma oil town of the 1930s. You could see it thirty miles before you got there – if you were looking – but most folks didn't look, because there wasn't much to see. The wind was constant and the dust and grit that the wind carried were also constant. There were no trees, no grass, no water. It had two gas stations, a Western Auto, a hardware store, a post office, a dry goods store, and a grocery store. The economy was oil and nothing but oil, and all the money was in the hands of half a dozen people. For a long time, there was no doctor; but some thoughtful citizen placed an ad in a medical journal, and in the spring of 1937 a – fresh out of medical school – handsome, single, and personable young man responded. His name was Doctor Adrian V. Brachitt, soon known to all as

Doc Brachitt.

He rented three small rooms upstairs over the grocery store. Two of the rooms he practiced medicine in, and one room he slept in. The rooms were only accessible by an outside stairway, and so he hung a sign on the side of the grocery store over the stairway that read,

Doc Brachitt –
Office Upstairs.

It could be said that he quickly became the most well-known and widely respected man within a hundred miles. He always had time; his hours were determined by his patients' needs – he never overcharged, never complained. Many of his patients were transient laborers and other offcasts of the oil-drilling business; they rarely had money for their bills – Doc never sent one. He always meant to build a new office, but something always seemed to interrupt his plans, and he never got around to it. He did eventually build a house about a block down the street.

About two years after he came to town, he met – and fell in love with – the daughter of one of the half dozen influential families in the community. They were to be married on a Saturday afternoon at five o'clock. About noon on that day, a migrant oil-field worker came to his office and begged him to come see his sick child. Doc went. The man spoke only a few words of English, and Doc misunderstood about where he lived. He didn't think he'd be gone long, and the case seemed urgent, so he didn't leave a message about where he had gone. It took nearly two hours to get there – the child was dangerously ill – there were no phones – he could not leave – and so he stayed through the afternoon and into the night.

The wedding was about the biggest event that had hit the town in a long time. Lots of money was spent – everybody from miles around was there – everybody,

except Doc.

When he got home late that night, he went straight to his fiancée's house. Her father came to the door and indicated that it would be best if he never came there again. When he asked if he could explain, he was told that no explanation could possibly justify the pain and embarrassment he had caused the family. When his explanation was finally heard, both his fiancée and her family were even more indignant that such an "insignificant" thing should cause them such humiliation. They broke their engagement, and Doc never married. Everybody thought Doc would leave, but he didn't.

He lived there forty-four years.

He was a town fixture. He attended all the high school athletic contests, the drama presentations, the choral concerts. He was a father to all the motherless or fatherless children and a helping hand to the town drunk. He counseled and encouraged the unwed mothers. He gave financial assistance

to every good community project – and some bad ones too. Whenever any-one was down and out, they always went to Doc. He never had a bad word to say about anybody, and he had a place in his heart for everybody – even the few enemies he had.

One morning he received news from the oil field that several men had been hurt in an explosion. He quickly gathered his things, rushed down the stairs, and ran to his car, which was parked at his house about a block away. Just as he reached it –

he collapsed and died.

They say it was the biggest funeral the town had ever seen. Everybody within fifty miles knew Doc Brachitt, and everybody had a story to tell about how he had helped them. Well –

almost everybody.

They buried him in the local cemetery, and there was much talk about erecting some kind of monument as a headstone. A citizen's committee undertook the project, but they couldn't agree on who was in charge or how much to spend, what to say or what it should look like, and in time, the idea gradually lost momentum and finally was forgotten.

No one knows for sure just who did it or when, but one day, somebody who was walking near the cemetery noticed a weather-beaten old sign posted over Doc's grave. It read,

Doc Brachitt –
Office Upstairs

The New Song

There I was, washing this tandem-axle, twin-screw, cab-over, eighteen-wheel, Peterbilt rig, when out from under November and December's accu-mulation of Chicago's white salt, Indiana's black dirt, Oklahoma's red mud, blue-grey, number-two diesel smoke mixed four-to-one with Kansas brown sand there appeared *The Newsome Truck Line.* It was startling how those words, painted in cursive white on a royal-blue, metal-flake base, jumped out at me when the jet-like stream of scalding hot, soapy water passed across the door of the Peterbilt –

"The Newsome Truck Line."

Something about those words caught at my mind and wouldn't leave. It seemed I ought to remember something or somebody, but I couldn't quite come up with who or what. I thought I had it when I remembered Bobo Newsome, a now-forgotten relief pitcher for the Detroit Tigers – one of my father's favorites – but that wasn't it, just a name. I tried to give it up and went on with my work.

I was washing the trailer and simultaneously admiring the fine spring day, warm and full of new life, when I slowly became aware that I was humming the melody of an old gospel song called "The New Song." That was it! It made me so happy, I could have danced – except I don't know how (fundamentalists like me don't go much for dancing). And besides, I had on some heavy rubber boots and a very cumbersome rubber suit, which would have seriously impeded my exhibition had I possessed the talent. So, with only a disinterested and totally unappreciative Peterbilt for an audience, I broke into a completely unrestrained a cappella rendition of the song. I even remembered all three verses, and I was absolutely ecstatic with the boisterous enthusiasm and exhilarating expectancy raised in me by the spirit of it. And as the song proclaimed, it did

"thrill my soul."

As I sang the second stanza, a warm and precious thought came to me. The words of the song are,

"The greatest joy that I have ever known,
Is praising Him in song.
I know some day, when I have older grown,
my voice will not be strong;
But if good seed for Jesus I have sown,
With angels I'll belong.
They sing in heaven a new song,
Of Moses and the Lamb."

That part about getting older and losing my voice hit me hard. I thought, "Lord, don't let me outlive my voice. What would life be to me if I couldn't sing?"

Heaven

♦

Then I thought about my mom. The last few years of her life had been very hard for her. She had had a light stroke, and it had partially paralyzed her vocal cords. What had once been a strong, vibrant alto voice had become gravelly and raspy. I had watched her often – especially while I led singing – trying so hard to sing, trying to clear her throat, struggling to produce the old sounds of praise; but they wouldn't come – they would never come again. So she would slowly close her book and her eyes, then fold her hands on top of her songbook. As she sat there, trying to be content with listening, I think she drifted away to where she could hear it again – the way it used to be – because I would see her smile and nod her head in approval. Mom really loved to sing, and our home was often filled with it. I have precious memories of her at the piano – with Dad, Jary, and I – singing her favorite hymns.

But Mom was gone.

My song ended – just as her life had ended – very suddenly. I didn't feel like singing anymore. A cloud passed over the bright sun, and the soft spring wind that had warmed me turned chilly. I hurried my work so I could go home. *Home* – what a warm and wonderful sentiment that word aroused in me. I thought of the words to the song again,

> But if good seed for Jesus I have sown,
> With angels I'll belong.

That part about belonging with angels could only mean one thing – *heaven*: no more hunger . . . no more thirst . . . no pain . . . no dying . . . no sickness.

They sing in heaven a new song.

Now it didn't take me too long to put two or three ideas together in a hurry. If there's no *sickness* in heaven and if they're *singing* a new song there – then my mom's standing in the front row.

Praise God! Mom's got her voice back, and she's singing the *new song!*

Praise God!

God continues to find ways of reminding me of his gracious promises and of filling my heart with thanksgiving for precious memories, for promises already fulfilled, and for the hope which is mine

when I come to the end of my journey.

Going to Heaven

It was Christmas, 1987. It's funny how thoughts come to your mind totally unbidden – with no planning and under circumstances that don't seem to be connected.

I had been hunting in West Texas. It had been a very cold, windy, blustery day – what else would it be in winter in West Texas? We had had a very successful hunting trip – my two sons and I. We had gotten home after dark, and I was in the utility room cleaning pheasants. Like the wind in West Texas, there are some things that never change. It's true – I had killed *some* of the birds – but I got stuck with the task of cleaning *all* of them. Where were my boys? Their enthusiasm for hunting never did extend to cleaning whatever we had killed. As soon as the car hit the driveway, they had *very important plans* – in this case, showers, phone calls, and wrapping presents.

I was alone in the utility room, but the sounds of the activities from the rest of the house drifted in. I don't know how long it was before I noticed the blend. In the living room, Kristen was playing "Moonlight Sonata"; in the family room, Judi was putting ornaments on the tree. The boys were giving her advice while they wrapped presents. The stereo was playing Christmas music softly, and my very all-time favorite – "Silent Night" – was on. There were good smells coming from the kitchen, and occasionally the telephone would ring and then there would be laughter. I was overwhelmed by an unparalleled feeling of *wholeness, completeness,* but it had a small tinge of sadness hanging around the edges because I knew that it was passing away –

I could not hold it.

At that moment, going to heaven became so important to me. I knew that only there could I recapture and hold on to that sense of wholeness. I thought –

"Dear God, I must not lose this."

That evening I caught a glimpse of one of heaven's greatest treasures – something I had never thought of before.

I don't think I'll kill pheasants there – somehow the idea of killing something doesn't click with my concept of *everlasting life* – but I don't have any problem imagining that Kris will play "Moonlight Sonata," and I'm sure we'll wrap presents and sing "Silent Night" and celebrate the birth of our Lord.

Heaven
is being able to hold
those precious moments
of wholeness
forever.

We Dream of a Place Called Heaven

His name was Al – short for Alvin. He died one day – which is to be expected when you're eighty-three years old.

He had been lying in the intensive care unit with more IVs, wires, hoses, lines, and monitors taped to his body and plugged into various holes than an automobile engine. He had been dimly aware that he was surrounded by his wife, children, and friends, who were grieving and praying. He had felt very tired,

so he decided to just go to sleep.

The next thing he knew, he was swimming, struggling to reach the bank of a great river whose powerful current threatened to carry him away. It was all he could do to stay afloat, but just when he had lost heart, it seemed that the current actually began helping him toward the bank.

As he relaxed, he gradually became aware of the fact that the riverbank was lined with people who were yelling encouragement to him. He wished that they would come to his assistance or throw him a rope, but no one offered. At last, his feet touched bottom. As he staggered, sopping wet, up the bank, he was greeted by the deafening cheers and applause of thousands of people.

It was quite a reception, but after the initial greeting and celebration, he was somewhat surprised to find that he hadn't changed much. He still walked with a limp, his back bothered him, his hair was thin and grey, and his digestion had not improved. It was obviously heaven, and he was enormously glad to be out of the hospital,

but it certainly wasn't what he had expected.

He was assigned a guide, to sort of show him around and acquaint him with procedures. His name was Mike – short for Michael – and he was an exceedingly pleasant fellow. When Mike asked him what he wanted to do, he was totally at a loss because he had no idea what his options were. He was pleasantly surprised when Mike suggested that he play golf. He had begun playing on earth when he was very young and had developed a passion for the game. Over the years, he had honed his skills and, for a period of time, was a "scratch" golfer. With passing years, his skills had faded, but he had played well into his seventies before physical maladies finally stopped him.

"Do you think I could?" he asked tentatively.

"I'm sure of it," Mike replied.

"I didn't bring any equipment."

"Oh, we supply all that."

The course was breathtaking. Only an old golfer could really appreciate it. Beautifully curved, tree-lined fairways; perfectly level, manicured tee boxes; exquisite, rolling greens; deep, strategically located sand traps; and occasional crystal-clear pools of water. He did notice that the holes seemed terribly short – even for his limited skills. He also noticed that there were no cart paths, and when he asked about that, Mike explained that in heaven everybody walked, because all of the lazy people were playing on a different course, in a

somewhat warmer climate.

When he was handed his bag and his clubs, he was startled. His face reflected his disappointment. They were *exactly* like the first set he had ever had – a discarded, unmatched assortment his mother had picked up at a garage sale. He took the driver out. The chrome shaft was pitted and rusty. The leather grip was worn smooth and frayed at both ends. The head was weathered, cracked – even warped.

"I can't possibly play with these. Haven't you got anything better?" he complained.

"Of course you can," Mike responded enthusiastically. "Let's get started."

"Aren't you going to play?" Al asked.

"Well, I don't think so, not today." There was something about his answer that made Al think it best not to pursue it any further.

He reached into the pocket of the bag looking for balls. He found one. It was an old Dunlop; the letters were nearly obliterated, and it was yellow with age. It was scuffed and cut so deeply from abuse that the rubber windings showed through the gap.

It couldn't possibly roll straight.

"Where are the other balls?"

"That's it; you only get one. But it lasts as long as you're here."

Not much consolation in that, Al thought. *The guy who used this ball before me must have stayed a long time.* But Mike was so cheerful and encouraging that he said nothing and determined to make the best of a bad show.

"What happens if I lose it?" he asked – almost hopefully.

"That never happens here; nothing is ever lost. You'll understand after you've been here a while."

He did not wish to appear ungrateful, and so with a heavy heart, he began. His first drive was so feeble that even on this short hole, no more than a hundred yards, it took him seven to get to the green. The lopsided ball was so unpredictable that he putted four times and took an eleven. He was nearly in tears.

"Hey, not bad," Mike said. "The last guy took fifteen." Al did not feel any better.

The next hole was about the same and the next and the next. He gradually lost track of his score and the number of holes he had played. He plodded along, miserable, disappointed, and not a little confused. Gradually, he lapsed into a sort of semi-conscious state of deep thought, in which his immediate surroundings – the sights and sounds and smells – blended together and faded into the background.

It was like time passing,
but not the same.

He didn't really know when he first noticed it – it was like waking after surgery or after a long, deep, drug-induced sleep. His first conscious awareness that things were different came with the realization that he was playing better and that he felt – well, he felt *different*. He was enjoying himself. In quick succession, he noticed that his drives were much longer, his chipping form had returned, and his putting touch was the best he could remember. And that's when he noticed that the ball was rolling straight and true. He examined it and found that, although it was definitely the same ball, it also was much improved. He also realized that he had not spoken to Mike for a

Heaven

♦

285

long time. Somewhat embarrassed, he asked, "How many holes have we played?"

"Oh, five or six hundred, I guess." Mike responded, as though that were nothing unusual.

"Five or six hundred!" Al was incredulous. "How big is this course?"

"I really don't know, I've never seen it all; the recreation department handles that stuff."

"How long have I been playing?"

"We have no way of determining 'long,' as you mean it. It simply isn't important. All that matters is how much better you are."

"How come the ball seems different? Did you switch it on me? And my clubs – they're . . . well . . .

they're better."

"That's it! That's it, exactly! That's the word I wanted you to say." Mike was excited. "It means you're growing, and I can begin explaining things to you. You see, in heaven, the Father has reversed what you experienced on earth. I guess you've also noticed that you don't limp anymore, your back doesn't hurt, and you're feeling stronger. It's not because you're younger, it's because you're *better.* As long as you are here, you will improve.

The more you use whatever is given you,
the better it will become.

"While on earth, you supposed that there was no time here. That isn't exactly true; time is sort of reversed here. On earth, you knew time had passed because things broke down and decayed. Here, time does not measure what has passed or how close to the end you are; it does not tell you that you are late or what the boundaries of your expectations are.

"Here, time *expands* instead of contracting. Rather than limit, it creates endless *possibilities.* Time does not point to a conclusion, but to a new beginning – a place from which to grow. Today you saw an old ball become new, a bag of useless clubs become objects of craftsmanship. Even in this simple thing, endless possibilities for improvement yet remain. Can you imagine putting a ball into a hole that is exactly the same size as the ball, on a green the size of a soccer field, which is covered with flower beds, shrubs, and running water?

"You have experienced within yourself a growing feeling of health and strength. In heaven, we always start everybody out with some simple, familiar activity, because they can't understand how things work here until they've actually seen the possibilities. What you've experienced so far is the most simple and insignificant of heaven's wonders. You can return and play

whenever you want. We have holes here that are miles long with endless variations and hazards, but most folks don't come back very many times.

They go on to more significant things.

Now, in our music department we have a piano that has three thousand keys and thirty-nine foot pedals; we have a trumpet that is ninety feet long and plays four hundred octaves. We have an organ -

A Fiddler on the Roof

The play closed on Saturday, June 24. We had rehearsed since the middle of April, and there had been seventeen performances. We began as a group of strangers, and we had become not only friends, but Jews – Russian Jews – and Anatevka had become our home. Leaving was very sad. During the last scene, I cried – not actor's tears, but human tears – as I left Anatevka for the last time. I said good-bye to the people I had known all my life – to my sons-in-law, my daughters, to the house my father had built and I had been born in. Then I loaded my wagon and left. We will never do it again and I

will never see Anatevka again.

It was a reminder of passing time, of the passing of things – things that are good and lovely and things bad and ugly. We were forced to leave Anatevka by the Russians, and we left to find new homes. Most of us were going to America. We didn't leave because we were seeking a better place; we left because – *we were forced out.* They gave us three days. We would have preferred to stay – even though we were very poor and even though Anatevka

"wasn't much of a place."

So we all cling to what we know, to what is familiar – to faces, towns, jobs, to *life*. And if we weren't forced to leave – we would never seek better places. It was hard to leave Anatevka. We tried to put a brave face on it. We said,

Heaven

♦

288

"What do we leave?
Nothing much –
a pot, a pan, a piece of cloth."

But it was hard because it was home – and it had been home for a long time.

We must leave Montgomery, too, and Lubbock, San Jose, Wetumpka, Idalou, and Pocahontas. We are being "forced out." It's not the Russians this time – it's God. He says, "Sell your house; pack your goods; you must leave this place – you have three days." Sometimes the notice is much shorter –

and we'll know He means business.

We don't want to go. We drag our feet and whine and cry. As sorry as this life is – and it is very sorry – it's home, it's familiar. It's not exactly the garden of Eden – but it's home, nevertheless. And if he didn't force us, we wouldn't go.

Leaving is sad, but there is a new land to which we must go. For the Jews of Anatevka, it was America – the land of the free and home of the brave. For us, the new home is *heaven* – and it's much better than America.

Heaven is the land of the free – those made free by the truth and by the blood of Jesus. It's the home of the brave – those brave enough to set out on the most daring venture ever imagined, a venture from which no one ever returns – or wants to. It's a new land of constantly changing possibilities, reserved for those who – knowing they will someday be called to a new home – do not try to hold on to the past; but looking ever forward, by faith they constantly visualize the Holy City.

And we are all closer than we think.

"Listen, I will tell you a mystery!
We will not all die,
but we will all be changed,
in a moment, in the twinkling of an eye,
at the last trumpet.
For the trumpet will sound,
and the dead will be raised imperishable,
and we will be changed."
—1 Corinthians 15: 51–52